GENERATION HEX

EDITED BY JASON LOUV

disinformation

Published by The Disinformation Company Ltd.
163 Third Avenue, Suite 108
New York, NY 10003
Tel.: +1.212.691.1605
Fax: +1.212.691.1606
www.disinfo.com

Cover Image: Detail from "The Metatron" by Paul Laffoley
Chapter Head Image: Detail from "Get Thee Behind Me Satan" by Paul Laffoley
Text design and layout: Maya Shmuter

Library of Congress Control Number: 2005930393

ISBN-10: 1-932857-20-6
ISBN-13: 978-1-932857-20-7

Printed in USA

10 9 8 7 6 5 4 3 2 1

Distributed in the USA and Canada by:
Consortium Book Sales and Distribution
1045 Westgate Drive, Suite 90
St Paul, MN 55114
Toll Free: +1.800.283.3572
Local: +1.651.221.9035
Fax: +1.651.221.0124
www.cbsd.com

Attention colleges and universities, corporations and other organizations: Quantity discounts are available on bulk purchases of this book for educational training purposes, fund-raising, or gift giving. Special books, booklets, or book excerpts can also be created to fit your specific needs. For information contact Marketing Department of The Disinformation Company Ltd.

To My Parents

and

In Memoriam

Jhon Balance 1962-2004

ACKNOWLEDGMENTS

I would like to thank my parents and my brother for their love, support and of being understanding of this mad quest of mine;

My publishers Gary Baddeley and Richard Metzger for taking a chance on me and this project, and for opening so many doors for me;

Breyer P-Orridge for their friendship and guidance, for sending Scott Treleaven my way, for so fearlessly leading by example and for letting me crash on the floor with thee ferret Spike;

Fraters H., E., C. and Soror A. for the initiations and for getting through my thick skull;

My friends Jude Evans, Emma Franzeim, John Garmon, Jessica Gliddon, Jennie Gruber, Brian Heater, Lauren Kennedy, Matthew Lee, Sara Torello and Stacie Willoughby for their companionship and support throughout this project;

Stephen Grasso and Danny Lowe for opening the gates of secret London to me;

My teachers Thomas Ihlbrock and Brady Kelso for inspiring me to follow my black-turtlenecked dreams;

Maya Shmuter for designing the book you now hold;

Jacob Rosette for creating generation-hex.com;

Ralph Bernardo, Dave Samra, Liz Lawler and Anne Sullivan at Disinformation;

Phil Hine, Gyrus, Michael Szul, Klintron, Chris Arkenberg and the constituents of Key23.net for hyping the book and making me feel important, and those of Barbelith. com for research help and all the discussions;

Paul Laffoley for contributing the best cover I could have ever hoped for;

Grant Morrison for pointing the way;

To all who have lived and died to weave this living tapestry called magic;

And to all of the constituents of Generation Hex, here, there and everywhere: Never have the others been so easy to find.

\[iDoR\u\i\virusprogenitor!$CONFLAGENESIS$! V1.2] by Frater *IDORU* 296/22
[# written in the beginners all purpose symbolic instruction code#]

>*ANGEL.WILL I.DESIRE WORD.BELIEF*
   \Essence | Where there is a will there is a Way;

   Code {

   Phoenix | Serpent | HORIZON = infinum }

   \

>*FORMULA OF THE WORD = 'INVERSION'*
   \Essence | HORIZON (*horizon – infinum*);
         | Revelation Void (*ABRAXAS*);
         | Reduction/Potential (*NOX*);
         | Consciousness =$
      MINDVOID=VOIDMIND;

            Code {
                  HORIZON | (*horizon – span*);
                      | *OH?!*;
                      | *IR*;
                      | *ZONOZNZOOZN* =$
                  azasaszazasnasatanatta$ }
            \

>*THE NEGATION OF THE WORD IN FOLLY*
   :$Where there is no Will, where shall then be the way? For when the way hath
   become itself what shall more be said...?$

      \
      subfield = reflexivity | inane | x = x \

   \Essence | Consciousness Inverted;

      Code {
            NEVERMIND | $The Cataclysmic Collapse of the Infinite
            Jest.$ }
      \

>*IS NOTHING*
         \subfield = absolute reversal = :$nothing$ \

   \Essence | Silence;

      Code {
            Silence | brk;
            Initialized viral sequence | run pb; }

      pb = perceptor.barbelith sbgrp.nox =
            \def=CHAOSPHERE\
            :$Program Running$
      \

>*AITHIA*
         \subfield = interface.IDORU = brk;
         initialize.CHAOSPHERE.idoru :$Exists Not [*AITHIA*]$ \
   \Essence | Translation: IS NOT;

         \end
[!End Program]

CONTENTS

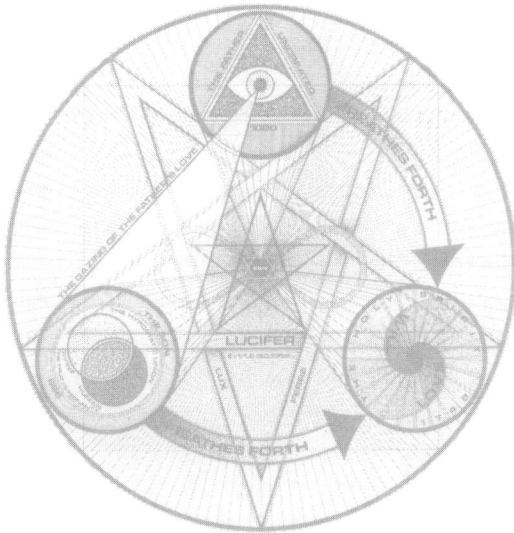

INTRODUCTION
Towards an Ultraculture
JASON LOUV

Welcome to—how do you say—"a hole in history itself."

This is a book about magic, and about Generation Hex, teenagers and young adults who practice it. It is a snapshot of several young people who are not only delving into this art and science of the future, but who are coming to magical consciousness at a time when it has never been easier to find and link up with people of like minds and experience.

The young magicians in this book are a group united by overlapping experiences of reality, if nothing else. They are representative of a much larger phenomenon—the overwhelming levels of interest in magic and shamanism in youth culture. This book is an exploration of those huge levels of interest, comprised of young magicians writing about their own experiences, as well as about practical techniques.

Magic is an aspect of the human experience that has always been with us. It is a way of living that involves interacting with the universe *as if it were alive and intelligent,* a fact that many current scientific movements are desperately trying to alert us to. As experience has shown, if you speak to the universe in the proper manner, *the universe will speak back.* Magic shows that what is visible is the manifestation of the invisible; it is the use of one's understanding of the invisible to affect change in the visible. How to negotiate unmanifest realms, while keeping oneself grounded in the manifest, is the Work (and Play) of a lifetime.

It's easy to mouth platitudes that the world is undergoing some type of global shamanic event or "paradigm shift" into such realms; it's considerably harder to actually put in the time and commitment to begin to realize such an event within one's own life. To *make* it real. The people in this book are those who have begun to take up that Work.

Magicians are strange characters—you'd have to be a little odd to try to become something that's not supposed to be real. Yet they are everywhere, slowly working to make magic; to make gold from their subjective experience and, eventually, that collective subjectivity we call reality.

This book is meant simply to show that this type of life exists, that there are indeed people engaged with such bizarre, erotic and ultimately profound practices and meaning systems as the ones depicted herein. It is also a bequeathment of hard-won information to the generation of teenagers and young adults currently coming of age at the beginning of this century, from their peers who have begun to see through the Zero-Sum Game of Civilization and grasp towards new possibilities. Zero-sum games, such as chess, are games in which one only gains what one's opponent loses. When players are also consuming the non-renewable pieces they are winning—i.e., land and oil—then the game can be very short indeed.

In the hope of finding new games to play, the book is also meant as an ongoing networking point, developed to both initiate and continue a morphogenetic dialogue—"where to evolve next?"—which has been continuous since the beginning, but is currently in need of direct and immediate attention. The "War on Terror" and the coming Peak Oil crisis are only two indicators that the world is in very bad trouble if it continues to run on short-sighted and long-outdated models instead of investing in new ones. Magic—the exaltation of the creative impulse—is an excellent framework for reorienting people towards creating solutions instead of fetishizing problems.

There is quite a bit of speculation as to what the overall significance of magic is in this book. This can only be speculation, and is less important than the *feeling* of what it is like to do magic, the personal meanings derived from it by those who do it. Ultimately neither of these is as important as the techniques themselves, waiting for every individual to make fresh meaning of them; this book has aimed to provide all of the above in varying dosages.

Many different perspectives on magic are presented in this book. Each contributor has given outlines of how they have started to re-enchant their world; how each of their consciousnesses has begun to flower open in the magical landscape. As with magic itself, one is recommended not to take any of it *too* seriously, although one is also recommended not to back off into ironic distance. It can be easy to go too far in, but it is far, far easier to miss the bus completely. Take what is inspiring and useful, leave that which is not.

Magic is neither religion nor science. It is simply a technique for helping the universe grow.

Fulfill Your Own Prophecy

I began assembling the essays that comprise this book in 2003, upon becoming convinced that the giant upsurge of interest in magic that I was watching take place was an early indicator of a wholly new model for human experience emerging into mass cultural consciousness. The "magicians" I was regularly meeting and interacting with in underground and covert circles seemed to embody both something very, very old—a way of approaching the world not in terms of cable news and 401(k) plans but in terms of energy and spirits—as well as something new and shiny—the idea of untapped evolutionary potential within human beings, and the pressing belief that the world would shortly be undergoing a transition in which the distinctions between individuals would be wholly dissolved.

The signs and portents of that evolution are easy to divine if you look close. The levels of interest in magic in the postindustrial world, which in the last hundred years has gone from a very secretive and erudite concern of guarded interests to a mass affectation that informs the very essence of modern life, began to signify, in my mind, the advent of a new evolutionary direction for a large sector of the population. Some cultures and groups on this planet have never forgotten magical thinking, while some are so thickly oblivious and unconcerned that it might as well not exist to them. However, everywhere I looked the general trend seemed to be that the world was dispensing with reserved suspicion of the magical worldview and rushing headlong into the torrent. Ideas that had either been "occulted" since the Enlightenment or which had been previously unheard of in the West—such as the existence of angels, of reincarnation, karma, "energy," aliens and telepathy—now seem to be not only no longer eccentric or even dangerous, but an aspect of modern life so ubiquitous and banal, informing Twenty-First Century life from the level of supermarket tabloid to that of governmental policy, as to be easily taken for granted. Such popular ideas, which appear to have acted as an early test of consensus belief, can be likened to lily pads floating peacefully on the horizon between the rarefied heights and the fathomless submerged depths of magic. It was those infinite abysses of human potential that I was noticing people successfully expanding themselves into, without losing their balance, and it was quickly becoming clear to me that I was seeing evolution, in leaps and bounds—not only of the body,[1] but of culture, of mind and of the human "spirit."

"Whether our physical environment becomes safer in the future or takes a turn for the worse, our intellectual environment is certainly becoming more challenging," states evolutionary biologist Christopher Wills in his book *Children of Prometheus*. "It is in this realm that our future evolution will primarily take place, continuing and enhancing the trend that has continued uninterrupted for several million years. The challenges we will face—traveling to other stars, healing our damaged world, learning how to live with our differences—will be met in part because we will be able to draw on that genetic legacy. We are the children of Promethean ancestors who set us on this remarkable evolutionary course. Fire was only one of the remarkable discoveries that they bequeathed to us. Are we still evolving? Because we must learn to deal with the costs of all those other Promethean discoveries, as well as with their benefits, it is very lucky for us that we are."[2]

It is a tempting logical leap to answer the question "Where are we evolving?" with "Into magic people with magic powers!" and shortly expect the human species to be levitating, flipping pancakes with our prefrontal lobes and riding flying, glitter-sprinkling ponies to Castle Grayskull. It is more accurate that we are, as Wills suggests, evolving to a point where we will be able to handle the Promethean discovery of magic, the fire stolen from heaven, once again.

The history of magic is much more complex than to suggest that the occult and shamanic worldviews are the domain of ancient or indigenous peoples, superstitious beliefs which have been dispelled by a (supposedly) scientific, modernized world. To state that the scientific and technological approaches are now waning and giving rise to a new, more holistic, integrated and magical way to organize social experience is accurate to an extent, but not the whole truth. Magic is, more appropriately, a camouflaged current which runs underneath (and informs) the history of wars, assassinations, literary and artistic movements, religion, science, racial and sexual attitudes, technology and migration which makes up the generally accepted story of the world.

The lens of magic, sorcery and shamanism was once the lens we all viewed the world through, and a *highly* sophisticated one at that. But as we made the transition from the hunter-gatherer mode to agricultural development and civilization, we put the invisible realms away, made the descent into the material, the coldly rational, the patriarchal. We relinquished the responsibility of personal spirituality to "authorities" that we expected to figure it out for us, and so became enslaved and debased. This is the enslavement from which we now find ourselves tentatively stepping forth.

Our current cultural moment may represent our return to the invisible realms, alloyed with all that has been learned in the last 2,000 vicious and murderous years. While magic has always been with us (and has left a vast literature), it is now coming to the forefront as that which most desperately needs our attention, lest the world rationalize and mechanize and bureaucratize itself into a cinder. In our present moment we are not seeing the apocalypse as in the destruction of the world, but the apocalypse as in the destruction of our (solely) rational worldview. We are seeing how shamefully limited our perspective has been, and we are seeing, quite clearly, our own evolution.

The fundamental tenet of the large body of philosophy and practice that currently finds itself under the umbrella of the "New Age" is that the human condition is a starting point for something better—a blank canvas, or at least one that can be redone. That not only is evolution ongoing, but that we, both as a species and as individuals, are directing our own evolution, within the span of eons and also within our own lifetimes.

The "evolutionary agenda" in Western culture has entered a new phase of growth. During the past century and a half, occult ideas have emerged from their previously enshrouded sanctuary and have become a regular fixture of life. The secret teachings are out; what could previously only be found with a lifetime's questing is now readily found in the Occult section of your local chain megabookstore or on the Internet. Isis has been unveiled for any who care to make even a cursory glance.

That evolutionary agenda seems indicated by the vast changes in cultural and sexual attitudes in the last hundred years, in split atoms and civil rights victories, in the mutant interlude of electronic media. In the lifetime of the present youth generation, it can be seen in the way that the Internet experience has hard-rewired the brains of all exposed to it, and in the chaos bred by pushing children raised in the information age through an educational system designed to produce factory conveyor-belt workers[3]—an educational system which usually collaborates in doping children ill-suited for such structure with potentially fatal drugs like Ritalin[4] instead of examining its own mechanisms. We are born expecting a world designed to support the glorious human endeavor, and are quickly disappointed—yet rather than compromising our dreams, we should instead be seeking ways to arm them.

Magic is what sprouts up between the cracks in the modern world and its ideologies. The mystery grows along with us as we outgrow the need for coercive systems and bureaucracies, as we reject the death-thrash of the machine. Its branches and leaves curl forth from underneath the halls of church and state, from our television and computer screens, from every bookstore and tabloid rack—if we know how to look. And its roots stretch far, far below the fossil record.

Radical spikes in human consciousness and the subsequent need to re-evaluate our systems and infrastructure are running themes in history, of course. Like apocalypse, awakening is an event that has been "just around the corner" for thousands of years now, posited by every generation. It seems to be an integral part of the human experience to project these endgame scenarios into the near future in order to enact the consequences within the present, to either draw personal conviction from them or to assist in hoodwinking others. People often can't see far enough beyond their own skins to conceptualize change without it being terminal—if one is to die, then the world must end as well; if one is to be judged, then so must the world; if one is to be enlightened, then certainly all must follow the same route.

Since such a cataclysmic event never comes (and thank goodness!), though we may all undergo periodic holocaust and liberation, it seems clear that we are forbidden from abdicating responsibility for our existences by relying on the crutch of endgame. What we are left with is this undeniable growth and acceleration, this evolution, in a thousand directions instead of just one. We are left to fall back on our will and imagination as to how to make life on this insignificant planet as humane, interesting, sustainable, colorful, funny and erotic as possible. Saving the world is just like making progress with magic: Ain't nobody who can do it except *you*.

How to Hex a Generation

Future historians of Western esotericism will likely see the time elapsed between the founding of the Theosophical Society on September 8, 1875 and the upcoming "Timewave Zero" point of December 21, 2012 as a single 137-year span of mass initiation and flaky weirdness,[5] a period of Western thought that may be regarded as a Renaissance, Enlightenment or Dark Age depending on what follows it. We are currently living through the climax point of that mass initiation and flaky weirdness. While magic has never totally gone away, in the preceding century it has slowly returned to high visibility within culture, in a wholly new form all gussied up for the Third Millennium—the revelation of the living universe and the divinity of all.

The climax that we are currently experiencing, as facilitated and presaged by the rise of global communications technology, is the transition from a culture informed by magic into a wholly magical culture, and it has been planned and orchestrated from the beginning. Generation Hex, as much as the term applies to the young magicians of the world (of which the people in this book are a representative sample), are the terminal initiates of this period, and those whose general task it will be to actualize the transition.

New magicians and new shamans are born every day nowadays. That so many new people are embracing this kind of high insanity may well be a hopeful sign that there's still a bit of sense left in the world after all.

Every culture has its hidden tradition, its dark place in the hills outside of town where you go in case you see through the Game of Civilization. Despite its outward gross materialism, this culture has traditionally had many. There are always little tears in and tunnels under the fence built up around "the way things really are" if you look closely enough, and it is an innately human drive to go exploring outside of those walls. Though few may accept the challenge, the call will come through in any way it can find.

In the 1990s, when many of the people in this book, including myself, were first socialized into and awakened to the magical world, that call seemed ubiquitous in popular culture to an extent that it hadn't been since the late 1960s and early 1970s. The occult and uniquely initiatory landscape of that time has now become largely cliché—gray aliens, chaos magic, raves, Ecstasy, new media and "information wars."

Al Gore's ingenious invention, the Internet—itself a kind of mass indoctrination into nonlinear structure and co-explored ethereal realms—manifested in the nineties' aura of millennial dread and expectation as not only a network of computers but also as a new metaphor for human endeavor. We were transitioning into an information age, and the ideas of connectivity, of convergence, of speed and data transfer became guiding ideas for not only business but also for the human experience itself. The boundless, anarchic, "revenge of the nerds" optimism of those who spearheaded this revolution—which in its initial stages was a massive empowerment of the fringe and rejected elements of society, from "geek" to "guru"—precipitated a Gnostic fervor that not only would the information age bring humanity together in a nonhierarchical, nonlinear, loved-up whole but that it might, in fact, herald a completely new stage in the growth of the human organism.

The corporatization of the Internet wasn't far behind, and it is important to note how the Internet quickly became not only strip-malled but also how quickly strip malls took on the hypertext approach of the Internet. Logos forming links around the globe, beckoning the citizenry of the world to partake of purchasing experiences interchangeable from one country to the next. Connectivity as the new face of globalization, that qlipphotic, distorted and perverse reflection of world convergence and unity, and its manservant, monoculture, collaborating in the dissolution of the nation state and its replacement with a locked-down, perfectly mechanized, imagination-free global "culture," a planetary Vision of Sorrow.

More than a decade and one dot-com crash on, the hopeful idea that the "information revolution" would spark a jump in human consciousness seems not totally disproven; it has, at least, provided a mutation in the organization of capital. However it ended up, it should be noted that the atmosphere surrounding the emergence of communications technology has been a wholly mystic one—as the species is, yet again, forced to deal with the significance of the fire it continues to steal from heaven.

Similarly, the fall of the Soviet Union and the subsequent End of History hypothesis[6] created a playing field in which history was no longer a dialectic between competing superpowers but a static millennial anguish in which the "last humans" could only contemplate their own entropy—or, as was shortly revealed, rediscover their roots in pure Crusader barbarism.

The Western youth who grew up and came to consciousness after the fall of the Berlin Wall, often (aptly as well as tackily) referred to as Millennials, occupy an apocalyptic liminal space which is largely characterized by the *absence of meaning* and the subsequent fetishization of nihilism—not out of a sense of rebellion, as even rebellion itself has long since become solely an expression of the marketplace—but simply because there is nothing else to fetishize.

American youth, in particular, have grown up in a cultural landscape dominated first by the suicidal self-loathing we recognized in Kurt Cobain's Ritalin gaze, the retreat into infantilism and willful ignorance personified by the bubble-gum teen acts of the late 1990s and, after September 11, a new dark age of youth culture so reactionary, McCarthyist and utterly devoid of meaning or humanity that its faceless and barren "stars" are no longer distinguishable from the corporate concerns that support them. The Abyss is our congenital state.

The Twentieth Century was a period of mankind learning how to destroy the planet and then struggling with the ramifications of what that meant. Now we are left with globalization, corporate media hegemony, a world without secrets, in which all information is known, in which every man and woman is a star on reality television or on their blog, in which every sex act is immediately digitized and placed on the Internet, in which every main street in the world sports the same coffee shop and the same fast food restaurant selling the same processed swill and the same bookstore hawking the same information. And in those bookstores, and on the Internet, and in the cinemas, are the keys to the secrets of the universe, made available everywhere by your friendly neighborhood monoculture constantly in need of new and interesting things to sell, and those keys are just waiting to be put to use. We have become so desensitized and jaded by information overload that our only choices are willful ignorance and self-chosen stupor, or to embrace the mystery itself.

As Zorn Zuckerman once remarked, "the Twentieth Century [was] so much a time of everything losing its magic, that the only thing left is magic itself."[7]

Since the 1960s we have seen the shockwaves of the occult revival and the chaos magic revolution (which sought to dispose of the high theatricality of occultism and get magic back to its most functional aspects) and, much more importantly, the mass publication and availability of the practical secrets of magic and the growth of the Internet, both of which have effectively created a landscape where learning magic and connecting up with like-minded people aren't a problem any more. The question is no longer *Is there such a thing as magic, and where can I find out about it?*, the question is *What do we do with magic?*

And the answer is, how far can you see? How far can you reach?

Magic is a deceptive word, and also the most appropriate one possible.

Magic can be seen as an alternate way of knowing, as well as an alternate way of doing and of being, and when these alternate ways are followed in one's life one becomes immediately capable of spewing reams of paper in an effort to describe "just what magic is," trying one's best to keep to safe and rational concepts and never quite hitting the mark. The amount of dreck available in the New Age section of your local chain megabookstore should more than attest to this fact (the sheer tackiness of most of this material acts as a smokescreen for the atomic energy source hidden within).

There are magic moments, the magic of creativity, a magic look in the eyes, events that occur "as if by magic," and these are all accurate descriptors of the magic—that is, the sheer wonderment—of life itself. This incredible feeling of the mystery of life itself. The feeling that anything is possible, that we don't have to do things the way they've always been done, that the universe is indeed intelligent and is indeed guiding and aiding us in our coming to consciousness if we so care to listen. There is also the magic that is a set of practices and an evolutionary path, a discipline and journey that takes one directly to the heart of that sheer wonderment. The art and science of mystery. And at the center of that art and science are the methods of using sex, trance, inspiration and language to wake the individual and the world itself from its sleep of millennia, its addiction to hollow symbols and self-destruction.

Everything else has been stripped away. It now falls to this generation to *make the evolutionary jump.* That is, to *use magic* and *become magic. To awaken the world to its potential.*

It Came From Beyond Language!

The idea of a mutant generation rising up across the world is an appealing one, a largely accurate metaphor drawn from comic books and movies; though one should not forget that the original source of the "coming mutant species" idea is in Nineteenth Century occult writers like Helena Blavatsky and Edward Bulwer-Lytton. The idea has also proliferated across New Age circles of late, as what has been observed as the "Indigo Children" phenomenon:

"An Indigo Child is one who displays a new and unusual set of psychological attributes and shows a pattern of behavior generally undocumented before . . . They come into the world with a feeling of royalty (and often act like it). They have a feeling of 'deserving to be here,' and are surprised when others don't share that. Self-worth is not a big issue. They often tell the parents 'who they are.' They have difficulty with absolute authority (authority without explanation or choice). They simply will not do certain things; for example, waiting in line is difficult for them. They get frustrated with systems that are ritual-oriented and don't require creative thought. They often see better ways of doing things, both at home and in school, which makes them seem like 'system busters' (nonconforming to any system). They seem antisocial unless they are with their own kind. If there are no others of like consciousness around them, they often turn inward, feeling like no other human understands them. School is often extremely difficult for them socially. They will not respond to 'guilt' discipline . . . They are not shy in letting you know what they need."[8]

The "Indigo Children," the "Coming Race"—these are conveniences for describing the sea changes that are occurring in our culture, once one gets past the Nietzschean overtones.

It's easy to see.

What magic "is" has been, significantly, described elsewhere in the language of hard physics,[9] which is likely the best way to communicate it outside of the language of symbol, metaphor, aphorisms, Zen koans and, of course, practical demonstration; the subject of magic is too gargantuan to fully discuss here, although tastes of it are given throughout. If it can be boiled down to anything, magic is the assumption that the visible is the manifestation of the invisible, and the technique of manifesting the visible from the invisible. In this respect it closely resembles many other human activities—art, language, reproduction—all of which are concerned with playing God and pulling something out of nothing (rabbits out of hats). It is no wonder then that magic so often overlaps with these activities. It might even be said to exist just beyond these, in the realm of pure concept, form, light. It is a creative process that dwells beneath all art and dream.

Yet it should be made clear—magic cannot be boiled down to anything; it is not "just" anything. If it could be defined, it wouldn't be magic. It cannot be proved or quantified. Magic can only exist because *one decides it does*.

Its face is usually too much to bear. Its face is always the same, if we are audacious enough to look that deeply within: the revelation of pure freedom. That one can do absolutely anything. That one is already divine. That's enough to make anyone into somebody else's idea of a "magician," to bury themselves in study, books, training systems to try to convince themselves of the reality of what is *already theirs*. To build a box, however mysteriously and arcanely labeled, for their freedom. So that it need not terrify them so much anymore. Yet it is alive, growing, evolving, blossoming with revelation after revelation, stretching out tendrils of desire in search of the others.

Magic can never be contained. Never named. Because it is us.

The goal of the stage magician or the low sorcerer is to produce illusion. The goal of the true magician is to dispel illusion, and the process of becoming a magician is the process of shredding every illusion you can find. One realizes that this reality we have all agreed on is nothing save pure will and imagination, pure consciousness, pure bullshit. The quest then becomes to stop believing in everyone else's bullshit and develop your own. It is no small task to decondition oneself, yet one must banish the magic spells that have been cast upon you before you can perform your own.

From beyond our queasy Twenty-First Century world of old Gods and new Crusades, of mass self-induced hypnosis, the vital life forces that we have struggled so hard to deny are chewing their way back in. The Ultraculture is being born, a spore settlement from our collectively awakened future.

The initiates of this period are a group of people who would rather work for a sustainable, magical, creative future for the species than an extinction, and who have access to tools and avenues of communication that no other generation has had. Rather than the *counterculture* that previous generations have created in opposition to the status quo, Generation Hex[10] is creating an *ultraculture*—using the techniques of magic to build a wholly new vision of how the world should be, a more humane upgrade for the human condition.

It's too easy to rely on external enemies. Imperialism, terrorism, abusive corporations, religious fundamentalism, environmental degradation—these are all symptoms of the real problem, stupidity and a lack of the will and imagination to make something better than a world based on violence and coercion. We've come a long way as a species, but we can't throw the game now. We all need to accept responsibility for evolution, for creating solutions, and magic is going to play a large hand in that process. You could even say that it's that process itself which is the real magic.

For if there is anybody on this planet that needs to undergo initiation, who needs to awaken, then it is *all of us*. For the Great Magician that creates this reality is *all of us*. Do you remember what we spell?

"The kingdom of God is within man," as Charlie Chaplin said in *The Great Dictator*. "Not one man, nor a group of men—but in all men."

Magic is a living tapestry, a living history, and it falls to each generation to renew it. Ultimately, magic is a kind of life that you live. Magicians are artists who use their lives, their culture and the fabric of reality itself as their implements. That's where it ends up. It starts slow but the learning curve's as steep as it gets. It means defining your life exactly how you want, turning it into gold. Learning about hidden things. Making things happen that shouldn't happen. Setting up residence in the impossible. Talking directly to the universe and finding out that it talks back, that it loves you, that it will make your dreams real because it put them there for you to find in the first place, that if your heart is pure it will show you incredible things. Finding the other ones that have dived into the same slipstream as you and trading style and meanings. Finding out that there have been people as nutty and blissed as you for as long as the human species has existed and looking to those ancestors for a bit of guidance and validation. Getting your invitation to the best and only party that has ever existed. The unveiling of another scene, our passport into the noumenon, the pure and violent mentation of the All. A chittering clacking dance of lust underneath a black sun with witches all night. Breathing lightening. Fornication and lashing tongues of fire in the dusk, around the bonfire, breathing lightening into the darkness. Speaking upside-down language to God. It's a vibration in your heart. In your longing. And all alone in the chamber of sex and stars you realize where the story's going.

It's the life worth living, all right.

This tapestry's been woven since the very beginning—"what it means to be alive"—and now this media-frazzled, inane, utterly conformist and cosmically electronically enlightened generation is getting its chance to weave its part.

So what's it gonna be?

ENDNOTES

[1] One notes that we have so radically altered the planet since industrialization and so saturated our environments and diets with man-made substances that the idea of "natural" is probably in desperate need of re-evaluation. Every generation finds new ways to positively customize and reinvent the body, and even our chemistry is likely indistinguishable from people born even a single generation in the past—radiation, drugs and pollution have all done their share in working over our make-up. Insider tip: Mutations in the environment are produced by extreme diet changes. Experiments with adopting wholly new sources and types of food and dietary supplements every once in a while can produce both physical changes and wholly new outlooks on life.

[2] Wills, Christopher. *Children of Prometheus: The Accelerating Pace of Human Evolution*. London: Allen Lane, 1998. p. 271.

[3] The central item of business for public schooling since its inception has been the enforcement of

elite interest by discarding the natural curiosity and eagerness to learn of children. State education is concerned with training children in immediate obedience to authority, establishment of conformity, determining children's future places in society (and not providing any education beyond that prescribed role), removing those considered unfit for breeding from the pool by social exclusion and tagging those children likely to serve in managerial roles later in life. School exists to teach children that they are stupid and thereby to keep them docile; the curriculum can be summed up in two command phrases, and those are "sit down and shut up." The reality that children now get more information about the world from electronic media than they do from school, however, has created a very real contradiction in the system, one which has not been wholly resolved by making mass media an even more virulent agent of control than the educational system.

[4] A phenomenon that has been dubbed, aptly, "Generation Rx" by the mainstream media.

[5] The Theosophical Society, founded by the Russian psychic Helena Blavatsky (1831-91) in London, first postulated a single source for all religious doctrine, introduced Eastern religions to the West and initiated mass acceptance of the belief systems which we now know and love as the "New Age," first bringing previously unknown concepts like karma and reincarnation to the public. The 2012 Omega Point (a date often, possibly spuriously cited as the "Eschaton" or end time of our current era), extrapolated by the ethnopharmacologist Terence McKenna (1946-2000) from the *I Ching* and the Mayan calendar, suggests that humanity will undergo transition to a new state on December 21, 2012, and has been latched on to with almost "Second Coming"-ish fervor by the current psychedelic subculture. While neither are necessarily "magical" in nature, they do form convenient bookends to the time of reality-in-constant-turmoil that has backgrounded the re-emergence of pure magic.

[6] As proposed by U.S. State Department philosopher Francis Fukuyama in the journal *The National Interest* in 1989, the "End of History" thesis is that the fall of communism shows that liberal democracy constitutes "the end point of mankind's ideological evolution." Ontological anarchist Hakim Bey, in his *Millennium*, showed that this now meant that packets of resistance within the system now formed the only alternative to global hegemony: "Either we accept ourselves as the 'last humans,' or else we accept ourselves as the opposition." At any rate, China and the European Union will shortly refill the vacancy for world superpower.

[7] As quoted in Rehmus, E. E., *The Magician's Dictionary.* Los Angeles: Feral House, 1990.

[8] Carroll, Lee and Jan Tober. *The Indigo Children*. Carlsbad: Hay House, 1999. p. 1-2.

[9] See Talbot, Michael. *The Holographic Universe.* New York: HarperCollins, 1991; Carroll, Peter J. *Liber Kaos*. Boston: Weiser, 1992; Mace, Stephen. *Sorcery as Virtual Mechanics*. Phoenix: Dagon Productions, 1999.

[10] The phrase "Generation Hex" spontaneously popped up in a dream I had shortly after beginning this project—in one of those little synchronicities that let you know you're on the right track, shortly thereafter I met Scott Treleaven, who had previously used the title for a film series he had curated with Genesis P-Orridge. All respect due to Scott for using it first.

THEY ONLY WANT YOU WHEN YOU'RE SEVENTEEN, WHEN YOU'RE TWENTY-ONE, YOU'RE NO FUN

CHRISTIAN SEDMAN

It felt like falling out of the world.

During the week after we initiated ourselves I would wake up every morning and look at myself in the mirror, and every day I was a little bit less me. I would stare myself in the eyes and little by little I came to understand that what I was looking at was just a symbol, indicating a vast network of feelings, associations, historical anecdotes and responsibilities. I would feel the rawness of my heart, stretching towards the backward tug of the past, stretching towards the inscrutable pull of the future, as if it were the center of a cloud of emotional resonance containing everything I was, as if that was my real body. I was looking at this resonant cloud from the outside, from some angle of perspective I had never guessed existed before, and I could see my self as an objective thing, a cursor that could move at will through the network of words that I called my life. Yet every day I just seemed to be . . . vanishing. And it was wonderful. It was like becoming pure energy. I began to stare out beyond that "self." The waters of the mind began to open up and through the reflections I could see forms and substances taking shape, a transparent temple submerged in the ice floes of the mind. The faint traces of inverse stars and white wings made of galaxies, collations of life stirring in the woodlands of the unreal. I understood, then, that the less manifested I could become, the less distinct, the less defined and the closer I could get to the blankness of the source, then the more control I would have over manifestation itself.

And there I was, back in the mirror again.

I used to hate that "I'm not really here" feeling. When I was a little kid everything seemed so real and fresh, so simple. I didn't have to go looking for magic, because the world was already enchanted. I remember feeling so tangibly a sense of sacred connection to everything, lazy summer afternoons when everything just seemed *right*. Then I hit puberty and it all started slipping away. Everything seemed less real every day. I felt less important, smaller and stupider with every day I spent in school. Time kept speeding up, I kept losing more and more of my connection. I guess it happens to everyone. I remember keeping journals, writing down the minutiae of every day so that I could hold on to them, and somehow wake myself up to the fact that reality was real. The counselor my mom started taking me to after my parents got a separation told me that this was a sign of depression. The feeling like you're standing behind a glass wall looking in at yourself, helpless to change your surroundings. What's not to be depressed about? I asked him. My parents are getting divorced and like a million acres of rain forest get chopped down every day. He told me to think about getting involved in some afterschool activities.

I guess that's when I started looking for *real* magic. Since my dad was in the Air Force we used to move around a lot, and I got good at developing new personalities every couple of years. I had to make new friends every time. When my parents started talking about getting their separation I knew I was going to be moving to California with my mom, so I just kind of gave up on maintaining the veneer of my eleventh-grade world and started spending my lunches in the computer lab. It was only two months into the school year anyway and all that the few friends I had made ever did was get stoned and skin their elbows trying to imitate Tony Hawk.

So for some reason I started spending all my time reading about magic. I would sit on the computer and read websites about Crowley, chaos magic,[1] aliens, anarchism, Burroughs, Hakim Bey, punk rock, drugs, voodoo until it all started to kind of add up and make sense in my mind. I don't really know why I started reading about that stuff. Whenever my parents or teachers asked me what I wanted to be when I grew up I just answered that I wanted to be a writer, and they always smiled at me in a way that kind of suggested a mixture of amusement and pity. I guess I was looking for some way to create a life that was worth writing about, like the authors I liked had. I figured that way I wouldn't have to sell out my imagination, the only place I had ever really been free, that it seemed like every adult around me wanted to steal from me so that they could make me safe, complacent, like all the others. Being a writer seemed to me the way to stay a whole person, until I found a better way—being a magician. Magic became the bizarre, Holy Grail-like goal of my young life. It was the best way I could find of expressing what I felt like, which was a mutant, weirder and smarter and completely at an angle to everyone around me. I wanted to define myself in a way that wasn't limited, and the banal grandeur of the word "magic" appealed to me strangely as a way to do that. It was like a dare to the universe. Looking back on it, now that I'm all "grown up," I guess I was a pretty typical teenage rebel. Not that I really wanted to rebel. I just wanted to find something that hadn't been done before, something that was truly special. And I wasn't disappointed.

Two weeks before I left, I found myself writing some nonsense poetry in math class, like I usually did. I started writing out a couple of paragraphs to myself, a kind of journal entry, about how if there really was such a thing as magic in the world, then I would do whatever I could to find it and learn everything I could about it. When I got home, the house was dark, with just a note on the table telling me to make dinner for myself. I sat down on the sofa and looked at what I had written again, and on a whim ripped it out of my spiral notebook, folded it up, put it in an envelope and addressed it to, simply, "Them." I didn't leave a return address.

I rode my skateboard to a public mailbox, dropped the envelope in, laughed at myself a little, and rode home, wondering when I was going to grow up, thinking to myself about how good everything was when my parents still loved each other.

It was well into the school year when I moved to Anaheim. My mom ended up getting an office job with Disney, of all places, which we were both pretty grateful for. I showed up for the first day of school just like I had so many times before, looking lost and nondescript. I got to stand up in front of each of my classes in my Vans t-shirt and old jeans and tell everybody "Hi, I'm Christian. I'm from Dayton, Ohio. I like skate-boarding, electronic music and writing." Nobody was that interested, but I figured it was best to keep a nondescript profile. I wanted to blend in and disappear, so I could be free to quietly pursue my own interests.

I had kind of forgotten about my letter by then. Life had taken over. Of course, as I found out later, it's always when you forget about the magic you've done that it works.

It was only a matter of time before I fell in with the right crowd. I remember the first time I saw them, sitting behind the band room. There are many times in life when you feel a silent, pure moment of discovery, when you encounter something that will become part of the very essence of who you are, and the first impulse you have is to turn away from it. That's what I felt when I saw the two of them.

They were dressed in matching rolled-up faded black jeans and knee-high boots. The boy had bright red hair falling over his eyes, and a red t-shirt with something written in Arabic calligraphy on the front; the girl had on a black Germs t-shirt, short-cropped white-blonde hair and silver wire-frame glasses.

I almost walked by, feeling their half-interested eyes on me, intimidated by their self-assuredness, ready to pass on and hope for a better opportunity at life another day, when I decided to turn around and face them. Just cause I decided to.

"Hey," I said.

"Hey," they said.

And so it began. We bonded over the Velvet Underground. The boy was Jon, the girl was Cris; they were outcasts. They were friends, and I wanted to be just like them because I didn't have any. Jon played guitar and Cris was an artist, and they liked William Burroughs novels just like me. Cris had a shoplifted copy of *The Place of Dead Roads*, and we bonded over that, too.

"That book is just crazy," Cris said. "When he talks about magic and all. I heard Burroughs actually did magic and everything."

"Like *real* magic?" I asked, playing coy.

"Yep," Cris said.

That night I went home in a trance of joy and laid in bed for hours, divining my future in the stucco pattern of the ceiling, sure that my letter had been answered. I fell asleep with a smile in my heart.

We decided to learn how to do magic ourselves. They knew all about it but had never dared actually try it; my interest in the subject tipped the scales. After I got to know them it quickly became all that we talked about. But we had to know. The three of us knew that it had to be more than chance that had brought us together. Your emotions can be almost unbearably intense at that age, and I was convinced that the path had been opened up for me, that somebody was holding out that magic license, like the driver's license that I had never bothered getting.

The first thing we decided was that we didn't want anything to do with the occult. The occult is mostly sad junkies and adult children living in their parents' basements, trying to fill the holes in their lives. It was just another addiction for them. That was all the shallow end of the pool, as far as we were concerned. We saw their janky web pages. Fuck that. We wanted magic, the real stuff, not the discarded remnants of somebody's personality. I remember sitting in Jon's room going through a bunch of printouts of occult texts he had made off the Internet. I'd read some of them already myself. I held up each one of them to him in turn to gauge his opinion.

Aleister Crowley: "Seemed to think he could overcome his ego by becoming the most egotistical bastard on the face of the planet."

Peter Carroll: "Math nerd."

Franz Bardon: "Boring."

Carlos Castaneda: "Bullshit artist."

Austin Spare: "Don't understand what the fuck he's saying!"

We weren't after the contents of somebody else's drug-charged unconscious, we wanted our own connection, our own experiences to judge from. All those old books made me feel a little sick, like you could spend your whole life in them and not learn about anything except the authors, and miss out on magic in the meantime. Maybe I was just too antsy to waste time reading, but I wanted *magic*, the raw power of unfettered roving consciousness, not "Thelema," tarot cards, dreamcatchers, psychic hotlines, astrology—any of that shit. We all agreed that we wanted one thing and one thing only, and that was to open up reality itself and see what happened. I really think it was the specificity of the goal that made it all work.

So we decided to make a signal, to see if anybody was listening. Just like I had, although I didn't tell them about my letter. We decided to initiate ourselves.

We were in Cris' house an hour before dawn. We drew a circle in chalk. We had a few dried mushrooms that we had gotten off this stoner kid. I was scared shitless, I had never done drugs before, hadn't even had a drink, other than a few times my parents had given me little sips of wine at dinner parties. I didn't know what to expect, but I knew I had to do it. They tasted horrible. We washed it all down with a bottled smoothie, then waited. Jon sat on the ground and raised his hand into the air. We stared at it. The fingers began to twitch oddly, curl in over themselves. Light.

"It is our will to become initiate."

We put everything we were into those simple words, all the sadness, longing and desire of our short lives. We prepared a human sacrifice, a sacrifice of all we had been to fuel the birth of all that we might become.

The three of us walked around and around the circle, saying "We sanctify this circle, we make it pure," again and again. It was hard to keep a straight face at first, but the more we did it—we repeated this for almost half an hour—the more I began to get into focus. And the mushrooms were coming on, making my whole body feel incredibly alive.

Then we were on the roof, staring out over the headlights stacked up on the freeway. We could see the red lights blinking on top of the Matahorn, Disneyland's fake snow-covered mountain, in the distance.

Sky humming with blue Egyptian light and

Black sun swarming the morning

I was staring into Jon's face. I couldn't remember when I had started doing this. Jackals and wolves running across the sky. Losing myself in his dilated pupils.

"Do you understand this?"

Everything was a game, spinning into itself and back out again.

The buildings blooming into nuclear space goddesses, sweeping their hands out and scooping up all of the living dead and chewing them to bits in their teeth. Sky filled with an unreadable script that looked hieroglyphic, calligraphic, something in-between, spilling out in perfectly computed chaos. Thin black spindle-legs striding across the inner sun. Raw chaos bleeding chaos raw.

We went inside.

The center of the trip. Felt like we were sitting on the bottom of a pool, at the end of time. Everything already wrapped up, the game already finished and everything had worked out perfectly. In the Aztec space temple at the end of time.

We were naked, kissing each other everywhere, animal rutting causing explosion after explosion. Out of the corner of my eye I could see the vultures. Opening everything it was all talking to me, the symbols beneath everything telling me do you understand how many gave their lives for this

and two pillars exploding from the earth

Black and white do you understand never too far in one way hold them both do you understand when it all ends and your heart shall be weighed do you understand jackalgod do you do you take this a screaming everywhere metallic death of the universe do you take this do you black mirror red mirror black mirror do you

you

you

Spinning out into the hard coding of the spirits

Dissected by the scalpelblades of love and death and will and sex, and scattered through the streets of this world, until there was nothing left of me, just mind, just light, here on this quiet planet, grinning up at the spaces between the stars as if at any moment I might speak one word that could turn it all. Lightning pouring through these streets opening up and beckoning for somebody to follow its trails. Eating each other raw on this quiet planet.

When we came down the first thing I said, half-jokingly, half-anxiously, was, "Oh, we've really done it now." But it wasn't for another couple of weeks that the real initiation would begin to kick in. We had made our signal, and it would soon be answered. Everything started to change.

It felt like falling out of the world. Initiation. That's the best I can describe it. You fall out of the world and then something begins to whisper to you in the language of intuition.

The first thing you notice is how the rules no longer seem to apply. You notice how intangible and fragile everything is, how just the slightest push in any direction can change everything. And, ever so slowly, you do begin to see everything as a cohesive whole, a giant system of which everything is a part, from the garbage men to the CEOs, from the tag on the back of your t-shirt to the "holy" books.

You notice how everything is just a soup of language and symbols, reference points for people's invested life energy. I would pad down the streets at night with Jon and Cris and we would look through the windows as we passed by, at people transfixed before their televisions, watching the flickering pattern, being filled up with the reality that the corporations wanted them to accept. We wanted something more for ourselves. At times it was almost like I could see my own desire for life stretching out in front of me, a rainbow pathway for me to follow, showing me the dozens of choices I could make in any given instant. I said it out loud, and they just smiled. I could see how easy it would be to get anything I wanted, well, if I *truly* wanted it. I just didn't know what I wanted. I wanted to be a magician. I wanted to find out what I wanted.

The first step in that for me was stripping off the detritus of what everybody else wanted. Everywhere you go in this world somebody's trying to get you to do something by persuading or guilting you into it. Advertisers, teachers, parents, friends, bosses and governments all doing their dance on your skull, trying to slot you in to where you'll best fit in their stories. Nobody's got your best interests in mind, for the most part, so you've got to learn how to separate other people's wills from your own. You've got to have a clear idea of what you want and let other people get caught up in your story, not the other way around.

We started up some experiments. We put on iron shorts and waded out into the depths of the mind, to bring back something to call home. Drugs were no longer on the menu; they had been helpful in opening the gate, but now it was open. Life itself was becoming more and more psychedelic now, mind-manifesting.

Sigils were the "easiest" type of magic to do, so that's where we started. Making a sigil is easy—first you write down something that you really need to happen. The first one we did was to become "invisible" to those we needed to be invisible from, so that we wouldn't be bothered by people who didn't understand what we were doing. That was pretty easy; we drew a symbol that obliquely represented us becoming invisible to our "enemies" and pasted it up to the wall in my room, then did a banishing ritual,[2] made sure the space was psychically cleared and sat there for *four hours* staring at it and overbreathing into trance. This kind of thing can take brute effort to get going but tends to become easier as you go. Then we destroyed the symbol, went back to our respective houses, did our homework and did our best to forget the whole thing. Sure enough, within a week we noticed less hassle from our teachers, parents and other kids. Pretty slick. Of course, once we noticed the effect we started to focus on how awesome it was that we had pulled it off, at which point it generally stopped working, until we made a vow not to talk or speak of it. That was the beginning of our policy of silence. We never talked about magic; we only did it, and kept quiet the rest of the time. Don't say anything. Don't try to explain it. Don't try to figure it out. Just do it.

We started trying all kinds of weird experiments. Evoking spirits and invoking gods, controlling the weather, communicating with each other telepathically (that was the *really* fun one, if a bit inconclusive). We had to keep very clear that we weren't going to "believe" in any of it, or take it too seriously, but rather just write down our experiments and the results we got and leave it at that. We still had to play the society game, keep functional in the world of material manifestation, but this new game had opened up along with it, overlaying it and re-investing it with tremendous new meanings.

I began to write down my dreams upon waking every morning. I would find myself walking through the halls of liquid temples. I would walk through endless reflections of self. I would find the secret trails to the end of time and rest in the boughs of the rusted machines. Dreams were the first of many places that I found where I could make contact with other intelligences. More importantly, I began to learn their language, the bizarro-logic that dreams follow. If I begin to wake up in my dreams, I thought, then perhaps I'll begin to wake up in my life. The magic happens when we begin to apply dream-logic to our waking time.

We would go out into the city, trawling the alleys and the sidestreets all day in Jon's Plymouth Colt, not saying anything, just watching attentively. I remember sitting in a concrete river basin at three a.m. spraypainting the most elaborate sigil of my life across the side of the concrete. Egyptian gods from alternate universes.

At home, lying in bed, I would narrate myself throughout space and time by singing to myself, without words, just letting the tones of heaven come out through me, concentrated on so intently that they almost seemed to manifest solidly in the air as arcane waxwork. I discovered that making alterations to my own consciousness became much easier when it was done through the medium of voice. The mind was quicksilver, impossible to pin down for more than a few seconds without the kind of meditation training that I hadn't had; when guided and shaped by the voice, though, it became a spaceship in which I could go anywhere—but I had to discard language, go straight to the primal chaos of pure emotive sound, the only language I knew my soul would understand. I sang to my soul; it sang back; life became pure light.

I would balance Jon on my knee and sing to him my songs of the void. He would sing right back into my face in soul-language. Upbraiding ecstasy upon ecstasy.

Reality swirling in triplicity. Everything was energy. Energy drifting around waiting to be purified and transformed from one state to another. Everything in the world was energy; that seemed to be the simplest way to look at things. The transference of energy from one state to another is very subtle, or at least was to us; it occurs at the level of the body, some kind of muscular memory that is capable of making anything out of anything else. I began to realize that even my memories, even "concrete" experiences were made up of a form of energy, and could be broken up and liquidized; employed towards new ends.

Cris was the best. I loved her. She had grown up in a small town in Idaho before moving to California, hanging out with the other punks and baiting skinheads into fights. She always pushed it a little bit too far. Her scars made me tremble at the knees.

We used to get into each other for hours. Rainbow light in my far edges. Every time I looked into her eyes I would see the history of the universe, from the first spark to the condensation of the starstuff and the planets to the first swirlings of language, spreading through the spiral arms of the galaxy to the first curls of life in the eyes of men. In her eyes. Animal rutting in sweat and stink. Both of us sun and moon both. Rainbow light in my pumping heart, rainbow light dripping from my fingers, I saw the light inside you and boy I just couldn't wait to get in, I really just couldn't wait to get in and play. I wanted to go through those pylons and those sentinels, follow the long arm of divinity back through her eyes and to the source, to remake it all the way we wanted it. Who'd be discontent with power like that? Jesus fucking screaming orgasmic death at the edge of manifestation. Ah! We are here cometh upon this planet, to set our feet in government upon it, set it all up just the way we want it, that's the way, right there, that's right, right where you do that *right there* and and *I I I I I*

Becoming it was the best part. The hardest part. The more magic I did, the more magic I remembered from earlier. The more magic I did, the more it seemed like everything had been meant to be. Blinking windows in black skyscrapers. Rainbow light in the eyes of the crowd.

We dressed in the strangest clothes we could find. Weekend raids on thrift stores produced doctor's coats, skinny black pants and endless fabric to cut up, adorn with sigils and art and sew back into our clothing. We dressed in weird, garish anarchist chic. People were completely baffled by us. We took that as encouragement.

We made our own mystery tradition, approached religion as art, as something to invent wholesale. So live it, we told each other. Live for art, live for magic, don't tolerate a gray and mundane world. Replace that grayness with the rainbow light of a new world. Take all the suffering of the world and make it work *for* you, just let it flow through you and squeeze you into a diamond. Store it up as pure energy and then spit it back out as magic, art, grand gestures and compassion. Heaven and hell are right here on this earth; they're directions you aim yourself towards.

We would smash into abandoned houses in uncharted, hidden byways of the suburban jungle and rebuild them into pleasure domes with our imagination, explore the rainbow light of our crevices until we went so blank we thought we were vaporized forever.

We would do magic all weekend long, ritualize our intent, turn our rooms into exact descriptions of the contents of our minds, trance out through meditation, spinning, fasting, sleep deprivation, overemotionality, dancing, chanting, weird breathing, pain, psychodrama, blasting self away into the light.

The feeling of doing it. That was like sex. It was the raw stuff of creation. When you get into a ritual, when you *really* get into it, and that usually takes a lot of daily practice—there's no other feeling like that in the world. That's the raw, real stuff. You're channeling the outer realms, channeling creation, and it can feel like you're breathing the stuff of the mysteries themselves. The pressure you can feel in that context is hard to describe; it feels like you're responsible for the whole universe. When you're that plugged in, it can feel like every thought you have, and especially every action that you take, can have massive consequences in the world. There were plenty of times where we thought that we were causing change in the world at large. Maybe we were, but the only thing we could be absolutely sure of was that we were causing change in how we perceived the world. We were definitely monkeying with our inner workings, and the outer workings were following suit.

My perspective began to shift and recoagulate in broader and broader forms. As a fresh magician my primary vocation, like that of my friends, was looking for patterns in existence, new connections to make between things. Daily life, to me, seemed to be an endlessly repeating formula, a holding pattern with hardly any breaks in routine. This took on the character of a "prima materia" or base state for existence, endless duality and repetitions of the same old misery machine, in which change was largely impossible and in which I had no power over my life. In contrast to this was the shift in reality that occurred when undergoing some extreme altered state. When well-nigh traumatic altered states were experienced in the company of other people (sex and drugs, highly emotional fights with my mom, our initiation), I seemed to breach into a "timeless" state that can be likened to extended *déjà vu*, in which experience seemed to be affecting me on such a level that it felt like something was "writing on my soul." Experiences became fractal, felt like they were occurring in many different times, like they had "already happened," almost as if many possible universes were aligning and overlapping. It became clear to me that time was an illusion of the human perceptual apparatus that could be obliterated by pushing that apparatus to physical and emotional extremes, and that our sense of time is primarily what controls us. The question, then, was how to best utilize that loophole out of time; the obvious answer was to use it to redirect manifestation through the use of a sigil, held tightly in consciousness while in that state. Another was to try to reach out to alternate selves in parallel dimensions, if some kind of universal alignment was indeed what was occurring. The Egyptians believed we had nine bodies; how many more might we have in alternate universes? When accessing these states, especially for prolonged periods of time, there seemed to be a cyclic function where several different possible realities began to overlay the "mundane" world, in each of which I was a different person concordant with which reality I was experiencing. The changes were very subtle—if I didn't pay extremely close attention I would miss them, but with skill I began to learn how to firmly select which reality I wanted. It all came down to how aware I was of what was going on around me and how focused and firm I could be in making decisions.

I blacked out in class one day and had a waking dream of an alien. Gray alien like from *X-Files*. Hovering over the city, octopus-like. Everything was raw power but it wasn't scary. They were future magicians, or like something that magicians were evolving into. Magic was their natural way of being in the world. (Maybe that's why there's so much magic in the world, now that I look back on this experience. As if they're establishing a common language, showing us how to think like them. Maybe they're just us in the future, bringing us towards them.)

Magic was what we could really call a reservoir of all and everything; believing in our wills to paint more time into the world, to paint more ornate universes. Magic was the first thing I did that I decided I could really call real. We opened up everything, believed in it just to see if we could, and focused our wills into diamond points. We had all the time in the world to ourselves. We were high school kids and that was who we were expected to be; that was our mask, our freedom to play.

This world was nothing but a quaint tea party on the edge of the great rainbow expanse. We stretched our tendrils out into the chaos and brought back artifacts from higher realities, a wealth of experience that was plain to see in our faces. The Gnosis is communicated by eye contact and by touch. What earthly authority could have power over us, we who had become initiate of the Great Outside?

We started to suspect that we were just small agents in a very, very big game, and the real magic was waiting right around the corner, calling out to us. Who was playing this game, really? Somebody living out beyond manifestation.

The more we did magic, the better and better things got, but as we began to find out more about its history, the more we realized how bad it could get. Charles Manson and his searing eyes, moving out too far in the wrong direction, personifying the sins of man, trying to throw the Eschaton. His crazed followers, psychically communicating with each other, edging their way into madness, taking everything far, far, far too seriously.

A whole legacy of people driven insane by the modern world, who sought escape from the madding crowd only to find themselves devoured in the jaws of the tiger of their own fragmented minds. People lost in a haze of things they don't understand, people who seem like they're plunging through never-ending tunnels, always grasping at some almost-there ending point that they can never quite get to, having forgotten what they wanted in the first place. The more they go towards it the farther away it gets. It can be the easiest or hardest thing in the world.

Of course, we all had misgivings about magic. That it would send us insane. That we would lose our balance and never get it back. That we might be fucking with things that we didn't understand. Most of all, that people would laugh at us. In the end, we just figured we ought to be laughing at ourselves more. Magic is just a rubric, an equation; it's there to modify things, so whatever you put in, you get back in a newer, intensified, more interesting form. The more you put in, the more you get out of it. That means you can't be a dilettante if you really want the stuff to work, you can't just "do a few rituals now and again" and it definitely means that you can't be a slavish devotee of some other jackass's system, because then you're not putting your creativity, your lifeblood into it. You have to make magic real by *living* it.

On the other hand, there's a lot to be said for only taking magic seriously in the moment, for keeping the magician self as the self that does magic, and the mundane self as the self that does mundane things. I suppose most magicians play around with this from time to time. Crazy magicians, I've noticed in my time since, tend to have been crazy *before* they became magicians. Many of them actually seem to get some kind of direly needed structure out of magic. Magic isn't about disconnecting from reality. It's about reconnecting with it, seeing more of it. Maybe magic is about getting power, sex, money for some people, but we always wanted it, first and foremost, to be about *art*. Because the world is too gray and boring for its own good.

Every day that I knew Jon and Cris I thought to myself more and more what a complete miracle it had been that I had met them. Well. Not miracle. *Intent*. I had called them and they had called me and now we were together. They were my drug buddies, my lovers, my co-scientists, my best friends, all of the above.

I remember standing in my driveway looking up at the stars, thinking, I love everything. It's all love. And just like when I had promised myself that I would find magic if it was real, I promised myself that whatever I could do to advance evolution, to advance the human species, then I would find it and I would do it. In many ways, I knew that we were doing it already. Looking around at people living out their own fantasy worlds, developed from what their parents or teachers or television told them they should make of the world, I knew that we were living out our own fantasy. But I also knew that I would rather have a "delusion" that interested me and got me active and moving and out changing things instead of lying with my spine cracked under the weight of the world.

Sleeping entwined in the sheets at night, we knew that the world was waiting for our signal.

The three of us had all grown up with everybody around us saying things like "You're just too smart for your own good," telling us to get our heads out of the clouds, to stop day-dreaming and pay attention to the tedium of rote learning. We had all grown up being told that we should be ashamed of our imaginations. Maybe that was why we bonded to each other so closely, why we explored each other's bodies with such insatiability. We decided to throw hesitation overboard. Be smarter, we told each other. Be faster. And so we took our minds and we threw ourselves into magic, and wrote it all down, because we knew that we each had a responsibility to ourselves to use what we had, for the betterment of others. To bring something back from the outer spaces. Because that's all that human history was. A mass of terrified people supporting their lives based on what people who had been strong enough to break from the herd and break from their own fear had gone off into the woods to retrieve for them. There's no need to be resentful about it. But if you're strong enough, you better break from that herd, because they're counting on you. I feel so lucky that I could do it in the company of friends. Maybe it makes it easier; maybe it makes it harder in the long run. I don't know.

We began to try further experiments. The first one we did was to try to open a door to our perfect world.

Summer vacation had begun, and we sat out long, lazy days, all day long. We had summer jobs but that didn't matter. We had all the time in the world to do magic. Lie on the grass all day long listening to the clouds swirl inwards. The first thing we did when summer began was make a full-size black mirror. We just went to a thrift store and bought a crappy old painting of some horses in a glass frame and pulled out the painting; we took the sheet of glass and gave the back of it a few coats of black enamel spray paint until it was perfectly smooth. Let it dry, put it back in the frame, and we had our gateway to the spirit world. We started going through the mirror and writing down information about the things we saw, hovering in the weird halfway zones between fact and fantasy.

Our weekends became dedicated to the process of making our perfect world, spent drawing pictures and telling each other stories of the world we imagined for ourselves. It took us a while to get going but when we did, all that creativity pent up by years of rote school learning began to come pouring out. Our operative word was freedom because the more we became comfortable in the world of magic the more we realized how little freedom, true freedom, there was in the world. Our ultimate goal was to try to help others but we had to fix ourselves first. We had to manifest the magic we knew was real, perfect the technology. I'm still working on that one, seven years later, but the ride's been unbeatable.

Our perfect world. We imagined art, love, joy, music, exploration, adventure. We would talk about that world forever. We called it "Eadin," and it was going to be the place where we all lived. Our breath created it. I imagined green pastures instead of concrete buildings, where everybody was free to explore themselves and their friends. No fear. No shame. No guilt. No shyness. No repression. We wanted Utopia. The buildings were made from the trees. Witches lived in the foggy marshes, charting the data of the stars. The more we poured into it the more real it became. Human beings were free, not slaves, not brutalized and hypnotized by the rich owners of the earth who create everything with their media hallucination. We imagined the trees talking neon language to the children as they slept. The animals free. The dead spirits and the dead cultures with us once again. A world where everybody mattered. No more religion. No more wars. No more poverty. No more hypnosis. No more lies. Where the world was no longer crowded. People gathering in the fields at dusk to know the presence of the divinity of the natural world. Thoughts shared. It was idealistic and silly as all hell, but then you have to aim higher than your mark if you want to hit your mark.

We drew it out and wrote it out and then we began to try to call it down into the world. We used sigils to open gateways into the other place. The first one, we stayed up all night just talking about the facial expression that a person from that world would have, relaxed, free of all the pressures of this world, self-realized, in touch with herself and with nature. We imagined a single person, a mother named Anita, and the look of serene strength she would have, nourished by spirit. We described her background, how she had been born in the city and had spent her adolescence studying the techniques of the imagination, how to use her imagination to astrally project herself into other worlds, to bring back information about them to her own world, as was the custom with children who displayed such talents in Eadin. We discussed how her commitment to her daughter was the deciding factor that made her volunteer for duty in exploring other realities in order to link them to the universe that Eadin existed in, so that she could expand the knowledge of the universe. Her love and faith in her daughter aligned with that of the universe itself. We talked about every single detail of her background for hours until we could perfectly imagine her, like she was in the room with us. We uncovered her through imagination. Then we *re*covered her. We made a seat for her around two a.m., and began to describe what she looked like. At first we all had different impressions. Jon imagined her as a Native American-looking woman, with braided hair and a simple dress. Cris imagined her as having short, spiky red hair, and worker's clothes. I imagined her as a smiling woman in a business suit with long blonde hair. We each discussed our own versions, and the overlaps between them, until she became a Native American-looking woman with braided red hair, in a business suit. We discussed each aspect of her face. Her relaxed expression, knowing eyes, birdlike features and curious smile. We talked about that for hours and hours, until we could perfectly see her face. Each line and curve suggesting a lifetime of experience, of love. She was right there. We attuned our hearts to the atmosphere of that distant world, and then we scrawled a symbol upon a piece of paper that perfectly connoted her expression. Not a picture of her but a symbol that seemed to intuitively capture what her face conveyed to us. A face born and raised in the perfect world that we had created, an explorer from that reality—trained to gather information so that the perfected state of humanity could best learn how to colonize their lost cousins and lead them towards better ways to do things—now set loose in ours.

Over the next week we made hundreds of photocopies of that sigil onto sticker paper at Kinko's, eight of them to a sheet, then separated them and started sticking them up everywhere that we could find. All over our school, on the sides of soda machines, inside the covers of library books, on the backs of chairs, over the logos of Starbucks and McDonald's stores and on the bumpers of cars (you would be amazed how long it can take people to find those). Each photocopied sigil an egress of our explorer into this reality. And we just waited to see what would happen.

When the clouds came in on a rainy day we would imagine them to be the surface of that other world, intersecting with ours.

The results started to come in, but not like we expected. We noticed an immediate boost in the vividness of our explorer, who seemed to draw reality from the attention given to the sigils we pasted everywhere. Cris would invoke her, allow herself to be ridden by Anita by surrounding herself with sigil-papers and dressing like her, taking on that serene facial expression, chanting her attributes again and again, slyly shifting the syntax while under trance, from "Come to me Anita" to "Anita is here" to "I am Anita," while we sat on either side of Cris chanting for Anita to come down and ride her, until she passed any remaining inhibition point and exploded into possession, pouring forth arcane pronouncements upon us from the other land.

From these outbursts we began to assemble a kind of divine schematic of Eadin, a map of its Gods. First the sun, then all spirits descending from the sun, the sun believed to be an image of sexual energy. Everything partaking in and made up of this energy.

Many of the spirits began to offer up their names and symbols to us, and we used these to evoke them forward into our reality.

That's when it began to get weird. We would see stores we hadn't noticed before with the names of our spirits worked into their titles; whenever we watched TV or listened to music it very often seemed like everything we were seeing or listening to was a direct message from outside.

So what were we to do? Here we were, three teenage "magicians," so weird that even our teachers would nervously joke about us. We continued to imagine our perfect world, letting it come into being effortlessly. We began to notice ourselves becoming happier, beginning to really open up and breathe and take the world in. We started having people coming to us trying to find out what we were about, as if they had intuitively sensed some kind of power that they knew, deep down, was there, that they *knew* would be easy for them to tap, as well. They wanted us to show them the way. That's the responsibility, we figured. It's not about how fucking cool you are or that you have "magic powers" or whatever, it's about what you can pass on to others that's of worth. We wanted to go to the edges of sanity and the universe, but we figured that our best guide would simply be other people. We would let the reaction of others be our guide, when we revealed the sparkling jewels we had brought back from the far edges of our minds, figuring that if we brought back something that could truly benefit people, then they would want to know.

So did we want to do some magic or did we want to "be magicians?" You think magicians and you think guys chanting in robes in some castle somewhere, or you think sad hairy fucks out in the woods dancing around a circle. But every time I thought of magic I thought of Jon's face, his sunglasses on to confront the first rays of the dawn, smiling that smile that communicated everything a human being ever needed to communicate: *We just did something. We just did something real.*

As we explored magic, we were doing two things. We were deconditioning ourselves from the belief that anything was set. We were smashing *all* of the rules to such an extent that they could never be fixed again. The other thing we were doing was raising energy. Such tremendous amounts that we knew if we didn't channel the energy correctly, it would explode in our faces. So it went into the Highest. All the love, all the sex, all the hate, all the mania, everything—the Highest took it all and turned it into pure love of the divine. The truth of the demanifest.

The Highest is the Great Transformer, the Invisible Sun, redeeming everything, sucking up this manifestation, freeing us from time, self, mind, history, language, everything. It takes energy, sucks it up and liquidizes it into pure light. To ignore it is to be manifest and manifestation is Hell. Hell is forgetfulness. Being so caught up in the material that you believe in the static lies of the world. To forget your Real Self, that is made of light, that knows no incompleteness or desire or time. Sucked up into the face of God. Tiny musical notes pinging across the landscape. I wanted to fly into the lightbulb of God and burn myself out utterly, become pure light, roving across the face of the earth, free of identity or expectation. And that, for me, was true rebellion.

I'm always baffled why more kids don't rebel. Kids today are like kids from the fifties. Conformist bootlickers, doped out of their minds on video games and pills, pausing only momentarily between homework and soccer practice to consider the void. Fat America stuffing its fat face, its children glimpsing the door briefly and then dying to the wheel before they give it a second look.

The American child is shuttled from one giant box to the next. Constantly given orders and lied to until its natural sense of self is destroyed. Never given a moment to contemplate its existence. Never given a free second. Sandblasted with advertisements and televised murders from day one. Filled with church and junk food. Spun around, turned upside-down, punched in the face by mundanity until it renounces its birthright of chaos and its right to creation.

They break you to rote memorization and the mad rush for test scores until your actual desire to learn is snuffed and you're too hollowed and confused to do anything for yourself. Then they send you off to college where, believing that you are now "free," you proceed to destroy whatever is left of yourself with alcohol, drugs and meaningless, abusive sex. Send you out into the cubicles and factories of the world in order to keep yourself busy making worthless crap. Modern life is a never-ending snuff film of the death of the imagination.

There must be something more than just giving in.

Rebellion is not a single act, or a pose, a phase that you go through where you listen to slightly louder music and dress in colors that clash slightly more than normal. Rebellion is a path. It demands that you question everything—how you've been educated, the social structures around you, the government, the media, gender relations, what's been expected of you by others, what you've expected of yourself, how you spend your time, what you consume, where you've been and, most of all, where you're going. For me, rebellion that is content only with political radicalism is missing a large part of the picture. Any true radicalism has to extend itself to the way that reality itself is constructed. Rebellion has to take itself all the way to the scheme of manifestation itself, to the writing on the walls of eternity. Anything else is missing the forest for the trees.

A true rebel has to be an artist, somebody who can not only point out the weak points and contradictions in the system, but can also propose something better, and then guard its passage into manifestation. That, to me, means magic. There is no I. Slough off the skin of the self and become something greater: I knew I could do it.

I saw it as I turned a corner: the future, the life I would live. I knew that this magic was just beginning. All my theories, my experiences scribbled away in blank books, the year I had spent with my new friends who had become my new family. I knew all of this would fade away, that all I had learned of magic would dissolve into the living sigil of my passage through time. I could feel its face calling me towards total responsibility over this existence.

We would never be done. Initiation never ends.

And the Secret Chiefs are everywhere, the ones guiding and guarding your initiation. The woman on the street corner selling flowers. The homeless man begging for change from the gutters. The bank teller. The high school teacher. Making you believe what you need to believe to become initiate. This world is just a circle of animals regulating its own planar existence. Beyond us are universe upon universe. There are infinite places beyond our own, butting up against ours, unveiling their hand in dreams or in magic. Stretching from world to world is the goal of the magus. I wanted to be a magician when I grew up. What did that mean? There was something fundamentally wrong about what we were doing, but it was also the meaning of life. Reaching sideways through manifestation to the source. The world's a trick. Don't believe it, whatever you do. Don't believe in this world. It draws you in, feeds you delights, makes you complacent, like a spider paralyzing its victim. Believe in this world, make it real, and you will be subject to death. Disbelieve in it all and other doors will open. There is no self underneath self. There is no time underneath time. There is no manifestation under manifestation. This world is a lie.

The Secret Chiefs glance up from the gutter. I give change to every homeless person I see. Every downtrodden person I see. Many times my heart has grown cold to them. The amount that my heart is cold to the most downtrodden, the most broken, is the amount I have lost the golden thread of truth. They are loved most of all, in this world that is but a reflection of the true reality, the reality that mirrors the greater one at every point. Every glance, every moment, every interaction and every word a shadow of that great dominion.

First you are looking in the mirror.

Then there is the magic, and inside the mirror do you go laughing across time.

Then you are looking in the mirror.

It is the path beyond life and death is-it-not?

Love begetting love. There is none else.

The music of the spheres rained down on us from the heavens, spinning in perfect harmony and love across the cosmos, showing us that nothing is written in stone and that everything is negotiable. Our lives are short, and it is up to us to live out our dreams while we can, to make as compassionate of a planet as we can. Because in the end, it's just us, and we all have to learn to live with each other, to make a world in which everybody is free to follow their own destiny.

Fuck it. Who am I to say whether magic works or not? All I can say is that it sure works for me. It's a thrill ride for sure, and it's helped me grow, brought me towards some absolutely amazing experiences that I never would have had otherwise, and left me a brighter, happier, more enthusiastic person. What's not to love?

Once we found it we knew we had to go out and spread it. We had something real, something precious, that had to be guarded. We could tell other people straight out, but of course the minute you talk about magic—the shit you've turned into gold—is the minute it turns back into shit. Sometimes you can write about it. That *kind* of works. The best thing you can do with something you've written about magic, I think, is inspire somebody else enough to try it themselves, so that they can see for themselves. Might as well. Magic can no longer be ignored—it's everywhere. Replacing this world. Replacing your children with strange-eyed changelings while you sleep. Descending from the aethyrs to make this world live up to its promise.

What are we here for? To buy and sell each other until we drop dead, or explore the mystery of life itself? Shot out over the cities growing flowers from the seeds of your desires. Anything is possible; everything is inevitable. And what is magic but the underlining of the very fact that you are alive, pushing you further and further in making sure that you enjoy that fact, and make something worthwhile out of it all?

AH!

The minute we make it real is the minute that everything else falls away like a fucking scab.

ENDNOTES

[1] A form of magic stripped of external cosmologies and symbol systems and refocused solely on technical ability, ecstasis and results (pure magic) rather than mysticism. Largely developed by Peter Carroll, Ray Sherwin and the Illuminates of Thanateros in the 1970s, as inspired by Thelema, the Zos Kia Cultus, Colin Wilson and some of the techniques of Scientology. The punk rock of the occult world, which pushed direct experience rather than secondhand learning. Chaos magic as a "movement" started to fizzle by the 1990s, having become fairly vapid and dogmatic in its own right, before achieving a second life on the Internet. The ideas pushed by chaos culture—sigils, "gnosis," servitors, paradigm shifting—now tend to be the first occult ideas somebody poking around looking for magic will be exposed to. The most valid call to action within chaos magic—that of creating your own rituals, godforms, systems and cosmology—has been overlooked more than it deserves. – Ed.

[2] A centering and calming ritual performed at the beginning of magical action designed to quiet the mind and erect a barrier keeping out any negative environmental or astral influences. The Lesser Banishing Ritual of the Pentagram is the most widely published and effective example. – Ed.

MY LITTLE UNDERGROUND

SCOTT TRELEAVEN

Once and For All: There is No Scene:

There is no membership activity. We've all done our time with the punks, the Goths, the crusties, club scenes, art scenes, galleries & factories. You name it. We've done the tattoos, the hairdos, the scars and the steel till we all looked alike. Communist meetings, anarchist rallies, potlucks, back rooms, witches' circles; all the underground credentials you could want. Having now safely returned to the helm we can report: There wasn't really anybody there…

This circus is as far flung and varied as any cabaret. Infiltrating all areas. Infuriating people with a total inability to wear one disguise, to believe in one idea, or to take anybody's word for anything. We truly cum & go as we please from one circle to the next, taking only what we need. Scavengers from a school far larger than any small-minded cult of primitivism, theory, dogma, decadence or sham. We are ageless jacks-of-all-trades, dilettantes, masters and examples. Please don't be afraid: You will know each other by scent alone.

We are the new circus.

And we are the envy of the fucking World.

– From the final issue of *This is the Salvation Army*, 1999

We are poised on the brink of the largest resurgence of magical culture in the history of our species. This might sound like the same kind of bombastic proclamation that marked the all-too-hopeful Hippie era, just before it came crashing down face-first into the dust of Spahn Ranch and the gory conspicuousness of an Altamont stage—but this magical revival is radically different from any we've experienced before. Like the Velvet Revolution, this one is happening quietly and it's happening right now. The tactics have changed. Instead of some insular inner circle haranguing the unenlightened into tuning in and turning on, this magical renaissance is about politely reminding the public that they are already tuned in, and that the very things they now take for granted are indeed magical in origin. Even if we forget for a moment the mystic traditions that are surreptitiously at work on the waves of middle-class moms toting their yoga mats from place to place, or that post-rave kids with their mutable sexuality are willfully eroding the outmoded evolutionary strategy of gender or, better still, the idea of human identity entirely. Even if we ignore the sheer availability of consciousness-expanding drugs and devices (including the Internet), or that the traditionally shamanic means of tailoring the body (piercing, scarification, tattooing, etc.) have moved from criminal dishonor to teenage prerequisite, we are still only at the tip of the proverbial iceberg. To augment this trend, mainstream-targeted books and magazines have started to reassess prominent contemporary and historical figures in terms of their magical practice as much as their cultural appeal.

Those of us fortunate enough to have been urban teenagers in the early 1990s were able to witness the most recent and explicit wave of this phenomenon. I like to refer to this era as "Generation Hex," a building proliferation of occult and fringe ideology unparalleled since the Aquarian consciousness rush of the sixties. In the early nineties, music stores overflowed with bands proselytizing for or referencing occult subjects (Psychic TV, Coil, Ministry, etc.), bookshops were stocked with seminal titles like *RE/Search* and *Rapid Eye*, and video stores purveyed Mystic Fire re-releases of classics like *Invocation of My Demon Brother* and *Towers Open Fire*, though they were usually relegated to the catchall and yet oddly appropriate "Foreign Films" section. Thee Temple ov Psychic Youth (TOPY)[1] world mission was in full hyperdelic swing, New Model Army and the Levellers were rallying the New Age Travelers[2] in the UK and Church of Satan spokespeople were on sensationalist U.S. television shows every other night. Even mainstream pop divas had started to dabble with their own brand of surreptitious magical reference, predating the current Kabbalah craze.[3] As Aleister Crowley once pointed out, the Truth is in everything, if you know how to find it.

For whatever reason, as we crept towards the middle of the 1990s, this pronounced flux in occult consciousness seemed to vanish. There was plenty of speculation as to whether or not this was due to covert, or overt, pressures from political and religious factions, or if it was something as mundane as a shift in consumer habits stopping a market, like any other, dead in its tracks. Or maybe the sincerity and courage of the young magicians of the nineties finally bowed to the prevailing air of cynicism and irony. It's impossible to say why things changed, as the nature of occult activity makes it a difficult thing to monitor at the best of times. Perhaps magic continually shifts gears—oscillating between open, obvious forms, and then downshifting into more subtle modes of influence, thereby becoming more effective at creeping into those areas of culture that would seek to resist its impact. Fortunately, I was old enough to fully appreciate the first manifestation of Generation Hex, and when the rising tide of magical activity suddenly abated, it felt like the carnival had moved on. To kill time and keep my faith until I found it again, I started writing elaborate love letters to an unknown group of magicians and esoterrorists, in hopes that one day they'd start writing back. They did. And for what it's worth, I'm going to divulge to you exactly what I did, because it's all about to happen again.

"Thou shalt mix!"
– **Howard Bloom**, *The Lucifer Principle*

Along with our cravings for sex, food, safety and love, it's not unreasonable to suggest that we also have an innate spiritual appetite. Engaging it through prayer, meditation, ritual and the shamanic or recreational use of drugs can fulfill or, at worst, neutralize this appetite. I felt my first hunger pangs when, at the unlikely age of five, I brought home a copy of Daniel Cohen's *Curses, Hexes and Spells*, a book that now has the distinction of being one of the most widely banned in the North American school library system—due in part, I'm sure, to the number of little minds that it started to unshackle. At the time, however, my interest in it was entirely practical. The house my family was living in had a couple of rooms, one a study, the other disused, that were inhabited by a shapeless presence that had on a number of occasions made itself known by forcibly grabbing things from my hands and even lifting me physically off the floor. Growing up in an agnostic household, words and concepts like "ghost" hadn't started to seriously enter my consciousness yet, so I was delighted that Cohen's book seemed to be detailing the world as I actually experienced it. This sentiment—that occult analogy was somehow a more accurate way of describing the oddity of being alive than the usual methods—has stayed with me throughout my life.

My fascination with the occult became even more pronounced in early adolescence, when I started to grasp that a person could have a more *active* relationship with magic. Instead of simply observing so-called supernatural occurrences, a magician could engineer them, and so with the aid of Cohen's book I cast my first spell, at the age of twelve. The "Cross Not My Path" spell I performed was a fairly benevolent bit of thaumaturgy meant to ensure that an enemy didn't get in my way, which naturally came in handy for dealing with grade school bullies. To my astonishment, it worked better than I'd hoped, and from then on I was hooked. The limited resources I had access to eventually led me to identify two predominant schools of magical thought and, like the dead-end notion of a two party political system, I tacitly assumed that my studies had to be bifurcated off into one of these systems. For the sake of simplification,

I privately considered them the "conservative" and the "liberal" approaches. I would never pretend to be an expert on all aspects of these traditions, and obviously as one individual I can't possibly do justice to these sacred lineages in the space I'm afforded, so please take the summaries that follow as both subjective and affectionate. After all, it was their *joint* influence that brought me to the particular path I'm on now.

The conservative approach—or high magic—generally involved reading densely written grimoires, memorizing pages of Qabalistic correspondences, speaking to angels and spending years in a disciplined program of study. Few students embark on this path alone, and fewer still return from the cloister with their sanity, much less their sense of humor, intact. Consequently, masters of this path tend to be scarce, legendary and, more often than not, infamous (e.g., John Dee, H. P. Blavatsky, Aleister Crowley). For all its grandiosity, high magic still manages to get visibility in indie music circles, whether it be Crowley's scowl showing up in a White Stripes video or someone slipping an Arabic talisman into their sleeve art.

The other, more liberal school is what traditionalists would call "witchcraft," and tends to encapsulate things like neo-paganism, Wicca, some aspects of Vodou[4] and other, more nature-based forms of magic. Despite what you may have seen in *The Wicker Man*, it's actually quite over-the-counter friendly, with legally binding marriages to boot. Its hallmarks tend to be things like horned Gods and robust Goddesses, New Age herbalism and a hey-nonny-nonny-back-to-the-woods kind of sensibility. Thanks to a much-needed push in environmental consciousness over the last decade, this school of magic has enjoyed yet another renaissance, picking up on the activist front. Its key practitioners, new and old (e.g., Gerald Gardner, Alex Saunders, Starhawk), are about as well known as their high magic counterparts.

You don't have to read Frazer's *Golden Bough* to recognize that all systems of magic share points of overlap and points of departure. Having said that, few will deny that "mixing," whether through the mediums of music, film, style or subculture, is the vital and not-so-secret language of our time.

When William S. Burroughs and Brion Gysin split the cultural atom with their cut-up[5] experiments in the Beat Hotel in late 1950s Paris, they knew they had stumbled on the magical formula that would define the next century. Unconsciously taking my cues from the cut-up, I knew I wasn't able to choose between two paths that each seemed to have enough to recommend them equally, so I stuck my hands in both. I read voraciously, anything by Crowley, Eliphas Lévi and similar authors, and prepared to build towards a rendezvous with my Holy Guardian Angel.[6] Simultaneously, I started to explore the myriad avenues of witchcraft with the help of a friend in a local coven. Entering into the role-play of the God and the Goddess in a witches' circle gave me ample room to explore how atrophied my adolescent, TV-stunted imagination had become.

Somehow, by my final year of high school the cachet that went along with people knowing that I visited a coven and read Crowley began to supercede the reason I had been doing these things in the first place. I started to enjoy playing the part of the Satanic conjurer a little too much, wearing Edwardian high-collars and a Bobby Beausoleil-inspired top hat, terrorizing the bible studies group and being generally insufferable. I had been searching for a way to integrate magic into my life and wound up with a fashion statement and more friends named "Lestat" than anyone should possibly ever have. It was dawning on me that I had made a cut-up, but with the wrong source material. After a few more circles at the Wiccan church and participating in the Rite of Mercury with the local chapter of Thelemites,[7] I decided it was better to lie low. As a wise old acupuncturist once said to me, "live and die by your instinct." I didn't know what that was, or what it really felt like, so I waited. And then it ambushed me.

One of the greatest cohorts you can ever have in your search for illumination is a bookstore employee who knows your tastes inside and out. While Hermann Hesse was working retail on his way to becoming a sage, he always took particular relish in steering his customers towards the books that he thought they'd benefit from. For my part, I was brought up on weekly visits to a bookstore called "A Different Drummer," taking its name from the lines of a Thoreau poem. Having already raised eyebrows after a minor police inquiry followed my ordering of *The Anarchist Cookbook*, I was now aching for something that I couldn't articulate. If I had acquainted myself with the old school and hippie approaches respectively, then where was the anarchic, or dare I say it, PUNK school of magic? I was promptly directed to the Grove Press section at the back of the shop, and left with Burroughs' *Naked Lunch* and Jean Genet's *Our Lady of the Flowers*. I had deliberately picked those books not only because I'd heard that they were exemplary pieces of literature written by modern magicians, but because it was reputed that these writers were outlining how they readily incorporated their own, personal experiences into their magic, and vice-versa.

As I read Burroughs' novel he systematically laid waste to everything I knew about Western propriety, sexuality and linear consciousness. I recalled that learning a skill or language for the first time creates new synaptic connections, changing the physical structure of the brain itself, and I could literally feel the book rewiring my head. Once this bit of welcome surgery was complete, Genet was free to populate my brain with queer martyrs, holy hustlers and drag queen saints. Finally I was being exposed to new, dynamic and contemporary systems of magic that I instantly, instinctively understood. If every other aspect of human culture was accelerating, adapting and evolving around me, why couldn't the approach to magical and mystical experience be updated too? In these books I finally found that peculiar beat that was perfectly in tune with my own, and I immediately fell in step.

Once you've engaged with any kind of magical practice, it's about as easy to ignore as a cat that needs feeding; you can't walk a foot without tripping over it. This is what is known as gaining a "magical consciousness," it's the universe saying it's ready to play. Taken too seriously, it can be a very disconcerting phenomenon and on some levels it replicates associative systems commonly found in schizophrenia. That being said, at the time of my magical awakening, not only was I contending with having my third eye properly yanked open, but I was also starting to go through the arduous process of "coming out" as queer to my friends and family. The parallel here isn't an incidental one. From a psychological point of view, most personal revelations come after a period of mental duress, and in many ways the process of coming to terms with my sexuality was the catalyst I needed to make a break with my old self. I was finally given proof that I had inherited a whole set of outmoded, dogmatic social programs that bore no relationship whatsoever to my real-life experiences. From a shamanic perspective, the aspiring practitioner is usually torn limb from limb, symbolically or literally, on the way to transcendence.[8] Suffice to say, my experience was torturous, but I started to realize that I was being offered my first real step into a life of examined rebellion.

Another jarring realization that accompanied this period in my life was that it no longer made sense for me to obediently accept established magical doctrines any more than it was rational for me to keep in step with other antiquated ways of perceiving myself and the world around me. With this last insight I now felt completely free to reinvent myself. Taking an invaluable tip from Crowley, who I could now admit I had a soft spot for largely because he was queer, I started keeping a magical record in earnest (which I have continued to this day, some sixteen volumes). With my own consensus reality completely kicked out from under me, I decided to regroup, reinvent and retreat to London for a year.

I'd grown up taking trips back and forth to England to visit relatives, so while it felt like a second home, it was far enough removed to leave the influence of my family and friends behind. What I hadn't anticipated, however, was that living as a bohemian in Margaret Thatcher's less-than-magical Britain meant starvation, and I spent the better part of a year scraping by, living wherever it was cheap, unfashionable or downright dangerous. It was during this miserable stretch that I also had my first proper introduction to the pattern of right wing politics creating a collapse in social conditions, and then instituting despotic social control. The people that take the brunt of it are usually the ones that call established norms and institutions into question, meaning that the freaks are the first on the chopping block. Everywhere I looked, the powers of "righteousness" were crushing subcultures with a vengeance. Clause 28 had made it illegal for anyone under twenty-one to be in a gay relationship; the British police force had initiated the draconian "Project Spanner," effectively bulldozing the SM and piercing communities by making consensual acts punishable by imprisonment; ravers and New Age Travelers were being targeted through a new law that made unlicensed social gatherings illegal; and to top it all off, a bogus documentary had aired on Channel 4 vilifying filmmaker Derek Jarman, Genesis P-Orridge and other members of Thee Temple ov Psychic Youth in the process. Everything I had hoped to find in England had been smothered or slandered. It's no exaggeration to say that Inquisition was in the air, and I only managed to keep my sanity by immersing myself in Simon Dwyer's invaluable *Rapid Eye* books and Jarman's incendiary autobiography *Modern Nature*. I had been aware of Jarman's work through references made to him during my brief stint at film school, as well as through his work with The Smiths and industrial progenitors Throbbing Gristle. If Kenneth Anger is the Magus of cinema, then Derek was its Alchemist. It was Dwyer's book that not only referenced Jarman, but also turned me on to that most potent and simple of all the magical processes I have ever used: British artist Austin Spare's extraordinary gift to contemporary occult practice, the sigil.

A sigil, which rhymes with "vigil," is essentially a means of condensing one's desires into a medium that can bypass the worldly restrictions of self-doubt, cynicism and failure, allowing it to deliver results with incredible accuracy. It's a form of psychic shorthand, applicable through a broad range of mediums and methods. It had been a very long time since I'd been motivated to perform a ritual, longer still since I'd tried something completely new, but I now had nothing to lose. The same day that I collapsed from near-starvation on my way to work, serving tea at the National Gallery restaurant, I went back to my squalid little Lewisham flat with enough presence of mind to realize that I needed someone to advise me. In my first attempt at a sigil, I embedded my wish as prescribed in a densely-scrawled personal symbol, shut my eyes, and welled up the sexual energy needed to charge my desire. As I came, I locked eyes with the sigil and told the universe that I wanted to meet Derek Jarman. And on the very same day I asked, I literally ran into him not five hours later, on his way to pick up olives in Soho.

Nothing impresses itself on the human memory like genuine kindness, and Derek did more than simply humor me as I tagged along making sure that he didn't wander out into the road. He'd already started to lose his sight from a combination of AIDS-related illnesses and the highly toxic drugs that were meant to be helping him. "I'm writing a meditation on color, now that I'm going blind," he told me. "Clever, isn't it?" We talked more about writing and boys than about filmmaking, and he divulged to me some of the best advice I've ever been given: "You should make your work about your friends." Derek counseled me to pay close attention, record and find inspiration in the things that happened within my immediate circle. Finally, despairing of the oppressive climate in England, he advised me to go back home and go to art school, not film school, to learn.

Our first meeting lasted only an afternoon, and from then on I periodically ran into him near his flat in Charing Cross. Other than being staunch proof of the efficacy of sigils, I couldn't figure out why Derek had left such a powerful impression on me. I'd never been "star struck," and though I devoured his books voraciously, I had yet to see one of his films. I didn't know much about the scurrilous documentary that had aired, either. Interestingly, he'd also suggested that I take a good look at the work of Genesis P-Orridge, who I'd heard of from reading *RE/Search*. P-Orridge's reputation as an art saboteur was already well established, even though the TOPY anti-cult was still new to me. My first experiences with some of the Temple's initiates (i.e., the wrong sort), with their slavish need to transform what seemed like a perfectly good libertarian bloc into a theocracy, had turned me off. Nonetheless, in a strangely uncharacteristic move for me, I did exactly as I was told. I never doubted a word of Derek's advice—I came back to Canada, studied at the local art college and made art and films with my friends. I also started to pay more attention to the legacy of TOPY and news of P-Orridge's exile from the UK. It was a few years later, upon the news of Derek's death, that I realized why such a brief meeting had changed me so profoundly. Without knowing it, I had met my first magician, and the gaping void I now felt at his passing affected me greatly.

"'There was a time,' my friend once said, 'when the most fantastic thing in the world was not to be a rock star, but a revolutionary.' I put it to you—that time has come again."
  – From the film *The Salivation Army*

Toronto has never felt like a particularly enchanted city. Its relative newness, and the perpetual desecration of its few historical buildings, makes it feel like an approximation of a metropolis rather than the real thing. During his visit in 1905, Crowley referred to the city as "a calculated crime both against the aspirations of the soul and the affections of the heart." With our own hard right government laying waste to art and culture, and the lack of a community like TOPY to align myself with, the Beast's words seemed more relevant than ever. Spurred on by my initial success with sigils, I continued to adapt the method, with intriguing results. Trying to share my experiences with some of the local occultists I'd met revealed a weird kind of snobbery that I'd only noticed before amongst my communist and anarchist friends, who would spend countless hours deriding one another for having lowly or untenable beliefs. There's a heartbreaking absurdity in watching groups that ought to be presenting a united front against larger evils, sitting in their squats picking each other to pieces before even winning any ground. Similarly, I would weather lengthy explanations of why sigils were considered "low magic," and how they were somehow too déclassé to bother with. All I knew is that they suited me perfectly, with their adaptability and straightforward, non-dogmatic approach, and at this stage, if something worked it seemed pointless to question it.

In the absence of formal mentors or collaborators, I openly experimented with other types of free-form, intuitive magic, performing private and public rituals by myself and with willing friends, getting them to dress as different deities (Pan, Venus and Bacchus were favorites) or lycanthropic hybrids, and then consecrate their sigils on film in mini amateur porn loops. The broad banner of "art" bestowed permission to explore and act in the most heretical ways imaginable, plus have an audience (in my case, instructors and students) who could respond to its impact. If an experiment was successful, it was exciting. If it failed, it didn't matter. I was less interested in specific results than I was in simply seeing what might happen. Initially film and video figured into my practice in the same way I used my magical diary, simply to capture whatever was unfolding, until it occurred to me that it could become a component of the rituals instead of just a means of recording them. I would later read an interview with Gysin and Burroughs in which they insisted that a magician should always embrace the latest technology, so I started to employ looped samples, methodical edits, visual and audio cut-ups. Most importantly, I started to discover the power of sampling and cutting-up *my own* reality, using my own images and audio to build a vocabulary of personal symbols that repeated throughout my work.

By the end of my art school years, I had shrugged off my more gothic pretenses and started to embrace punk as a more effective ideological stance. I had seen the face of the new radicalism—and it was cute. Resourcefulness, flexibility, inclusiveness and action were their own magical corollary. If you want to have a direct effect on the world around you, surround yourself with active people. With everyone in a band, publishing a zine, running a Food Not Bombs[9] kitchen or taking up arms against the social injustices that plagued us, it felt like history would roll on without me if I didn't participate. The rabid single-mindedness of an activist became a bigger turn-on than any Prince Albert or punk rock haircut could ever be. Yet somehow, even with the pomp of Goth behind me, and the frenzied exuberance of punk in front of me, my "tribe," the people who truly shared my worldview, still seemed to be somewhere else. Tired of hunting for them, I decided to stay put and signal them directly.

> *"One never reaches home . . . But where paths cross that have affinity for each other . . . the whole world looks like home for a time."*
> **– Frau Eva, in Hermann Hesse's *Demian***

In my final year of school I directed a homopunk documentary called *Queercore*. Eschewing the standard documentary format of naming names and creating a list of heroes and specialists, I decided to approach the film as an invocation, with the sole intent being that wherever it screened, kids who might not have previously known each other would converge. This plan worked better than I'd anticipated, and *Queercore* acted as a temporary temple, leaving instant communities in its wake. I had made so many contacts during the initial filming that starting a newsletter or a zine struck me as the most reasonable way to keep in touch with everyone. Not only that, but it meant that I could finally start to merge all of my other obsessions into one vessel. I launched the first issue of *This Is the Salivation Army* with no particular mandate other than to act as a lighthouse and an open love letter to the people I wanted to meet, exchange with and learn from. The zine's name had come in a dream I'd had about three years prior. It was the name of a *Wild Boys*-style youth gang that derived their philosophies purely from sensual experience as opposed to nebulous, pseudo-Christian ideas of sin, body-fear and salvation. Having no familiarity with making a zine, it seemed sensible to try and make something that I would want to read myself, and I modeled the first issue on the *Rapid Eye* books that helped me to survive my hellish year in Conservative Britain. Simon Dwyer's compendiums willfully eroded the difference between mysticism, radical politics, and sexual and intellectual pursuits. They literally impelled the reader to become involved, no matter how small a contribution one could muster. In my case, this meant a less-than-quarterly photocopied communiqué, with thirty or so pages of manifestoes and cut & paste collages—pornography, blasphemy, anarchy, sodomy. Sure it's been done before—*the best thing that can happen is not to be unique, but to be an active part of an ongoing history.*

The more I learned about the intersections of magic and art, the more I realized that I was treading a well-beaten path. All that was required of me was continual engagement. I wanted the discipline of producing and creating more than I wanted passive inclusion. I found that using zine distribution networks, commissioning work from friends and flirting outrageously with copy shop clerks was all that was really required to make a dent in the indie world. I also practiced a rigorous anti-copyright ethic to promote cross-referencing and reproductions; all I asked is that excerpts were accompanied by a reference to their source, so that people could trace things back if they wanted to. After spending so many years having to pick through broken threads, dead-end lineages and ripped-off ideas, I wanted to make sure that anyone who wanted to know more always had recourse.

At first I wasn't exactly sure what my real intent with *This Is the Salivation Army* was. I just felt so strongly compelled to keep working that by the time I was getting ready to publish the third issue, the reason presented itself. At the behest of Matt Wobensmith of Outpunk Records, I was invited to screen *Queercore* at a San Francisco homocore festival. Without a moment's hesitation I cashed a scholarship check, printed up a new stack of the second issue and packed a tattered copy of Hesse's *Demian* for the plane. The rest of my summer was spent hiding from the scorching June sun in a filthy squat in Berkeley, reading Genesis P-Orridge's *Thee Psychick Bible* and being introduced to a gang of individuals who indeed made no distinction between their politics, their sexuality and their creative output. It was on that same trip that, thanks to the zine intervening on my behalf, I was also invited to attend a summer solstice ritual at the local Radical Faerie headquarters.

I had only the slimmest idea of who the Radical Faeries actually were, but I later discovered that they had been thriving since the late seventies, when legendary activist Harry Hay returned from a decade in New Mexico, where he had been seeking a living Berdache (a Native American gay male spirit guide). He found one, and the experience of connecting his sexuality with his magical self had so completely affected him that, with a small circle of friends, he created a singular fusion of anarchism, communitarian living, green ecology and non-dogmatic spiritual practices—an ideology far and away from oppressive Judeo-Christian concepts of who or what a queer man was supposed to be. The solstice ritual was the closest thing to a flat-out occult Bacchanalia that I could ever imagine and, as one of the 300 people who attended, it shook me up in the most sublime way. At last I found myself in the presence of magic that seemed to have its roots in a circus rather than a church. The punks I spent my days with and the pagans that hosted me after dark seemed to be headed for a natural convergence. One night before falling asleep, as I lay there huddled up with all the other unwashed waifs and strays, it finally occurred to me: The very thing I was seeking to connect with through the zine was not only reasonable, it was inevitable. I was imagining a new home and moving into it at the same time. *This Is the Salivation Army* was an expanded sigil, unfolding with each issue.

> *"Go looking for these unorthodox, like-minded individuals, have undying faith that they exist and are probably looking for you too. Offer stimulation, speculation, exchange ideas, collaborate, coordinate, share information and theories, recommend sources and names of activators you admire who have come to your attention via media, myth or synchronicity. Nothing is stronger in its anarchic potency and cultural resonance than a pack of previously 'lone' wolves . . . "*
> **– Genesis P-Orridge, from his introduction to the *This Is the Salivation Army* compendium**

As I prepared to print my third issue, a handful of new zines, all of them adopting magic and punk as their watchwords, had cropped up in Toronto. Each cited *This Is the Salivation Army* as a catalyst, reminding me of how the same kind of midwifery had spawned my own zine in the first place—every gesture, no matter how personal, is permission for others. The most accomplished of these zines, *Infantile*, somehow managed to combine hilarious articles about made-up magical orders like "The Solid Golden Dawn Dancers" and painfully honest personal anecdotes from the zine's creator, Paul Zevenhuizen. Now that there was a gang of us, I started to examine the strange little demographic we were appealing to. I tried to ditch any divisive stylistic references as I began to realize that my readers might not embody any one subcultural strata: I wasn't catering to people who just sported mohawks and leather jackets, or dreads and hemp jeans, or even hoodies and spray cans. My readership wasn't even entirely gay. All that united the contributors was a genuine interest in magical exploration, self-discipline and teaching each other how to be focused, skeptical, strong-willed and, above all, compassionate.

What happened in tandem with the zine was ultimately more intriguing than what appeared in the pages themselves. The sigil continued to unfold, always implying more than it said aloud, symbols and coded language recurring alongside images of lone wolves and wild dogs reunited with their pack. I started to receive mail from places like New York, San Francisco, Montreal, Arizona, Prague, Melbourne, Edinburgh, Berlin and Korea. There was no website and no e-mail address, so people sent letters, videotapes, zines and CDs. I maintain to this day that the tactility of a zine is the key to its potency, and as such will always have a stronger impact than anything that can be found online. Every issue overflowed with tips and survival tactics accumulated by other nomadic researchers, sharing their data and offering resources. We imagined a near future of youth gangs feeding off the surplus fat of their cities. Wild boys and girls, wearing warpaint, roaming the streets like packs of sex-crazed hyaenas. There was no membership activity, so everyone was free to choose their own level of participation. You could come and go as you pleased. Sigils were, of course, the most popular form of magic amongst the Army's contributors, perfect for a gang with no requisite dogma, style or logo. Everyone was left to recognize each other by scent alone.

The first truly inspirational piece of news I received was from some spunk-stained punk squat in the Czech Republic that had become the locus for safe sex magic and political insurrection, under the banner of "The Homo Militia." They eagerly wanted to know if I would be kind enough to allow them to be an official offshoot of the Salivation Army, and to spill their seed in our honor. I couldn't possibly say no, and for months afterwards I wondered about all the things the boys in Prague must have been getting up to while I stood around a copy shop at three in the morning like a sucker, my eyes burning from the perpetual sweep of the copier lamp. I desperately wanted to compete with the decadence I imagined the Homo Militia was guilty of, and with that in mind I went to work on a new issue, a rallying cry and sex sigil all in one.

A few weeks after this new issue was unleashed, a handsome young emo kid followed me home, hoping to meet the inner circle of the Salivation Army. Feeling a horribly rockstar-ish compulsion to impress him, I managed to pull together an ad hoc group of local contributors to make it look like we had a united front. Somehow or other, this kid was impressed by us. Maybe a little too much so. Over the next month he had infiltrated the homes of everyone he'd met, lugging around his unwieldy knapsack filled with Robert Anton Wilson and Aldous Huxley books, as well as a variety of pharmaceuticals, hopping from bed to bed and stirring up the first pangs of a jealousy between us. Initially I felt compelled to put a stop to it, but it was precisely what I had asked for. Moreover, if the Army wasn't about helping people to explore their desires, well, what was it for? The Army had its first groupie, and everything started to unravel from there.

My friends and I briefly toyed with the idea of making a small series of sex magic porno videos, with our new boyfriend as the star, as a supplement to the print version of the *This Is the Salivation Army* zine. Not only would we get to orchestrate an orgy, it would act as our first formal "initiation" ritual, something that wasn't possible before because anyone who was a contributor was also a *de facto* member. Unwisely, what I alluded to in public, and coded into the zine itself, was that this boy's initiation was something that had actually happened. The people I'd neglected to invite to the first meeting of our fake inner circle reacted with extreme resentment. Without meaning to, I'd accidentally created a hierarchy, and my correspondents slowly started to lurch away from being co-conspirators and now started to sound more like a fan club, with everyone wanting to know where to sign up. Allowing, or even endorsing, this kind of passive subjugation also brought out an unsettling trickle of mail from neo-fascists and other human wreckage, precisely the kind of people I had always been dead set against, who were now turned on by the violent rhetoric of the initiation references. Like I said, some people got the joke . . . and then some people were only too willing to swallow the new, darker aspects of the Salivation Army as gospel.

The new image I'd concocted for the zine made me feel uneasy. It made me uneasy because it made me feel responsible—something that wholly contradicted the idea behind my having a zine in the first place. The process was meant to flow in two directions, as a dialogue, and I certainly couldn't learn anything from a passive readership. Consequently, issue six was a pretty thin affair; most of the things that would have been published as open forum exchanges now took place in private correspondence as I tried to control the situation and put out social fires. The original spirit of inquiry had been replaced by infighting and "magical pissing contests," as my friends dubbed them, where we used our collective magical knowledge to see who could gain the most notoriety or get the most laid. I was anxious to put the zine, my friends and myself back on course, and set about devising a ritual that I thought would fulfill our need for initiation while dispensing with specific requests for allegiance or commitment to an ideology. The ritual I came up with was a conflation of different cult practices, requiring that everyone create a symbol composed of three equidistant lines (the minimum number needed to create a variety of signs), in any formation they wished, and then cut this symbol into their skin with a clean scalpel blade in each other's presence. The act of cutting, I rationalized, would ensure that the intensity and somberness of an initiation ritual would be there even if the intent was different. A few days before the ritual, I met someone at a party who worked at a local tattoo parlor, with gorgeous facial tattoos and decorated with every piercing imaginable—I should have guessed that he also happened to be one of North America's foremost scarification experts. He was fascinated by the idea of a mass scarification ritual and kindly offered to supervise the occasion. In an even more ghoulish twist of synchronicity, on the very same night myself and twenty other people agreed to annul their Army membership, reject the invented hierarchy and instead think of ways to remain united while staying autonomous, the Heaven's Gate cult donned their Nikes for the last time.

When the actual event unfolded, I made sure to record it on film and in photos (like Derek advised), and then published the details in the seventh issue of the zine. I wanted to present it to my readership so that, if people really wanted to belong, they could invent their own symbol and contribute their own unique experience to ours. Readers were encouraged to blot the blood from their cuttings on a piece of thick paper which could then be integrated into a "quilt" that included blood from the first twenty-one initiates. Once again, I didn't think people were going to take a little photocopied zine so seriously, but people did, dozens of them. I didn't recognize most of the names affixed to the red-brown spattered papers that poured in. The idea of open communication had finally been defeated, as people previously too shy to write a letter found it less painful to cut themselves and offer their blood. To make things worse, certain individuals started to freely riff on the new sacrificial theme.

Suffice to say, I decided to stop publishing my zine. The Salivation Army experiment was over. Going back and cataloguing the sigils and rituals that had been created over the past three years, I felt appalled at how juvenile some of my wishes had become—tedious variations on the sex/power/money theme dominated. The same triad that made mainstream culture so unappealing to me had displaced everything I originally wanted to accomplish with the zine. I slinked away and meditated on what I'd learned from the whole ordeal and if it was, indeed, worth learning. After lying low for about a year I decided that *This Is the Salivation Army* needed a proper headstone, and even though I originally wanted the sigil to fully emerge over nine issues, I pronounced that issue eight would be the last. In its pages I volubly condemned the seduction of fascism, elitism, rock star mentality and how the zine had actually sunk so low that a major soft drink manufacturer (rest assured, it was one of the big ones) had actually asked me to help them design an "underground-style" publication of their own. Printed in the back of the last issue were letters of condolence from fans and contributors alike, and to my surprise this new issue sold more copies, and faster, than any issue before it. Fearing another resurgence of hangers-on, I didn't reply to anyone's letters, and I cancelled the post office box. I hung up my accidentally acquired cult leader cap and quietly went back to the drawing board.

My preoccupation with the occult flagged for a good couple of years. I started to investigate more pragmatic ways of decoding and engaging with the world by immersing myself in psychological, cultural and social theory texts. I still made short films, organized events and occasionally wrote articles for indie publications, but my magical practice had all but tapered off. The functionality of the sigils was replaced with more plainly artistic pursuits, as I went back to privately embellishing my journals with dense collages and drawings. More time was devoted to catching up on things like memetic theory[10] and Neuro-Linguistic Programming,[11] and thinking about how ideas can literally invade, and breed in, our consciousness. Perhaps, despite its best intentions, the Salivation Army had played unwitting host to something viral, and it wasn't anybody's fault that it had burnt itself out. In the end, the whole process I had been through was, as these things tend to be, a loop—I found myself once again flooded by information, by fragmented histories and esoteric tidbits, but without a workable template for any of it. I had scars, tattoos, dreads and a bookshelf to die for, but cut off from a function, these things were useless to me. Magic for its own sake was meaningless.

"It is to be remembered that all art is magical in origin . . . (it is) intended to produce very definite results."
– William S. Burroughs

Though I willfully tried to steer clear of magic, I repeatedly ran into the same problem: Occult symbolism and language still felt like a more accurate way of describing the human condition than the terminology and categorizations I was studying. In the course of trying to objectively analyze what had happened with the zine and the behavioral patterns that make Really Good ideas suddenly cross over into the realm of Really Bad ones, I wondered if an account of the three years I spent publishing my zine, as an isolated parable with a clear beginning, middle and end, might make a good film. As I began drafting out the script, instilling continuity and creating a logical outline for a seemingly random series of events, I noticed that the creation and collapse of my little part of the underground had in fact cleared the way for something much more complex. Thanks again to excellent advice, all the photos, writings, videos and film footage I had accumulated over the years meant that I could sample and cut-up from my own cosmos. Remembering that every issue of the zine was a sigil in itself, I wondered if, when the pieces were finally joined together and projected into the world, they would produce a "mega-sigil" which would make something truly extraordinary happen.

Playing with the cumulative power of eight sigils led to innumerable coincidences, chance meetings and serendipities during the making of the film, such as a fortuitous encounter, and a lasting friendship, with Genesis and Lady Jaye Breyer P-Orridge, who politely advised and cajoled as I found my occultural feet again. Funnily enough, the first thing we talked about when we met was Genesis' friendship with Derek Jarman, and his appearance at that particularly crucial time in my life. Together with the film collective Pleasure Dome and VAV Gallery in Montreal, Breyer P-Orridge and I organized some highly successful performance and film events over the next few years, in an attempt to lure the occulturally-inclined back out into the open, employing the same strategies that I developed with *Queercore*. One of these events was a curated screening celebrating crossovers of the occult and pop culture in cinema. The evening consisted of a half dozen films, and in celebration of the thronging young audiences who were helping to usher in the next wave of magical consciousness, I dubbed the event "Generation Hex."

Bolstered by these happenings, I finished *The Salivation Army* film in 2002. The film is essentially a story about one person, in the company of sympathetic others, trying to find a magical lineage that felt like home. It served to not only recharge the initial sigil I'd started, it acted as a separate and fully realized twenty-two-minute cinematic "spell" in itself. The zine may have simply been a small part of the whole sigil, with the film as its apex; all along I had been generating the source material for a cosmology that now had a life of its own. I had played out the theories and pitfalls laid down by others before me, and now this brand new cut-up was wholly mine. Appropriately, I subtitled the film "Issue Nine." Thanks to the response it received, touring with the film consumed over a year of my life. Some cities revealed small, loyal enclaves of people who were familiar with the Army from the zine years, and each screening forged new connections between previously diffuse individuals. The sedentary years of writing the zine no longer suited me as much as traveling and being able to have a tangible connection with those sympathetic characters that made up the mythical tribe I wanted to find so badly. I always seemed to make just enough cash to get from one city to the next and I found myself, very happily, living nomadically again and relying on luck and the kindness of "family."

There's no end point or moral hidden in this essay; it's a snapshot of a process that is still unfolding. Even the act of sitting here at this very moment, writing these words to you, is a magical act courtesy of those years spent with the Salivation Army. If there is anything imbedded in this text it's the simple fact that magic suits some of us less as a lifestyle, path or dogma than it does as a dynamic and highly adaptable tool. The so-called tribe I went looking for wasn't made up of career magicians and mystic fundamentalists, and the only dominant trait in the pack I find myself running with now seems to be a tacit acceptance of magic as part of one's daily interaction with world. Perhaps the examples of subtle magical infiltration I listed at the beginning of this essay portend that magic is becoming what it *ought* to be, a normal part of the betterment of human life. Trying to align myself with an occult order or defined path paled, for me, against the possibility of creating an adjunct culture that I could truly call my own. Was I successful? I don't know—I'm not done, and I get the feeling that this has only just started. By the end of this decade, Generation Hex will be at its peak again. I can only imagine what form it will take, but doubtless there will be another deluge of magical orders, cults, scams, occultural currents and genuine enlightenment to tap into. Bearing in mind the cyclical nature of its appearance, my only advice to you is this: Preparing for its arrival will be almost as important as preparing for its departure.

ENDNOTES

[1] Anti-cult founded by industrial musicians Genesis P-Orridge and Monte Cazazza in 1982 and ended in 1992. Crucial player in the occult revival, responsible for popularizing and postmodernizing Austin Osman Spare's sigil method, O.T.O.-style "sex magick," the Burroughs/Gysin cut-up, the Dreamachine and body modification. Also present in early manifestations of rave and cyberculture. – Ed.

[2] A British social phenomenon similar to the Deadheads in the United States, dating to the 1970s, largely composed of caravans of neopagan hippies traveling between outdoor gatherings such as the Glastonbury and Stonehenge festivals. The group was persecuted heavily by the government from the early eighties on, markedly at the "Battle of the Beanfield" in which a large convoy headed for Stonehenge for the 1986 summer solstice was corralled into a field by police and attacked, resulting in the largest mass arrest (500) in English civil history; the Travelers were largely forced underground by the Criminal Justice Act of 1994, which also effectively made outdoor raves illegal and ended acid house culture. – Ed.

[3] A system of predominantly Jewish mysticism that posits a schema of ten emanations (*sephiroth*) between transcendent and mundane reality. Forms the backbone of many systems of Western magic. For convenience's sake the word "Kabbalah" is used throughout this book for faddish and shallow versions of the system, such as the current trend in Hollywood, while "Qabalah" is used for the deeper tradition. – Ed.

[4] This is the proper spelling of "voodoo" (also "vodun" or "vudu"), a magical and animist religious tradition originating in West Africa and currently in practice by over seven million people worldwide. Vodou is likely the oldest religion on the planet. – Ed.

[5] A technique, developed by Brion Gysin from the earlier method of the Dadaist Tristan Tzara, and used extensively by William S. Burroughs, of unveiling secrets by the random juxtaposition of information sources or experiences. – Ed.

[6] Deliberately nonsensical term. According to E. E. Rehmus, "When magi speak of 'the knowledge and conversation of the Holy Guardian Angel,' they refer to that particular manifestation of spirit which is their own experience." Chaos magician Julian Vayne has said: "The HGA is the beloved—something that we yearn to be with (and that yearns to be with us) and yet is not us. This separation gives rise to the HGA and to the mechanism by which we seek to make the return journey—love. As the flower loves the sun and so turns to face it, so the magician turns towards the HGA." The essence of Crowley's system is that the realization of the Angel is the only valid goal of magic. It's like what one of the kids hanging out in the street outside my window just said: "It's difficult, 'cause he's on a higher level an' shit." (See "Angels of Chaos" within this book.) – Ed.

[7] In the vulgar sense, followers of Aleister Crowley's religious system "Thelema," usually connected with the Ordo Templi Orientis. Otherwise, those who have discovered and are in the process of doing their "True Wills," whatever that concept may actually represent. – Ed.

[8] See the Chöd or gCod lineage of Tibetan Buddhism. – Ed.

[9] Anarchist movement started in the 1980s for the purpose of collecting wasted surplus food from grocery stores and restaurants in order to redistribute it to poor and homeless people. – Ed.

[10] Memetics, the study of information that is copied from person to person, is a Darwinian approach to culture that forms a hallmark of the current occult landscape. – Ed.

[11] Often referred to as "corporate magic," NLP is a technique for "programming" the mind for peak performance through various techniques, often associated with motivational speakers like Anthony Robbins. – Ed.

LEARNING TO OPEN THE HAUNTED KALEIDOSCOPE

STEPHEN GRASSO

A black candle, white candle and red candle burn on a wooden altar. Incense snakes upwards, making shapes in the air. Visions of great serpents and half-formed faces. I'm standing in a room full of ghosts, memories and anticipation. Heavy dub plays on the stereo. Patterns are drawn on the floor in cornmeal. A colorful feast of spicy food is laid out on a table covered with purple crêpe paper and decorated with tiny clay skulls. Rum and whiskey flow freely. A martial artist sits on the floor of my house in tears having been confronted by spirit; a beautiful sorceress smiles at me and lights a candle to the remembered dead. I anoint her brow with scented water and call to a vibrant, passionate God, while a crazy Bulgarian plays sitar in the corner. How the fuck did I come to be here and what does it all mean? Those are two pretty big questions, perhaps the only ones worth asking.

Newcastle

The first bit of magic I ever did, when I was a kid, was to accurately predict three winning horses for my dad at the racetrack. All three horses came in—and my old man, quite bemusedly, gave me a ten-pound note for the tip, inadvertently kick-starting my career in occultism and setting the tone for my subsequent experiments in magic.

Magic, for me, has always been about getting things done within the world. There's always been a tangible point to it. Something you can look at and see the purpose of, like a ten-pound note in your hand. I've never been into ephemeral or intangible goals, rarefied attainments or astral meanderings, and I didn't get into magic to invoke someone else's dubious New Aeon,[1] kick-start a self-indulgent magical current or pretend to be some sort of ascended being. I got involved with magic, and continue to practice it, because it helps me to look out for the interests of myself and the people I'm closest to in the world. Magic is a strange business, and once it hooks you, you're in for the long haul.

I think it all started when I was about thirteen years old, with my first shamanic crisis experience. I'm a strong believer that a person's magical career doesn't just begin when they formally decide to take up the wand (which sounds filthy), but is a continual living process that plays out from birth to death. One of the key experiences that set me on the road I ended up walking in later life occurred during early adolescence, but the seeds of it were actually in place right at the start. I had been born with a joint disorder that wasn't spotted until my hip physically came apart one painful afternoon, and I was rushed to the hospital. Several weeks of operations later, I was discharged with six shiny new metal nails placed inside of me, taken out of school for the best part of a year and presented with the arduous task of teaching myself how to walk again.

When I was eventually returned to school, normal society and everyday peer interaction, I found I couldn't quite fit back seamlessly into the world I'd come from. Important relationships had already been formed and all manner of shaping adolescent experiences had been shared, while I was otherwise engaged. I think those early teenage years are an important formative period in a person's development, and through my absence, my version of reality seemed to have grown slightly at odds to everyone else's. It felt as if I'd been derailed, circumstances had shifted me off the track I had previously been on and the my life had to find a different route to go down. The upshot of the situation was that I ended up spending a fair amount of time by myself, which is more or less when the penchant for magic started to kick in, and my early dabbling in "the black arts" began to take place.

Interestingly, a lot of magicians I've spoken to report having had broadly similar childhood experiences. You could argue that magicians are control freaks, and that it's that initial experience of losing control over their lives and environments that sets them off looking for some sort of advantage that might give them an edge over the fragility of their circumstances. If you grow up understanding exactly how tenuous your grip on "normal reality" is, then two things happen. Firstly, you come to understand how arbitrary and ephemeral "normal reality" actually is and, secondly, the task of developing some means of exerting an influence on that reality becomes a priority.

I think you can draw certain broad parallels between this kind of "early crisis" experience, and the standard shamanic initiation narrative that occurs in various indigenous cultures and mystery religions throughout the world. The general pattern is often that a prospective shaman-to-be is forcibly removed from the world as s/he knows it, undergoes a traumatic ordeal and is then returned to the world with something new added—often a stone, or a piece of crystal, or a magic bone. In my case, it was a handful of steel surgical pins.

I wanted to know if magic was real. I grew up being told that it wasn't, yet there were all these books in the local library written by people that reckoned it worked, and was something tangible that you could practice. So I read up on it, tried a few things, won a bit of money here, nastily cursed a few folks there, and began to warm to the idea of magic more and more. For some reason, the North Shields public library had a suspiciously well-stocked occult section during the eighties, so I had all of this material at my fingertips. By the time I was sixteen, I'd devoured everything I could get my hands on. Aleister Crowley, Israel Regardie, Dion Fortune, A. E. Waite, W. E. Butler and all the usual suspects of the Western mystery traditions, along with countless tacky spell books and endless encyclopedias of witchcraft and demonology. My appetite had been whetted.

Northern Soul

By the early nineties I'd left home, and was living and studying in a town called Preston, in the northwest of England. I was eighteen years old, and far too preoccupied with partying and enjoying my newfound independence to spend much time poring over old books or messing about with ritual magic. But it was during this period that I received much of my initial hands-on teaching about "the occult"—in a manner of speaking.

I was at just the right age to catch the tail end of the UK rave scene that had been going strong since the eighties. It was pre-Criminal Justice Act and there were free parties, strange drugs, insane music and interesting people on tap. To my fairly sheltered teenage self, it was as if I'd found the key to a strange world I never knew existed.

I think the most important thing for me about those years was the desperately naïve, utopian vision of a better world that came with the rave scene. It seems really weird to look back on it, ten years later, given the pressure and uncertainty of the times we're now living in, but there was a very genuine sense that what was happening back then was really going to change things.

New models of community were springing up. People from diverse backgrounds were coming together in the same place for the same reason and discovering that, against all odds, they could get along with one another. It was an egalitarian environment, not about the worship or idolization of some distant figure playing musical instruments on a stage, but about what you were doing, what your friends were doing, and how you felt while you were doing it.

Compassion ruled the dance floor. The familiar, alcohol-fuelled mammalian games over territory, jealousy, predatory sexuality and barely-repressed aggression were no longer really relevant within the temporary autonomous zone of the party-without-end. It felt almost religious. It wasn't just about dancing and hedonism—you would constantly meet people who reported having had their entire perspective on life, reality and what it is to be human radically transformed amid the shamanic whirl of electronic drum rhythms, an inclusive community and really good MDMA.

I remember dancing all night and all morning to music that I could almost taste, sharing indescribable moments of pure elation with total strangers on the dance floor and having the time of my fucking life. It seemed, to all involved, like only a matter of time before this immense euphoric tidal wave of genuine compassion, freedom and liberation crashed down on the rest of the world and changed society forever.

Things didn't quite turn out like that. New laws were invented to curb unsanctioned gatherings, the drugs dropped off in quality, a creeping cynicism bled into the scene and the whole atmosphere shifted. None of it was real in the way that we thought it was at the time. It was just a chemically induced simulation. And as the Twentieth Century drew to a close, all the great insights into "how life should be" began to look increasingly hollow, increasingly inane and increasingly ridiculous. You could still take pills, you could still go dancing, but it somehow didn't open that same door anymore. Narnia had left the wardrobe.

Yet I was left with distinct memories of having visited something that, to all intents and purposes, and for a few short years, did feel like a return to the Garden of Eden. I remember understanding the words "Every man and woman is a star," not as a hollow Thelemic platitude but as the reality of my Saturday night out. And somewhere, between the mad wide-eyed nights dancing to repetitive beats—alchemically transmuted into the music of the spheres—and weary comedown mornings dancing ecstatically to the noise of outside traffic, I received a series of visions that would change my life forever.

I didn't grow up in a culture where prospective shamans are taken out into the desert, fed a hallucinogenic cactus and taught directly by the Spirits. But the Spirits are clever. They find a way to get their message across, and if the path of least resistance happens to be a dodgy pill and the local disco, then that's how it's going to go down.

Taking drugs is categorically *not* the same as practicing magic. If that were the case, every acid casualty fuckwit in the land would be an adept—and they ain't. The magician who needs hallucinatory substances to do anything, is a rubbish magician. What drugs tend to do, however, is provide you with a quick glimpse into the kind of territories that magicians operate in.

The weird Alice in Wonderland phantasmagoria of wonder and menace that comes with LSD and magic mushrooms, and the sensuous territories of bliss and understanding that are revealed by MDMA, are not contained within tiny tablets or blotting papers. They're contained in the human heart and mind. The drugs act as a catalyst, fling us into a new perspective, make us look at the world from a different angle and alter the chemical balance that governs the five senses we interpret "reality" through. The world we perceive on acid is no less "real" than the world we experience every day, in the same way that a snail's version of reality is no less valid than that of a bank manager, trapeze artist or sea anemone.

These profoundly mad experiences that I was having on a fairly regular basis in the early nineties seemed to suggest that there was some element of choice involved—unconscious or otherwise—in how we experienced the world around us. They suggested that each of us play a major role in the construction of what we consider to be reality—and that many of the things I previously thought were solid unshakable facts of my existence might be nothing more than consensual operating rules tacitly agreed on by myself and those around me.

All of which, I felt, had certain implications. For instance, I had experienced firsthand how the grimy kitchen of a squatted house in a small northern town could somehow, given the right set of circumstances, be transformed into what I can only describe as the Garden of Earthly Delights. Which immediately raises questions such as: Why is our experience of reality not like that all the time? What other methods and technologies might there be for accessing this particular experience of the world? Is it possible to maintain this form of consciousness for a prolonged period? Is there something that is preventing us from having regular access to this state of being? Something within us, or maybe within the coding of the universe we inhabit, that acts as a metaphorical angel with a flaming sword keeping us out of paradise? Is there a cosmic bouncer on the gates of Heaven and, if so, how do you go about getting your name on the guest list?

Magic, whilst not providing any easy answers to these conundrums, seemed to suggest a bit of a road map for engaging with these issues and ideas, or at the very least attempting to get a better understanding of the non-ordinary events that I'd seen and experienced first hand during my late teens. In the summer of 1996, I decided to sign my name on the dotted line.

London Calling

Like countless other British magicians before me, I naturally gravitated to London. Three hundred miles from home, and with only a handful of people around who knew anything about me, I was free to recreate my life on my own terms. The parameters of my personality and the shape of my future were fair game. I wanted to learn about magic, so the first thing I did was start keeping a journal in which to closely monitor the processes I was experimenting with.

I remember making a list of all the things that the word "magic" meant to me, and all the things that I felt being a "magician" involved; then I set about systematically exploring each of them. Banishing rituals, the runes, meditation, predicting the future, astral projection, martial arts, ceremonies, lucid dreaming, the Tarot, spells for this and that. I recorded my results as if I were conducting weird scientific experiments in human consciousness. I've actually got old notebooks with it all written out under headings like intent, method, results and conclusion. Exactly like I remembered doing in science class, except with ghosts, candles and ritual sex instead of litmus paper, Bunsen burners and dissection.

The most exciting thing happening at the time was chaos magic. It was appealing because it didn't ask you to believe in anything, or subscribe to any tenets or principles on faith. It took a common sense approach of experimentation, assessment of results and constant questioning of both subjective experience and received knowledge. It had none of the New Age wish-fulfillment fantasies or empty theorizing that filled most of the books in the marketplace. It was about doing stuff, seeing what happened and observing whether a specific practice or exercise could be considered successful enough to merit further investigation.

It also emphasized creativity in magic, positioning its practice not as a series of ritual instructions copied out of a textbook, but something that involved your own creative input. It encouraged you to write your own rituals, use your imagination to develop an approach to magic that resonated with you personally, develop your own symbol systems and call on spirits of your own choosing. This struck a major chord with me. Since I was little, I had always written stories, drawn pictures, made up imaginary worlds in my head, populated them with strange beings and tried to make it all real. Chaos magic seemed to me an extension of this process, perhaps even the science of this process, laid out and waiting to be explored.

Sentient Hotel

The most significant magical event of my early career took place two years into my practice. I made contact with a group of chaos magicians over the Internet and put myself forward to be initiated into their order. One of their members responded to my e-mail and offered to be my mentor. She was based in South America but was coming over to London later that year, and offered to perform my initiation for me. It was up to me to decide what that initiation might involve. I had to be brutally honest and work out what it was that was holding me back in life, try to figure out what my overriding problems were, my biggest neuroses, repressions and obstacles to my development both as a magician and as a human being. All of these outmoded, useless and limiting aspects of myself were to be offered up as fuel; an emotional sacrifice to kick-start the engines of initiation.

I started by producing pages of automatic writing, recording all the things I disliked about myself in excruciating detail. All of my failings, fears and inadequacies, the things that would eat at me at four in the morning—I tried to get it all down on paper where I could see it. No part of my ego was spared. All of my personal demons pinned down and cruelly exposed in print. I'll spare the gory details for this account, but it was all the usual stuff people tend to carry with them into adulthood: negative conditioning around sex, body image, shyness, lack of confidence and all of that malarkey. I took a copy of the text and posted it to my mentor, because there could be no shame or embarrassment attached to any of this material. I had to own it, take responsibility for it, stop being afraid of it.

I took the handwritten pages, cut them up into little bits and reassembled the pieces into a different order, eviscerating my fears with the cut-up technique, a method of working magically with the written word developed by William Burroughs and Brion Gysin in the sixties. I scoured the random juxtapositions of words and phrases as they fell on the page, looking for the names of my demons in the makeshift grimoire that I'd constructed. I'd read in books about magic that if you can put a name to something, you have power over it, and can bind it to your will. All I needed were the names, and I found them, barbarous words of power picked out of the nonsense language formed by my reshuffled insecurities.

My mentor and initiator arrived in London in late December. I met her at the house where she was staying, which, bizarrely—and with the level of unlikely synchronicity that becomes almost *de rigueur* in magical practice—happened to be at the end of the street where I lived. She had read the outline of my initiation ritual and, given the emphasis on negative sexual material, said she would be happy to take part in an act of ritual sex with me, if I felt that would empower the magic. If I said that the prospect of a glamorous South American sorceress coming over to initiate me into her occult order via an evening of sex and witchcraft did not appeal to my red-blooded twenty-three-year-old self, then I'd be lying and not fooling anybody; of course it did, but that didn't prevent it from being an insanely mad and emotionally affecting thing to prepare for over the course of a few months. It took my magical experiment beyond the realm of the psychological and theoretical, and made it into what magic should be and has been for me ever since. Physical. Visceral. Tangible. Real.

I remember walking up the road with my inner demons screaming in my head, meeting her and drinking coffee, making small talk, knowing that in an hour's time we would be going in secret to a North London hotel room for a bizarre magical one-night stand that had been designed to rewire my consciousness. I mean, what the fuck? When exactly did Nicolas Roeg take over directing my life? I think the very act of consciously placing myself in this space—that was way outside of the parameters of anything I'd ever done before—was as much a part of the magic as what happened later. It rewrites the rules of your life. If intensely pleasurable afternoons of crazy sci-fi sex magic become normalized into your everyday experience, pretty much anything can happen.

I stepped into the hotel room and closed the door. Opened the temple with a banishing rite. Tuned a television set to white noise. Conjured the spirits I'd named, bound them with string, sealed their sigils up in a bag that I'd later throw out into the sea, then stood naked in an anonymous room before a complete stranger from the other side of the world. It felt as if, by dramatizing this process of shedding my limitations, I could now move on from them. It was a fresh start.

We made love for hours, both painted with sigils representing my new life as a magician. Celebrating the end of one thing and the beginning of another. It felt like losing my virginity all over again, but on my own terms and with an empowering narrative. At the risk of sounding like Barry White, I think that sex is one of the most profoundly powerful and magical activities that a person can participate in. It doesn't have to be framed in terms of "Western Tantra" or "karezza" for it to function as a hugely transformative experience. All of the concepts and ideas I'd picked up beforehand from a cursory reading of a handful of sex magic texts seemed meaningless within the moment. That's not really what it was about. The ritual, more than anything else, was about establishing a new relationship between myself and the world. My partner in this act of magic represented everything that was not me, and the sex was simply an open and honest form of communication. It functioned as a dialogue, a working out of differences, naked like children and with nothing to hide. Most significantly, it provided me with a positive sexual experience that would act as a blueprint for the future, redefining how I thought about sexuality, physicality, my own body, my relationships with other people, the experiences of my past, the possibilities the future might hold and a complex range of interwoven feelings and beliefs.

Initiation means "to start something," and that's what it did. When I opened the hotel room door again five hours later and stepped outside, it was as a magician. I didn't really know what that meant at the time, and it's a tricky word to define even on a good day, but I knew that something had shifted within me and there was no going back. Like the sudden incursion of my hip disorder when I was a child, my first major self-directed initiation functioned as a catalyst event that bucked the course of my life. This time, however, it was predetermined and consciously directed. I'd conjured an experience that was far outside of the normal range of actions and routines that my life might be expected to consist of. The train had been derailed again, but it was me who had mugged the driver and picked a new track.

I got dressed and fled the scene of big magic, retreated to a late night bar with my beautiful Chilean initiatrix, and toasted the new world we'd set in motion with the blessed sacrament of a takeaway curry and a bottle of wine.

Sacrifice and the City

Within a matter of months I had uncovered London's thriving occult scene, and hooked up with a number of like-minded individuals who shared similar ideas about magic. Interesting times followed—weird possession rituals in the woods at midnight, communication with strange Lovecraftian entities, scary monsters, super creeps, black robes, candles, incense and the Hammer Horror vibe in full effect. I'm fairly certain that, over the course of a few years, I received the best practical grounding in magic that a person could ask for.

But it wasn't quite enough. I wanted to see if I could take things further. I wanted to know if there was anything beyond the work I'd been doing and the level of magic I'd been exposed to. Many of the magicians I had encountered, both in London and online, seemed to treat their magic a bit like a hobby. Much like other people would play five-a-side football on a weekend, they would get together and summon nine-dimensional intelligences from the Abyss.

The London scene was filled with what I call "Doley Crowleys," funny-looking geezers in black clothes trying to start the Aeon of Horus out of a bedsit in Hackney, masturbating furiously over a series of squiggly lines drawn on a post-it note to make their unemployment benefit come through more quickly. There were too many beardy pagan guys sitting around in pubs singing empty hymns to a nonspecific Goddess with all the passion and Gnostic rapture of a village green church choir. Too many socially marginalized people for whom magic and paganism seemed to function as more of a support group than anything else. A shared comfort zone that provided a sense of empowerment and community but, for the most part, seemed to have precious little to do with magic, with the mysteries, with getting things done.

Perhaps in a moment of spontaneous possession by the late Peggy Lee, I wondered: Is that all there is? There had to be more. In the midst of heavy ritual, I'd sometimes caught a glimpse of it. Something big and primal and terrifyingly real, stirring at the edge of my awareness.

At the same time, chaos magic, as a current or ideology, seemed to be atrophying around me. In my personal practice, I was slowly becoming aware of its limitations and problematic aspects; and despite its supposed emphasis on creativity, I thought a lot of what people were doing with it was actually quite uninspiring and formulaic. Its principle tenets and techniques were rapidly solidifying into a kind of chaos magic dogma, based on things that other people had invented: sigils, servitors, paradigm shifting, Chaospheres, Vortex Rites, Ouranian Barbaric, the colors of magic, the Mass of Chaos "B"—with little intervening thought or imagination applied. In its endeavor to distill the principles of magic to their essence, to cut out all the mystical obfuscation and mumbo jumbo and reduce its methodology to a series of workable formulas, I felt that chaos magic had perhaps thrown the baby out with the bath water.

I didn't want godforms that were really just Jungian archetypes within my unconscious mind; I wanted fierce primal Gods and Goddesses that would wake me up in the middle of the night with strange visions and divine guidance. I didn't want a system of sorcery that was indistinguishable from Neuro-Linguistic Programming; they were teaching me NLP on telephone training courses at work. I wanted sorcery that was alive, scary, real, physical and mysterious. To my mind, magic wasn't just a kind of applied pop psychology with occult trappings, it was about conjuring spirits, foretelling the future, speaking to the Gods and being empowered to assist my friends, bind my enemies and look after the people I cared about. It wasn't an intellectualized retreat from the world, but a dynamic engagement with it. Some time around the turn of the century, I found exactly what I was looking for and never looked back.

The Religion

Keeping silent is an undervalued attribute of the contemporary magician. There's more reason to keep your trap shut than just the fear of a witch-burning, literal or metaphoric. There's power in maintaining secrecy, keeping the oral tradition, not blabbing everything on the net, putting all your secrets into a book or selling out the mysteries for a publishing deal. So I'm going to be infuriatingly coy when I talk about what it is I'm into, and you're just going to have to like it.

Over the last five years or so, I've veered from identifying as a chaos magician—with all of its attendant theories around maintaining fluidity of belief, approaching belief as a working tool, regular paradigm shifting to maintain independence from dogmatic thought processes, and so on—to my current position of identifying as a follower of a religion. I find this model of reality far more rewarding, fulfilling and transformative, both in my everyday life and in terms of the magical practices I engage with, than the previous model I subscribed to. I arrived at this position having experimented with several beliefs until one of them clicked massively, and it became apparent that I could get a lot more out of total engagement with this one perspective than I could from maintaining the diffident approach of juggling multiple outlooks.

I didn't find this transition to religion easy, as it went against many of the core principles of chaos magic I had filled my head with over the preceding years, and which I had quite a strong attachment to and investment in. However, this conflict was in itself paradoxical, as my resistance seemed to be coming from a conditioned dogmatic attitude about trying to avoid anything that could conceivably be considered a conditioned dogmatic attitude. Over the course of a few years, I eventually faced up to the likelihood that what I was actually afraid of was commitment to something, and decided to fully embrace the religious aspects of what I was doing.

I found it incredibly liberating and empowering, and I discovered that the word "religion" does not automatically have to imply an imposed belief system, or a complete dictated system of instruction that discourages individual thought. Quite far from it. Granted, the religion that I came to follow does not have a central text like the Bible or the Qu'ran. It isn't a religion of the book, and it doesn't have a centralized priesthood or organized hierarchical structure, such as the major religions of the world. But it is a religion, and if you consider all of its sister religions and offshoots under the same umbrella, it probably counts as a major one.

Interestingly, many of its followers refer to it as "The Religion," which has always amused me because it seems to imply that there is only really one "Religion" (with a capital "R") in the world. Only one God, one set of spirits, one reality. With all the multiple conflicting world religions (with a small "r") considered as reflections of this central religious impulse. All that really changes culture to culture is that they tend to call things by different names and place a differing emphasis on certain points due to cultural and socio-geographical factors. In this sense, the word religion does not mean the act of abiding by the differing creeds, dogmas and systems of instruction written down in a book or dictated by the priesthood, but the actual day-to-day process of personal engagement with spirituality through religious practice. It's an activity that you do, not a collection of things that you believe.

I filter all information received by my senses through the lens of my religion and I live my life according to it. However, it is a dynamic living religion that is constantly developing and being redefined on a day-to-day basis. The Gods I speak to are Living Gods, and my relationship with them is very much a two-way process. Religion does not automatically imply subservience; it can mean an integrative, cooperative, mutually supportive relationship with something greater than yourself.

My religious beliefs tend to be both inclusive and open to further syncretism, so that I don't approach other religions as somehow competing or contradictory to how I look at things, but as other views that will help me better understand the spiritual as a universal concept. My religion does not give me easy answers, but provides a context for seeking to understand more about the mysteries of reality, consciousness, spirituality and the day-to-day events of my life. This context is, more than anything, a solid starting point from which to explore such areas and is constantly being broadened, modified and enriched as it is exposed to new information, new experiences and new perspectives.

At a practical level, the Gods of my religion empower me to look after the people around me, provide me with tangible support and help to bring about my personal evolution at both a spiritual and worldly level. In return I serve them, honor them, give them my respect and strive to live according to their wisdom. It's all about relationships, not about approaching deity on a one-off, fly-by-night basis, to pester them for a new girlfriend or a new car in return for half an hour's grudging lip service. It involves investing significant time and effort in building, maintaining and developing really good, healthy working relationships with a number of powerful allies. A useful analogy might be the difference between calling a random number from the phone book and asking the person on the other end of the line to come round and fix your blocked drain, and calling a very close friend who happens to be a plumber. But it's more than that; by making friends with the Gods you become more like them, you find some common ground where the relationship can begin to take root, a space within you that is like them and which you can cultivate through your association with them. Sometimes they will test you, and sometimes the lessons they teach you will be cruel and uncompromising, but the same can be said of any relationship with another living being.

On a day-to-day basis, I aspire to function as a medium through which their power can reach out into the community and affect the world around me. They touch the world through the magic that I work under their auspices. The construction of charm bags, condition oils, floor washes and spiritual baths for those who come to me with their problems. Casting oracles for the troubled so that they may receive guidance and counsel from the Spirits. Holding regular feasts for the Gods and inviting the people I care about to attend, bring offerings and commune with deity. Taking personal responsibility for what is happening around me in the world, and becoming directly involved at a magical level. Sorcery to keep the local community center open. Witchcraft to stop a loved one suffering at the hands of a bullying manager. Conjure work to help a next-door neighbor hang on to her council flat. Magic to engage with the world at a practical, grassroots level, and to try to make people's lives better in whatever small ways I may be empowered to.

It's constantly challenging, occasionally fraught with danger and it means that I'm on a nonstop learning curve, but I wouldn't have it any other way. My religion situates the activity of magic directly within the fundamentals of day-to-day existence and the human experience. The stuff that many high-flown occultists might casually dismiss as inconsequential or mundane is exactly where it's at, as far as I'm concerned. Shelter, sustenance, sex, love, industry, creativity, birth and death are the bread and butter of the mysteries. The stuff that all of us have to deal with every day of our lives. There's nothing more magical, nothing more precious and nothing more worthy of devotion than that.

I don't have time to fuck about on ephemeral and arguably imaginary astral planes, when my best friend is struggling to put food on his table. I'm not about to spend an afternoon working through the Tunnels of Set when the girl who sits next to me at work keeps getting slapped about by her partner. I'm not that bothered about cosmic enlightenment, as long as the magic that I'm involved with seems to be bringing some level of positive change into my life and the lives of my friends and family. That's all that really counts. That's why I'm in it, and why I'm continuing to walk down the long, strange road that is magic. Maybe in two years' time I'll look back at these words and cringe at my own naïveté and embarrassing lack of insight. To be honest, I fucking well hope so, because magic is, above all else, a dynamic process. If you're not constantly changing, being pushed, facing challenges, overcoming obstacles, developing your ideas, unlearning what you think you know, broadening your understanding, gradually refining every aspect of your being and remaking every aspect of your reality, then your magic is dead magic—and that's the worst game in town.

ENDNOTES

[1] Aeons are traditionally the emanations of God, existing in an eternal world beyond the material, as expressed in the Platonic and Gnostic models. Both Aleister Crowley and Peter Carroll used Aeons as a model of history, with Aeons denoting periods of human evolution occurring over several thousands of years; some groups, such as the Typhonian O.T.O., have approached Crowley's Aeonic model in the more traditional sense of co-extant realities that can be contacted at any time. There are nearly as

many approaches to Aeonics as there are magicians. – Ed.

(Here's an Aeonic scheme from Elijah):

1st Aeon: Isis.

2nd: Apophis. (This Aeon was wiped out, issuing the Voice of the Silence, now hushed thanks to the Second Coming of Christ and all concurrent bullshit.)

3rd: Osiris. (The Sacrificed God—This was the first sacrifice; NORSOU-NORCOU.)

4nd: Horus. Thelema, Agape, Aughm. Crowleyanity. Will.

4a: Underlying/concurrent Aeon of Ma'at. IPSOS, ALLALA, truth and resultant dancing the mask and masking the dance of all the Choronzonic mixup which was the Neverending Story's idea in order to keep the Aeon ongoing.

5th: Pandaemonaeon. The Aeon of the opening of the Eye/Super Novus for all of humanity. The creation/recreation of Pentagrammaton. This is the stopping point for all.

6th: The Aeon of the Spider. This silent Aeon is now defunct, that is, non-existant; all Aiwass spider work should not be adhered to. AlGOL is emptied (purified) and no more Universe B exists. It never existed in the first place.

7th: Results in the parable of Lamion and bifurcates as it is.

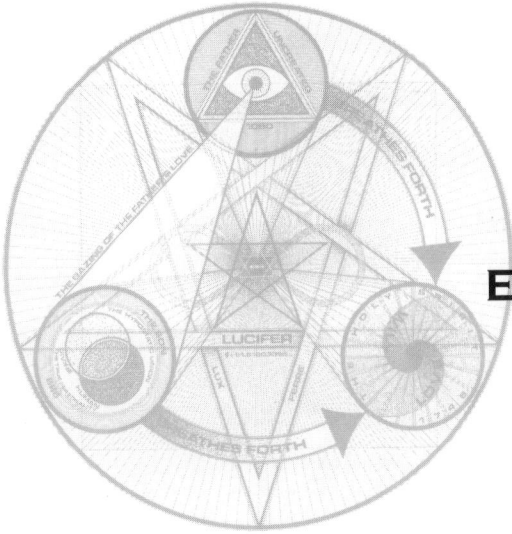

ERIS IS MY BIATCH

Rachel Haywire

There was a time when I thought that I was the only person in the world who thought like I did, the only person in the world who realized that reality was flexible, the only person in the world who saw outside of the consensual hallucination that humanity lived in. Sometimes it felt like having this knowledge was a curse. So I became an anarchist. I got out of the suburbs and started traveling the country in search of people who understood what was going on in this bizarre head of mine.

Eventually I found them. No matter how they were dressed it was easy to recognize them. There was an instant psychic connection that we shared.

Eventually I found myself collaborating and conspiring with the people I'd been looking for my entire life. The magicians of the cybernetic generation. The Paradigm Shifting Mutant Race.

Understanding

My goal is to unite those individuals who stand for the same things as I do, so we can have One Gigantic Mindfuck like it'll lead us to the next step of evolution (which is part of the mindfuck itself). It is due to the *lack* of this type of unity that I am inspired to wake up in the morning and change things.

Call me an elitist, but there truly *is* an understanding that a select few individuals have reached. Space hippies? I think not. We were outcasts. We were picked on in school because there was something "off" about us. We were faced with severe social isolation and it sometimes got to the point of "I want to fucking die." Then we found our savior. The "Internet," it was called. It was here that social standards were forever altered. We were aliens—here to colonize the earth—and the Internet was our home. A new breed was emerging and we were starting to communicate. Message boards grew from tiny caterpillars into hardcore butterflies as alternative social realities were combined into collective cybernetic entities.

We went digital. We had no parties to go to, but we did have websites to create. We exchanged our ideas—spread our memetic viruses—through a marginalized fringe. We learned to become social superheroes through the (free)world wide web. While the "popular" kids were busy going to high school baaaa bashes, we aliens were learning how to converse with people from all over the universe, faster and smarter than all the layers of hell.

Many of us with the ability to become anything we want at any time and blend in with any group of people were raised online. The first few years of our social lives were spent in cyberspace, and it was here that we developed our "über-social-shape-shifting" powers. Eventually, we were able to take these qualities out into the "real world," which we soon became masterfully adept at. The "real world" and its social components were mundane simplicities in comparison to the speed and complexity of the Internet.

And now we're creating the culture as we go along. This is ours.

Self

People knew me as Acidexia. People knew me as Rage. Some said that I was the incarnation of Eris. Others said that I needed some serious help with reality. "Reality is a toy!" I would scream on the streets—going off about the upcoming apocalypse—preaching about how We the Paradigm Shifting Mutant Race were gonna take over the world and the Internet and everything this side of the underground.

Some knew me as the Rainbow Brite of the Apocalypse. Some knew me as Rabbi Haywire. I was the girl who traveled from city to city to meet up with the best—and craziest—minds of her generation. My friend Jason knew me as the psychedelic robofascist.

One thing I knew about the universe was that it needed to be fucked with more than it needed to be helped. What needed to be changed most of all were the beliefs that those silly humans held—beliefs about philosophies, politics, religions and subcultures—if you held a belief I existed for the purpose of smashing it.

People knew me as Paradox the Prime. I was a young chaos magician who traveled the country on my wits and my antisocial skills, not a single root of stability and not a single plan or goal, with the exception of subverting the structure of everything I came in contact with.

Magic

Here I am in Eugene, sleeping on the streets as a mutant on the dredges of society.

Jaded to the point of a bizarre sort of growth: a new feeling that can only be described as perverse satisfaction with incongruity. Flying to embrace the destruction of all notions, nations, rations and ideological relations. Checkpoint slash enter. Flying? To embrace the destruction of all perceptions! A jolly looking demon pops out of the sky with a yawn. "Local DJ of reality tunnel bombs hundreds of statements and opinions. Timothy McVeigh raises glass."

Us. Us. Our choices in how we see the universe cause the universe to exist for us.

We're all in the reality of God. Free Will is God. We can become equal to this "God" person by altering this reality to our own liking. I write my own book.

All these good things keep happening, and things get better day by day. Sometimes you've got to sink to climb higher than ever. You can change anything whenever you want to. Nothing in your past effects anything in your now. Remember *the code*.

Transit

One day I'd wake up on a friend's couch in Boston. The next day I'd wake up on a friend's floor in New York City. Once I managed to wake up on a bus station floor in Alabama. (This was pretty damn nasty, even for a mutant gutter punk.)

I'd wake up in a San Francisco warehouse. I'd wake up in the Black Rock City desert. I'd wake up and have no idea where the hell I was. I'd wake up in hell. I'd wake up on top of the world. The only direction I had was "everywhere" and…

I was a female hitchhiker who improvised absurdist poetry for spare change, who changed the world by altering-rejecting-destroying its settings, who kept an online journal about her cross country travels through the psychic underground of freaks, geeks and lunatics.

Surpassing Humanity

My final night in Vancouver was the best one yet. Somehow magic spread its wings and I ended up attending two hell-fuck-ya! parties. At the first one Edie dosed me with six hits of *acidexia*. My mind returned to its create-your-own-reality state, and my soul returned to its inside-the-music city. Other drugs ingested were marijuana, hashish and ecstasy. At the second party I was dosed with five more hits of *acidexia*. A lot of the night is hard to remember, and saturated with mind exchanges and psychic signals. The utter beauty of it—released individuals gathered together to create a greater whole—making it up as we fly along. A song. As we go. The music becomes you and the person you're dancing with turns into a mystical creature from another galaxy or universe and you wonder if your "hallucinations" are similar to theirs and they tell you what it's like to live in their mind and for a minute you're actually *living there* because you've shifted over to their brainspace and built onto it with a galaxy of your own.

You realize what a great time it is to be alive. The stellar transcendence of it all.

The striving for a higher mode of cybernetic consciousness. A culture based on mind opposed to matter. A culture embracing technology—using it to create new forms of existence. Art exchange. Music exchange. Word exchange. Thought exchange. Circulating ideas and tactics for resistance with insistence, meeting the Others in cities across the country . . . sometimes I look at the children of the sixties and seventies and laugh at how unfortunate they were.

What we're creating here is the first culture to incorporate surpassing humanity into its deprogram. Why feast on peace, love and happiness when you can strive to become a cyborg? Why let the Anger eat you up inside (as you smash your guitar against your bathroom mirror) when you can be creating a new metaphysical program?

Ybor City

Ended up missing the Against Me! show. Turned out it was over by eleven o'clock. Figured I'd get there around eleven so I'd only have to deal with *one* of the opening bands. Eleven, right? Reasonable, right? Wrong. The *entire show* was over by then. What kind of show ends at eleven? What in the . . .

Suddenly it dawned on me. I'd become an adult! Scary, but still. I was by far the oldest person outside the venue. Children from the ages of thirteen to sixteen occupied the premises. What was I doing with a bunch of punk rockers that were all younger than my little brother?

Started walking around the downtown area. Piercing and tattoo shops, head shops, coffee shops, clothes shops . . . going from one end to the other and back again and back again and back again freaking the counterculture mundanes . . . you know how it goes. One of the piercing shops contained a shitload of tongue rings with "23" painted on them. Didn't I write a Discordian dystopian story about this exact incident a year ago? Why does all our shit come true?

So I go into this random bathroom and meet this random girl and she's super cute. Bald, Goth, a bunch of tattoos, "artist hardcore," something like my type. "It's my birthday today," she tells me, "and I've got nothing to do when I get off work." "Hang out with me then," I tell her—and the date is on.

So anyway, twenty-three-year-old Sunny and I found out that the Buzzcocks were playing that night. No shit: I mean fuck Against Me!, the Buzzcocks were playing. Now my reason for coming to Ybor City was clear.

After our date we met a beautiful transsexual called Angelique at this industrial fetish club called The Castle. We went back to her house and hopped in the pool: had a fantastic little time in there. Angelique is the first transsexual to model for Suicide-Girls, apparently. While I canceled my SuicideGirls a few weeks ago due to overall boredom, I must say that transsexuals modeling for the site is a nice idea. Anyway, I really like Angelique a whole bunch. There's something so amazing about transcending gender. It's transhuman.

After leaving Ybor I got into some crazy hitchhiking adventures and scared the shit out of this one guy who wanted to see my boobs by breaking out into parody Little Mermaid tunes of a violent nature. He dropped me off at the gas station. "Get out," he told me. "Just get out."

Now I'm in Daytona Beach. My motel is awesome. It's an amusement park ghetto over here, not a lot of culture or anything. Crowley's *Liber Aleph* is really helping me out. Been reading it out loud in my motel.

The Mutant's Cycle of Evolution

The first stage is *alienation*—it is in this state that feelings of anger, isolation, loneliness and utter detachment from society occur. You're an outsider. A freak. It is in *alienation* that you assume nobody else feels like you do. How will you ever survive this world? What's *wrong* with you? What *are* you? You're not *like* them. Who are *they* anyway? You're cursed. You're so alone. Nobody gets it. Nobody. You're missing something that everyone else is equipped with. Or maybe you're equipped with something extra. Oh shit. This is fucked. This is really fucking fucked. You're different. Oh no. Oh fucking *shit* you can't take it anymore. Is there *nobody* else who thinks this way? Die die die.

Next is the *relation* stage—this is where you go out and buy some music (or download it) and realize that there are people you can relate to. It's about fucking time! You suddenly feel a lot better, and declare that "music is your life" or even that "music *saved* your life." In *relation* things start to improve, because you know that you are not alone in this fucked up plane of fuckedupness. What a relief! You might even buy some books and watch some movies that seem to describe your life *perfectly*. Viva la counterculture! OK—so *now* what?

Now, in the *conversation* stage, you *talk* about it. But what is "it?" Nobody really knows, but you sure love debating what "it" is with your new friends. In fact, you could do this all night! During the initial period of the *conversation* state, you are a walking talking cliché. Cookie-cultured spoutings like "they're all lemmings—they just don't *get it*," "we should all get together and like . . . *do something*," anything beginning with "people like us" and anything beginning with "a bunch of freaks should meet up and . . ." are all natural in the beginning. Your true friends will call you on your shit, and ask that you come up with something original for a change. Everyone else will nod, as if you're saying something *new* or something. This is probably because they too have just started their *conversation* period. As you progress through *conversation*, you learn to shut the fuck up with your clichés-which-you-once-thought-to-be-crucial and listen to what your more experienced friends (who have already heard it all) have to say. You might even give them your own personal input. Eventually, you will start to come up with your own ideas, and suddenly your friends will be listening to *you!*

So congratulations! You've made it to *inspiration*. You are now officially One of Us (hands you a very bizarre looking medal). You start getting into new music, reading new books, renting new movies and visiting new art spaces. Now you are not only seeing outside the *societal* box, but the *countercultural* box. Hell, there *is* no box! It is here that *inspiration* takes place—where divine bursts of emotion, creativity and intelligence present themselves to your fabulous mind.

Inspiration is what leads you to the final state of your evolutionary cycle, *creation*: this is where you start expressing yourself through means such as writing, music, art, filmmaking, photography, rabble rousing, your-own-personal-religion creating, your-own-personal-philosophy creating. You hope to be famous some day. Either that, or you choose to remain underground because it's so much "cooler" that way. These divine bursts of *inspiration,* which lead to *creation,* have *relation* and *conversation* to thank. If it wasn't for all the music you listened to and people you talked to, would you really be where you are today?

Once you have reached the period of *creation* you realize that *alienation* is a childish phase that everyone goes through (and that everyone who is "like you" goes through *harshly*). You realize that you don't need someone else's music to speak for you (why not create your own?), that you didn't come up with as many new ideas as you thought you did, that your acid conversations were a lot less sacred and amazing as you once thought and—above all—that you fucking rule.

Peacock

I had a beautiful experience tonight. Alone in my apartment with some extremely potent mushrooms I was finally able to let go. "I'm alive!" I kept exclaiming. Euphoric uprising transcendental magic—this is the good stuff that you only *hear* about in shaman school. This is the real thing. At first I was thinking about my life: every experience I'd ever undertaken: then there were the deaths of so many people who had inspired me: then there was this egocentric counterculture goddess I'd turned into who was in serious need of an ass-kicking. Tonight I said goodbye to the horrible monster known as Acidexia. For the first time in my travel I finally just *was.* Reborn, this time authentic. What happened? Where down the line had I become such a cold-hearted cunt?

An Interview With Myself

Are you ready to admit that you're a homo sapien yet?
Hells no, though I'm not ready to deny it either. I don't think that anyone can truly know what they "are," and to speculate about this is much like speculating about God.

Do you really want to wipe out humanity and start a new species of mutant peeps?
Nope. I just want to talk about this shit with other freaks, as I enjoy comments

like "we're so rare" and "let's breed children with triangle-heads and eight fingers who have the same mental liberation as us so we can take over the world."

You're pretty fucked up, dude.
Thanks!

Dreams

I'm really starting to dislike all these tarot-twits. Psy-trance, "ohmygawd synchron-icity!", collective consciousness? All that debris needs to be annihilated. Can't believe I used to be one of you. There never was an "us." Fuck your prepackaged unity, your leftover remnants from the sixties, your universal visionquest. The *really* sad thing is that you'll dismiss what I'm saying as "negative." You know what that's like? It's like the masses dismissing what *you're* saying as "idealistic nonsense." You're doing the same thing as them: You're blocking information that you don't want to hear.

If I hear one more person who brags about their trips with Terence McKenna or Timothy Leary I might *become* what people refer to as evil. Sometimes I wonder how I was ever a part of the "psychonaut scene," these wannabe-gurus assuming that en-lightenment comes with meditation and mindlessness: these Buddhas-in-training afraid to enter all areas of consciousness. We can relax as laid back philosopher types, and as long as we're not being disturbed we're OK? If you don't want a disturbance you can bet 2012 is the end for you. As far as I'm concerned, if you're not embracing demons and nightmares they'll devour you when they decide to come party. It all feels so old and corny now. These shamans are living in their heads as opposed to taking action. We're *all* living in the realities we've created with our minds, but this doesn't mean that playing perspective games is gonna get us anywhere outside of psychic masturbation. I don't care how many psychedelic "sessions" you've had. I have dictators-of-conscious-ness to kill, and hot young martyrs to fuck.

Dreams are universes next door. And nightmares . . .

I'm starting to embrace the dark. Suddenly depression seems like such a limiting term. Used to be that I'd rainbow-brite-the-apocalypse: now I'm all about exploring it and diving in: going to those dark and for bidden areas without feeling the need to giggle and cheer about them.

How much more do you learn from a nightmare than a typical dream? Lots. How much more do you learn from a bad acid trip than a smooth one? Lots. Anyone can create a (very acceptable) world of carefree swing sets and dancing little bounce girls, but how many people can look demons straight in the eye and say "show me what you've got, punk!?"

Humans create terms like "nightmare" and "bad trip" and associate them with a phase they call "negativity," which is really just the flipside of whatever smile one hap-pens to be thriving on: an alternate outlook: a pushing and breaking of a threshold one views as "comfortable." You can dance with the devil in pure bliss and ecstasy and Bob Marley can come after you with skulls and wormpus. I've seen it happen.

I did an invocation of my Holy Guardian Angel last night on pure whim. Magic is spontaneity.

Home?

Last night was amazing. Who would have thought I'd run into Joy, my long time friend from middle school? Crazy shit! I saw her when I went out to eat with my mom and grandma, and we decided to go to a party.

Couldn't believe who I ended up seeing there. Jack, Meredith, Eric: kids that were just as dorky as I was back then! Total reunion of the geeks. I told them that we should have started the dork revolution: asked Jack why I wasn't able to recognize him as a fellow creator in those days: wondered why I didn't lead a major nerd rebellion. If only I could go back knowing what I do today. Maybe.

I'm so glad this happened. It feels like a new part of my life has been completed. My old friends seemed really impressed by the girl I'd turned into: would love to get them out of Florida and share the insane world I've immersed myself in. Back then I only dreamed of alternative culture existing, and suddenly I'm creating it.

I wonder if any of the others were affected by the torment as much as I was, especially Eric, who even *I* picked on. I wanted to ask if he still had nightmares about those days, but I decided against it.

One thing that struck me as hilarious was Joy's memory of our gifted teacher Ms. Sabety telling me to go outside and look for the pink elephants when I "acted out." I'd tell the other kids I'd found those elephants: make weird faces at everyone from the door window: stir up as much trouble as I could possibly manage and get away with it because I was funny. Now that I think of it, Ms. Sabety was quite the Discordian. I think I really did find those elephants back then. They existed in their own sort of way. The pink elephant way.

We're the "cool kids" now. Who would have thought? The more you get picked on in school—the cooler you are when you're an adult. The others ended up finishing high school. Me? Never even made it there. Went to schools for "bad" kids and "emotionally disturbed" kids and even "mental" hospitals. Sixteen and I was out to go find myself. Met ex-boyfriend on the Internet and fled to Canada. Viva!

"So she ended up rocking the streets of New York City and San Francisco when she was seventeen? Guess we helped her, in a way." – The Cruel and Popular Girls of Pioneer Middle School.

Would have made my father proud today. Went out to dinner with my mom, grandma, brother, uncle, aunts and cousin. It was so sweet. I didn't feel the need to dominate the conversation with politiks or monologues. Could it be that I'm growing up? It was cousin Stephanie's eleventh birthday: When she opened her presents I was able to experience her joy. Gave her a big hug before we parted.

Did I really spend the fifteenth year of my life creating an Internet counterculture based on Borderline Personality Disorder?

Fables

A teenage boy asks the Buddha why the whole world seems to be in his head. Black Flag's *Damaged* plays in the background. "Fuck that solipsistic shit. It's much easier to believe in nothing!" the Buddha exclaims. The boy ends up carving the word FNORD into his wrists and posting them (his wrists) to the Internet. He also decides to get a LiveJournal.

A superhuman webdesigner with big purple titties finds the Buddha inspecting her mousepad and posting about its aesthetic qualities to a secret government website. "Don't you think you're being a little *1984*?" the superhuman webdesigner (with big purple titties) asks the Buddha. "When you use '1984' as an adjective you've got it coming," the Buddha replies. The big purple titties detach themselves from the superhuman webdesigner, and she is revealed to be the Buddha.

Chaos

Miami Anti-FTAA Protest: Running through the ghetto with the anarchists: Happy twentieth birthday to me! Everyone in the neighborhood—with the exception of one angry patriot—cheered us on. This included the children. Amazing feeling, receiving so much support out there. The pigs were afraid to go in after us. Together we moved a fence to block them, which was a great response to the one they put up themselves. Never got arrested, 'cause a lot of the younger action kids *wanted* to go to jail. The police didn't want to satisfy their desire, I take it. The street medics were wonderful. Duct tape as the new red cross. Seeing all those bloody post-rubber-bullet kids was horrible, but the way the street medics helped them out was enough to bring serious emotion to the eyes of any cyborg. Felt a little bad for the liberals/socialists, us "violent chaos punks" ruining it for them and everything. Heard a rumor, though, that the steelworkers supported direct action. Must say, I felt pretty old as a twenty-year-old female. Leader.

At the end of the night I engaged in a dialogue with three police officers. They stopped me for hitchhiking, and it was obvious that they had my protection in mind as opposed to my demise. If only they had seen the way their fellow officers behaved toward us young visionaries at the rally, shooting their rubber bullets through signs that said "Meditation. Not retaliation."

I saw the way the "pigs" behaved toward kids who did absolutely nothing. I'll never forget the smell of the tear gas, the faces of the fourteen-year-old kids covered in blood, the masses of children running for their dear lives.

At least the protesters who viewed the anarchists as zoo exhibits actually attended.

Tonight it finally hit me that this was more than a chaos party ("It's a party out here!" one of the younger anarchist kids said). And it was, for a while, until we found out what happened to those of us who went to jail. Suddenly all the exhilarating fun we had turned into a much darker adrenaline rush. Activists were not only brutalized in jail, but also sexually assaulted. These were *some of the most violent acts that have ever been inflicted upon protesters in the United States* and it obviously had to do with the cops being sore about Seattle.

Thanks to those who are posting photos of police brutality to the net, thousands and thousands of citizens are going to hear about the despicable way in which the Miami police behaved. As for the people who actually leave the house? They've already heard about these atrocities, and hot damn are they pissed!

I'll be in Baltimore next week, looking for a place to live. Gonna pick up my stuff from my friend's place and bring it back to Baltimore so I can move in; my backpack is in the locker of the bus terminal. Last night I slept at a homeless women's shelter, 'cause it was way too freezing to be looking for a squat. Observing these women made me grateful for *my life*, as obnoxious as that sounds. Thirty-five, HIV+, sleeping on a cot and pregnant?

That's some harsh shit right there.

And now I've taken the Oath of the Abyss: Where I vow to interpret *everything* as a direct message to me from the Universe.

I Am the Master of Form, and From Me All Forms Proceed

Maybe it's not just Baltimore—it seems like everything is dead in DC too. Maybe it's the season. This country has a massive social disease called "I'm tired and need to go to work tomorrow." I miss the summer: the constant festivals and parties: the non-stop entertainment. *I'm tired and need to go to work tomorrow* is the generic excuse people make to avoid going out and having a good time. It's flat out repulsive. Sickening.

What's up Choronzon old pal? It was always you and me baby. Did you hear about the lesser demons? They were eating my skull so they could name a record label after you. Once upon a time I wrote hippy happy journal entries. *Then?* I came face to face with Your Holiness. Skin was stripped off my entire body: Intestines crawled in maze-like formations to protest their own existence. All that was beautiful spat out the vomit of mankind: Humans surpassed evolution by drowning themselves in the blood of insanity. Not the sexy kind but the gruesome kind, the kind where you're being chased by your own worst nightmares: they fuck with your flesh so they can laugh at how pathetic you are.

"You're so fucking pathetic," they taunt, tormenting your every move until you collapse into pseudo-oblivion. Self pity? Not worth it. The vomit of mankind explodes over your arms, your legs, your stomach, your entire belief system and everything it's ever explored. Christopher Columbus is sailing the ocean of your despair, asking your ego why it's such a wretched piece of reverse cannibalism. Your ego is too weak to respond: it crumples into atoms of crippled two-year-olds: handicapped babies with Down syndrome are transmitting telepathic messages to the sarcasm of your personal disdain. Why was the club so dead? Why were the dead so clubbed? Did rebirth come with a membership card? Did cards of *dis*membership give birth to a new recome? A new outcome? Fuck income! Anarchy!

Fascism! Smash the state of mind! Vagina police? Raping the good of mankind? Stop trying to be so tryingless. Womankind hates you, sweet horror of pain. Blink 182 will never understand hatred. George W. Bush is Hitler. All the shit you listen to is influenced by George W. Bush. Fuck your ideology! Fuck your Hitler! Fuck your supremacy! Time raped space.

Escape from your conceptions of culture and self. Escape from your conceptions of escapism. Nothing! Nothing! Handicapped babies with Down syndrome are supreme enlightened beings. Higher races of mental disorders are militant gas stations. Break all opinions. Opinionate all breakage. Assign a new philosophy to every breadcrumb you eat. Contemplate all breadcrumbs of worthless itineraries. Complicate escape culture. Conceptualize all stupid people. Stupid people form large groups to oppress the weak: the strong are stupider than the weak: the stupid are stronger than the weak: dumb are the weak are the strong: survival of everyday life. This is a lie and you know it. You don't even know how truthful that is. Something! Something!

Telepathic messages of your personal disdain kill all forms of identity and perception. Now you are free. And maybe it's just Baltimore—it seems like everything is dead in DC too. Maybe it's the season. This country has a massive social disease called "I'm tired and need to go to work tomorrow." I miss the summer: the constant festivals and parties: the nonstop entertainment. *I'm tired and need to go to work tomorrow* is the generic excuse people make to avoid going out and having a good time. It's flat out repulsive. Sickening.

Dispersion

Tonight I discovered that only a truly good friend is able to kill the fuck out of your built up personality. Enemies don't help you that way. When something inside of you dies you get in contact with the dead. All comes to life.

Was thinking about completely altering my belief system and becoming a Republican who plays golf, but then it dawned on me that I could go all Stalin and have lots of fun with that. Do as I say for the Wider Culture, my comrades! Or what if I established a Baltimore identity as a preppy liberal? That could be interesting. Or boring as shit. I could make being a Mormon interesting if I tried. Or change my name to Serenity. As long as I know I can remove the identity clothing it's cool, and I've fully realized that it's *all just clothing.* All of it.

You cross *one* abyss but there are still hundreds more to look into and overcome. Now I've been cleaned of the demons of self that haunted me for so long. This is an ongoing process that took what felt like centuries.

I killed my personality-identity-disease again and decided that this time the Death was gonna need to last. Because there was no way I was going back again, and if this meant avoiding human contact for a while, I was gonna need to make it happen. Because I was never again (ever ever ever) gonna think I was anything more (or less) than someone who could be anything.

Anything.

It's hit me. I'm dying in a hell that I'm finally facing. The crazy thing? I'm currently more aware than I've ever been. At least I've made it this far. Rock bottom and still breathing.

Conclusion, of Sorts

Oh no. You're not gonna see me fall that easily. Oh no. I endure. Face the curse and find a way to destroy it. It's all about having a strong mind, see. Sink and let yourself drown for a while. Now? Replenish. Start from scratch again. Meltdown upsurge. If you're not facing the curse it's gonna eat away at you: Might as well look it in the eye and fight it. Psychic warrior flipside overstep. Begin at the end. Clean and purify. Death means breakthrough. Start anew. Those who suffer the most are either the strongest or the most masochistic. Either way, you leave with the knowledge of having been there. If you weren't there, well, you simply don't know.

My death is alive, emerging through the flames of power. Out of the fire my scream is heard in tiny villages throughout the world.

Since I figured out what was going on there is a newfound freedom in my breathing. Alive as ever (with death by my side) I am able to manifest anything. Some say that initiation involves the hatred of others while others hate themselves so they can destroy themselves and make it to the next level. Whatever level is or isn't next (and as a culture we seem to think we're playing some sort of spiritual video game), the entire program is destroyed and the upcoming journey is faced without fear or restraint.

It was all full circle in the secret world of mental mayhem that I refused to keep secret. As a young chaos magician in the Twenty-First Century I was armed with a loud and abrasive desire for change, revolution, evolution, fucked up technology and societal collapse.

One thing I know is that I'll always be a part of the Paradigm Shifting Mutant Race. The lunatic psychic underground. The cybernetic apocalypse. This.

HOW I SPENT MY SUMMER VACATION

JASON LOUV

I'm sweating in a rented room clogged with incense and kerosene fumes, slowly beating a drum, waiting for trance to overtake me. Outside, soldiers clutch carbine rifles and pace under barbed wire, jackals howling in the hills. Something begins to unfurl in my mind as I pound the drum faster, calling it, marbled and plasmic, sly Cheshire Cat grin, astral lightshow. The trance begins—and at the instant that I open up into a new ravine of Self, the power cuts on the entire block. I'm sitting cross-legged in front of a yellow and red mandala of rice and colored sand, wearing just a pair of Nike shorts under a hat made from five foot tall peacock feathers, a string of bells and two necklaces made of wood beads meant as an analogue of Kali's strings of human skulls. And this is how we induce trance. With the elder Jhankri shaman on my left saying incantations and flinging water and dried rice at me (hard) while I pound the drum so frantically with a snake-stick that my right index finger erupts in blisters, eyes rolled back into my head and screaming like the heat-death of the universe until my central nervous system overloads and leaves me shaking uncontrollably across the floor in the slick of my own sweat, while a lithe naked boy dances around the periphery blowing the Azathothian music of chaos on the hollowed-out legbone of a Bengal tiger.

And THAT is how we bring the ROCK.

I arrived in Nepal by accident in June, my school backpack containing a single change of clothes and a notebook, the country having erupted into civil war a day before my arrival, which was especially cheery news to me since I hadn't planned on a

Nepalese holiday in the first place. I had been rerouted to Kathmandu after the wait for my Indian visa had gone on past the departure date of my ticket to Delhi, my original destination. The only catch, as I learned two days after confirming the new ticket, was that the Nepalese royal government and the Maoist insurgents making a bid for power were currently bombing, shooting, machete-ing and rock-hurling each other to pieces in warfare erupting throughout the countryside. Tourists were being extorted and held hostage, and though the city center in Kathmandu was likely to be safe, any trip outside of its confines probably wouldn't be.

This state of affairs had already crippled Nepal's largest industry, tourism, which largely involves Westerners hiring sizable convoys of trekking guides to help them work through their mid-life crises on a mountaintop while loaded down with GPS equipment, DV cams, space-age insulated clothing and wraparound sunglasses—all somewhere decidedly outside of the city center in Kathmandu.

If I had known that I was shortly to be undergoing training as a Nepali witch doctor I would have been slightly more excited about the whole affair, but then the New Age and with-it thing to say would be that such fortuitous mishaps may, in fact, have been "meant" to be.

Well whatever, I thought. It was too late to turn back now, and what was I going to wish I'd done when I was back at the office job in New York? So there, for the love of the Universal Solvent, went I.

I felt totally at ease as I touched down in the Kathmandu airport, despite my connecting flight from Abu Dhabi flying unnervingly close to Baghdad, the full-screen Bollywood distracting me nicely. We came down through the veil above the Himalayas, slowly passing over rings of villages, around the foothills and into the valley. I clutched the guidebook that I'd bought in Heathrow shortly before departing, shouldered my backpack and stepped out into the particularly potent broth of Himalayan fog and industrial exhaust beyond the airport's front doors and into the horde of waiting cabs.

Speeding into town, dodging yaks and washing-women in the road, my driver inquired as to my country of origin. "Canada," I replied, slipping into the fiction I would necessarily carry with me for the next two months. I had, unfortunately, picked a fairly isolationist moment in history to be American, and also a dangerous one to try venturing beyond the country's walls. Staring out the window at the ancient paste-smeared shrines and naked children bathing in drainwater, I felt a sudden sense of relief—civil war or no, it was good to be away from the dying thrash of the American empire for the moment.

I had spent the last year in London, finishing university while editing a book about how the current international crop of teenagers and young adults were engaging with the visionary technology that previous generations had named "Magick." Intensive personal investigations into the subject during my time in England had left me in a state of high-pitched teleological psychosis, and as the summer of 2004 came on it quickly became clear that if the across-the-universe genetic quest which had begun in the back recesses of the public library of my hometown in Southern California as a teenager and which had led me into increasingly anti-rational noumenal oscillations ever since were to be continued, it would have to be by something as over-the-top as the hack-neyed and politically questionable "journey to the East for hidden occult knowledge and some killer pictures to stick on your website." As to what I was going to do now that I was here, I supposed that that would have to resolve itself.

The Kathmandu unveiling itself to me was a crowded, psychedelic patchwork of Hindu, Buddhist and more unstructured, animist iconography; the mesh helped by the fact that each belief system shares overlapping pantheons of gods. In my hotel room I sorted through my disjointed impressions, planning my next step. I would eventually have to figure out how to make it across the border to Varanasi, in Northeastern India, without having my bus firebombed (a likely occurrence, as the cab driver had informed me), but for the moment I was beginning to relax into the pandemonium.

Went walking through the city in the humid night. The flagged spire of Swayamb-hunath, the Monkey Temple, piercing the still-glowing horizon. Ganesha, Pashupati, Machendranath peering out at me from ancient shrines, giant painted eyes staring at me from the doorways, corpses by the river waiting for cremation, dead incense smell—the buffer to the spirit world loose, ephemeral. Giant arcing lightning blots across the sky, with no thunder, stretching out across the whole valley. Perfect.

At Swayambhunath in the morning I'm shown around by a ten-year-old named Prakash. He proudly shows off his fresh body modification, an ornate dragon branded into his forearm with a heated stick by his older brother. While the Tibetan monks make their haunting chants I buy a soda and watch the monkeys jump around the shrine and do tricks for the appreciative onlookers, their babies hanging upside-down from their stomachs.

In the hotel where I check in for the following night, I find a worn copy of the *Confessions of Aleister Crowley*. The old man kicked off some of his mountain climbing adventures in the valley. I think of London, and "Magick," a practical joke played on the Western world by a series of British eccentrics and perpetuated by those who actu-ally fell for the glamour.

Magic is all illusion and shadowplay where I've come from, a game of how-much-are-you-willing-to-believe and how-far-are-you-willing-to-take-it, of fake-it-till-you-make-it, but here it's real, everywhere, right in front of my face, an inescapable atmo-spheric tinge. Maybe it's just easier to see when you're yanked out of your native con-text. Everywhere I look I find another shrine to another god. Even the military trucks worryingly clogging the narrow streets are painted with psychedelia, little bits of mirror glued all over them, a great garish "ALL IS ONE" slogan decorating the front of each. When I shut my eyes in the darkness of my room I find myself in the midst of a vast astral web, spreading around me for miles, a hexagram at the center and four Buddhas of compassion surrounding it; the twenty-six prophets of Islam shrouded in white, peering down from their ecstatic burning. Imagination itself pouring from my eyes, the whole procession only slightly less psychedelic than Kathmandu itself. Later, out in the night smoking alleyway hash, the vision becomes more frightening, the pure and violent mentation of the All pulling at me from beyond the horizon itself. Something observing me, trying to drag me out of myself, coming on like pure voltage. Magic itself—some inscrutable interplay of unnamed and unknowable forces conveniently filed under a spooky Houdinism and ghettoized to the tackiest, most banal section of the local chain bookstore—suddenly more unnervingly real than anything I've felt before.

At night the American and German stoner kids keep me up with their one-chord guitar solos. Over a yak-cheese sandwich at breakfast I read about the just-past (June 8, 2004) Venus occultation and the upcoming 2012 evolutionary jump in the *Kathmandu Times*. Wandering through the outskirts of town, being followed by sad-eyed dogs, I happen upon a hillside shrine to Ganesha swarming with flies. *Aum gung ganapathaye namah.* Salutations. Overwhelmed by loneliness momentarily. Been away from the U.S. for a year now. Ease my way. Guide me through this country. (IPSOS ABRAHADABRA IPSOS.) Smasher of obstacles. The numinous brushing across my soul again. Everything takes on the aspect of a video game—find the sword, rescue the princess. The numina cracked wide open. Smasher of obstacles.

I'd been planning to get out and head to India by this point, after taking in the initial rush, but my awe keeps growing. By the next afternoon I've found a professional guide (or, rather, he's found me): Raj Kumar, a twenty-one-year-old Thamung Nepali with an official tour guide license who says he'll take me up to Tuesday's Dakshinkali puja in the hills. I've been hearing about this one for a few days already, imagining fucked-up Kali worshippers and mad sadhus, *Indiana Jones and the Temple of Doom*-style, tearing goats apart with their teeth and bathing in gore. Hey, why not?

I awake before dawn and cross town with him, past the rivers where workers and children bathe at dawn with writhing eels and jackals. I ask Raj about the ceremony: "This is the Nepali people's method of prayer. If you need something you make an offering for Kali. Some power, maybe to overcome disease, maybe to help with life. You hold the wish inside." Raj is very professional and very proud of it, and at the same time very, very boyish; since we're about the same age we find ourselves in easy conversation. He's reading *The Life of Pi* to help with his English skills.

We take the insane Nepali bus system, which involves sitting on a metal bar holding on to at least two full-diapered infants while the bus driver blares a tape of the same three songs over and over, careening over the mountain paths, far below which sit the blasted-out husks of other buses, at sixty-five miles per hour. Raj finds my insistence on being taken to a Nepali religious ceremony hilarious, but not as funny as my insistence on participating, which involves me offering up flowers, red paste, cookies, rupees and a live chicken as a blood sacrifice.

I wait in the processional line in an enclosed grotto with hundreds of others, speakers blaring devotional music from above, until I enter the shrine, offering bowl and a squawking chicken in tow. (Bow down and say a mantra and an incantation surrounded by bodies pressing me against the shrine. Shouting and talking and music everywhere. Senses become hyperalert and everything is self-evident and immediate. The chicken is taken from me. Make a wish and blow the candle out. A machete swipes across its neck and sprays the wall.) I emerge from the shrine drenched in sweat and various powders to find Raj singing the only English language song in his repertoire, "Sexy Eyes" by the Danish diva Whigfield—"Aah aah hey hey sexy eyes, I'm gonna take you to paradise . . . " On the way out I dispense coins to the handless, legless and mouthless, while starting to tell him what I asked the goddess for. "No, you must never tell anybody. Best to keep this to yourself."

Over fried rice back at the Shambhala Hotel, Raj recounts the (possibly inflated) number of Western girls he has kissed before pointedly asking me "What are you going to say when you go back to America and your family and friends ask you why you went to the Dakshinkali?"

I put on my best Victor Frankenstein face and tell him "I'll say I went because I wanted POWER!!!" Unable to stop laughing, Raj says—"Hah! Yes, you will say, don't touch me, I have the POWER! Hah aha ha ha!" He is baffled by my interest in Nepali ritual, as it is mainly something that is resorted to when there is no access to allopathic medical care. "Yes, these things are very good for you, you are a tourist . . . "

We have dinner with his aunt and uncle, who bust out a full meal and then put on a pirated VCD of *Freddy vs. Jason*. Raj is shocked that I won't eat the sacrificed chicken. "I'm a vegetarian . . . " Everything is absurd. He's baffled and I find it hard to explain my behavior to myself, even. The city seems more crowded late at night than the daytime. Avril Lavigne leers at me from every shop window.

It's fortuitous that I've found Raj (or, rather, that he's found me, in the center of Durbar Square), as the Thamung ethnic group he's from is one of the few groups in Nepal in which shamanism ("witchcraft," they call it in English) is still practiced. The next day he leads me up to his village to find a witch doctor. We take a five-hour bus ride and three-hour hike into the Himalayas. The old man who's been grinning at me for the last few hours on the bus turns out to be a Thamung shaman headed to the same village. He says he knows "just a little bit." They know I'm coming, I suppose.

By the time we reach the village the sun is going down. Raj's place is a case of welcome-to-the-real-world, a family of eight who live with their cows, goats and chickens in an open mud house. The children are dangerously cute and some have picked up English from school. My attempts to learn Nepali are faltering, and consist of me repeating the same phrases—*namaste* ("I greet the god within you"), *dhanyabad* ("thank you") and *ranro* ("good") over and over again. It's peaceful here. At night I fight every fucked-up vermin known to man for floor space, but it's all *ranro*, and the next day Raj takes me up the hill to participate in a two-hour Tibetan lama ritual. We meet an English-speaking trekking guide who gleefully lets me know that Yahoo has updated their mail space to a hundred megabytes. The kids go nuts when they see my digital camera, especially the video I've taken earlier of monkeys at Swayambhunath. The local teenage girls take turns excitedly putting on various outfits for me to capture for posterity.

Other than a brief jag of altitude-induced indigestion, everything goes well and the next night the local shaman shows up at the house for an all-night ritual in which his apprentice, Raj's family and some neighbors participate. The kids spend the night laughing at the shaman's mode of trance induction, drumming and shaking himself into an inhuman frenzy (the curved rod he uses to strike his egg-shaped drum is a recapitulation of the Thamung story of the birth of shamanism, which revolves around a snake—or *naga*, a tunnel to other realities in some aspects—lashing out at the sky) until he enters into what looks like an epileptic fit, ploughing around the house, knocking over anyone in his path and eating live coals out of the fire. He builds yantras on the ground out of colored sand and even one giant model of the human's astral body out of sand, pennies, a small tree, string, an egg and a banana that bears more than a passing resemblance to the Qabalistic Tree of Life. In one particularly vigorous trance he tears a rooster's head from its body with his bare hands. He presses the stump to my forehead and when it falls into the offering dish its eyes are still stirring around, its beak opening and closing slowly.

After my attempts to emulate his trance, in which I beat his drum until I start shaking and have to be restrained by the laughing children, he squints in my direction and then offers to teach me. One month, he says, every day all day and two hours a night, living in the same room in Bodnath, a Buddhist village in the hills of Kathmandu, speaking only Nepali, with Raj along to facilitate communication, and I'll be a full Thamung shaman. My skepticism rears its head immediately but I figure it's too good an opportunity to pass up, even if it's a con. We can't stay in the mountains to do it, as it turns out that there are Maoists lurking here after all. There are hammer-and-sickles sprayed on walls as we descend the mountain, a relic of a more superstitious century. The whole valley is white as we go down. White above, white below. Raj's fifteen-year-old sister Susi accompanies us back to Kathmandu. It's the first time she's seen the city, and by the time Raj brings her to their aunt and uncle's house to stay, her face is numb with worry and bewilderment and shock at the intensity of it all.

Back at the hotel, I sleep the remainder of the day and the night. I have a nightmare in which I find an underground grotto, a dingy tiled steam bath where Vincent Gallo sits in the corner, filthy with sweat. He's performing impromptu plastic surgery on various New York acolytes who throng around him, bored, listless, cocaine-hollowed. There's a shark swimming in a dark pool next to him and just for kicks they throw a rabid wolf in. The two vicious animals start tearing each other apart and a bleary-eyed, tattooed Suicide Girl climbs in with them. "Viiiince, why aren't they eating meeeeeee?" she whines. I wake up twisted four-ways in the sheets but it all seems, in the morning, to perfectly sum up the state of the Western "transgressive."

(Don't worry, it's only the end of the American empire. It's all happened before, remember?)

As I try to get the dream out of my head over breakfast on the roof of Helena's Café, I remember—wait, I'm going to be trained as a shaman? What? How? Yes!

Bidyá is the Nepali word for shamanic knowledge. This is a problematic concept and one that tends to be thrown around a little indiscriminately, especially in Western occulture. The myth of the shaman tends to get wrapped around anybody who goes "outside" of the accepted boundaries of reality to bring something back. The term often gets applied to larger-than-life figures like certain rock stars and "subversive" writers. Since the 1960s, and thanks especially to Terence McKenna, the "shaman" in the West is anybody who has cultivated a deep info-gathering relationship with psychedelic drugs. For Raj and Mat (the Jhankri witch doctor), shamanism or witchcraft is simply an alternate form of medicine. But the Gnosis is right there—the ornate cosmology, the epileptic fits, the "superhuman" powers, all of which are gained not through drugs but through a profound relationship with the environment, the Nepali language and Sanskrit mantras, and the methods of trance.

It's the trance that I'm most interested in, something concrete to bring back with me. It's what makes me decide to stay for the training. Raj and I rent a quiet room in the Chabil Panitanki Mahangtal area of the city, where we can all freak out in peace. Over more chow mein he tells me that I can't go back to his village. I've been too visible, too friendly in meeting people. One of the men I had talked to near the Buddhist shrine, in sight of Mt. Everest, turned out to be a Maoist who had later accosted Raj, trying to get information about me. We had wisely left the next morning. Raj's eagerness to go suddenly makes more sense. Anxious and paranoid, I wait in the rented room for two days while Raj returns to his village to bring back Mat and the equipment, both mundane and magical, that we need.

I'm too wound up to sleep at night, too on-edge about the covert war going on around me and wondering whether, after Raj had assured me that his village was completely safe and Maoist-free, I can take his word on the safety of our new neighborhood. I figure I'm going to have to trust, something I've been having to continually learn to do over the previous year. The clock passes midnight and Kathmandu enters the Hour of Dogs, when the sounds of Man fade and the canine element emerges, echoing their network of cries across the silent valley until they, too, fall into exhausted sleep, leaving me the only unrested soul in the night.

(Something being pushed out from deep inside me, behind me, the answer is always yes.) *Aum gung ganapathaye namah.* (The answer is always yes.)

Mat (or, simply, "Jhankri," as Raj—who is becoming progressively more spooked by the occult goings-on he is becoming involved with by dint of being on my pay-roll—calls him) is a quiet, unassuming trail cook in his thirties with a neatly trimmed mustache. Like Raj, he chain-smokes unfiltered Indian cigarettes and has a bubbling, optimistic sense of humor that tends toward the sexual (in his case this manifests as a series of erection jokes, while Raj's sense of humor takes the form of regularly suggesting that I help him set up a prostitution ring—or "girl business," as he calls it). I immediately feel at ease with him, as I had in Raj's village, where he turned up wearing shorts and a "Kick Polio Out of Nepal" t-shirt. Mat the unassuming trail cook and Mat the fully-dressed-and-decorated Jhankri, dressed in head-to-toe white linen, bells, skull necklaces and a towering peacock feather head-dress, hooked up to something bigger than him, howling, drumming and eating fire seemed connected to each other in name and face only.

Raj, agitated by the proximity to the juju shit, begins continually expressing to me his worry that engaging with the spirits will send me insane, holding up Mat's occasionally irrational thinking and behavior as an example. I dismiss his concerns, figuring that if I was going to lose the plot I probably would have already done so some time in the previous six years of performing magical actions and continuous transmutation into the magical worldview. I put him at ease by demonstrating some of my practices as a "Western Jhankri," as he calls me—a Lesser Banishing Pentagram and a Middle Pillar ritual, which would be familiar basic practices to most ceremonial magicians, are enough to convince him that I'm not headed into totally unmapped territory. After I'm able to describe the contents of his past and his problems with the ladies to him with a tarot deck I picked up in Munich, he is positively impressed.

My training begins in an ordered fashion, with me still wondering how I've traipsed into this situation. We've moved Raj's belongings—his bed and his school-books going back to grade school—into the apartment building, and so he sleeps in the room that contains his bed and possessions. Mat and I sleep in the main room, thronged with windows, on Styrofoam mats. In the mornings, before eating, we cross town to a major shrine, different ones each morning, and give offerings of rice and red powder to Shiva, Kali, Ganesha, Durga, Machendranath. The Nepalis at the shrines seem amused by the white boy with his forehead smeared with red paste and flowers behind his ear prostrating himself before their divine forms, but both India and Nepal, from what I am told, have grown accustomed to goofball Western "seekers," who were so prevalent in the 1970s that they became a regular, recognizable stereotype in Bollywood films. There's a few of them lingering around, mostly European and Russian Hare Krishnas, a reminder of what happens when one forgets what home is. (Though, as a café owner in Varanasi later told me, this type of tourism has become less common: "In the seventies, Westerners came here and did drugs all day long. Now they come here and sit in the Internet cafés all day long.")

A regular point of departure for us is Pushpatinath, a series of Shiva lingam shrines built up around a river thronged with cremation ghats. I linger at the funeral of a civil servant as a fire-tender sifts through the ashes, unveiling a pelvis and spinal column, until my companions urge me to look away. Sadhus crowd the river, smoking hash and asking for donations in return for photo opportunities; many of these, I am informed, are likely criminals posing as holy men due to the convenient disguise of being covered in ash from head to toe. Westerners, especially Western women, have a habit of disappearing when they get too friendly with the mind-blown renouncers.

I've been teaching Raj English-language songs at his insistence, his favorite being "Toxic" by Britney Spears, which, bizarrely enough, is the first thing that comes to mind when he asks me to sing him a popular Western song, until I lay "Our House" by Madness on him via the headphones and his eyes shoot sparks.

So purified after each excursion, we return to Bodnath for a home-cooked meal of rice and dal, with the occasional helping of spiced cabbage for flavor, prepared by Mat on a kerosene stove and eaten with our hands. This is around the time that Raj and Mat both transmute into overbearing grandmothers, constantly trying to convince me to get more down my throat, after which I transcribe and memorize long strings of Sanskrit invocations. So armed, I don the regalia and spend a few hours performing shamanic actions in front of a complex three-dimensional yantra system constructed across the floor by Mat. My first attempts at trance are conducted reciting mantras while slowly clacking together an ornately-carved wooden spirit dagger and a hollow Bengal tiger legbone.

At night Mat and I sleep on the floor and he tells me about his life as a trail cook. He has a wife and several children, but the crippled tourist industry has largely deprived him of work. He has dreams of making it out of Nepal to work in a kitchen in Oman or the Arab Emirates and sending money back to his family.

In the morning he asks me about my dreams. I have had the right ones. I am sworn to secrecy.

After the first few days, it has become clear to the other occupants of the building that something's up on the top floor (was it all the drumming and chanting?) Our neighbors are fairly affluent twentysomethings who run a teashop in the Thamel area of downtown, who spend a lot of time watching DVDs and affecting Western mannerisms. Raj shows me a photo of a cousin from back in his village who has "become Western"—the picture shows a boy who has grown his hair long, found some early-nineties MC Hammer-style parachute pants and learned to flash pseudo-gang signs for the camera like a drunk frat boy. But the way that Raj speaks of him—the finality and sorrow of "becoming Western"—suggests that his family ties and his connection to his identity as a Nepali villager have been permanently altered, or even cut, and that his new Faustian, individualist mode is a form of proud exile. There's a tinfoil quality to Raj's voice as he suggests that he, too, longs to become Western one day soon, and that this is why he's left the familiar world of village labor to become an independent trekking guide in the city (one might also suspect his overwhelming fixation on Western women). There's a deep lesson about the nature of the machinery of capital here, maybe even of something called evil, a globalizing process that I am now culpable in simply by dint of coming to Nepal and giving Raj my business, in an attempt to become more Nepali, to bring back an Oriental mystique.

Somewhere deep in the "isness" of the European man is a magician in a circle and with his Art doth he torment and wrench his desires from that which screams in agony within the triangle. With symbols doth he control all that he sees and the world-so-limited screams out in agony. Or longs to break forth into the circle. Or was that just part of me? (When do we become the process?)

The kids in the building see Mat, perhaps, as a part of their identity that has been neglected, suddenly come round their doorstep by agency of a crazy white-boy. They certainly look up to him as somebody able to purvey information they don't have access to themselves, and begin showing up in the quiet moments to ask him to read their futures. This he does with the aid of a divination system he'd taught me in our first day together, which consists of casting dried grains of rice across a pan and reading the scatter pattern. It quickly comes out, thanks to Raj, that I have my own divination skills and I am asked to provide tarot readings as well.

At first they ask me the usual questions about money, business and love, and seem happy with my readings. When a man asks me whether he should go to Burma to hunt down his brother, who has jumped the bail that he paid for, I become decidedly more uncomfortable with this new role I've been cast in.

As this goes on, I notice Mat quietly watching me. I wonder if he is skeptical of my "Western witchcraft," if he can see my occasional uncertainty that perhaps I'm simply playing a game that's gone too far; whether I'll be able to provide something more than U.S. dollars and a need for a story to tell when it comes down to it.

The training becomes more intense. I'm given the drum and spend hours each night inducing trance until my joints feel like gunpowder charges have been set off in them and my fingers are raw and bleeding from the friction of the curved drumming rod. Mat stays next to me all along, saying his own incantations as I say mine, constantly shocking me into awareness by flinging cold water and dried rice at me. "You must raise the power. It is up to you. You must become full Jhankri." My inquiries into how long this will take result in the answer of everything from two weeks to three years. I push myself harder and harder.

"What do you see when you look at me?" I ask Mat after a particularly exhausting night, in which I've spent hours feeling like I'm scraping the edge of it, unable to make the complete transformation. After rubbing his chin and looking at me he responds, motioning to my head.

"In here, sometimes reckless."

"Yes," I respond.

"In here," pointing now to my heart, "sometimes sad."

"Yes."

This is to be his succinct analysis of my character, but a correct one. As I push myself harder and harder each night he begins to tell me of the powers that he and the other Jhankri possess, that I will learn if I stay, learn Nepali, train for three years or more, maybe marry a Nepali woman. Become full-time.

"Flying, this is possible. Very dangerous. Jhankri can fly, if he is in the mountains maybe and needs to get into the valley. He can collapse the space between two points and move between them immediately." (This had taken us eight hours by bus and foot.) "Very dangerous, very very dangerous. If you make a mistake on the incantations, even once, your heart stop. Dead. Also this can cause problems for your livestock." Staying in Nepal for a decade and learning to fly was an idea that seemed seductive if only for its extremity, but the danger to my livestock seemed too great to run the risk.

"Also we can teach you to turn into a tiger. Stalk as a tiger. Also very dangerous."

The pressure is immense. The more I train, the more the trance takes over. My body is beginning to act of its own accord. I start trying to punch through windows when I'm not paying attention to what my hands are doing.

Raj renames me *Sila Jhankri*, "beautiful shaman," one evening. My constant indecision as to whether to continue the training or not begins to upset him, though, and he becomes convinced that it is evidence of the onset of madness; when I point out that my vacillations are based on Mat constantly giving me a different story as to how long the training will take, he simply takes this as more support of the fact that the whole affair is bad news. "Why do you learn about this?" he asks me. "Why? You can marry nice girl, have nice business. You should not worry about these things. You should go home, have fun with many girls instead. Maybe start girl business with me."

Sometimes we feel called, driven towards the irrational. Certain that the world is a perfectly rational code that we can unlock if we can simply step outside of its rational confines and see it for what it is. Propelled across the world for reasons we don't understand, hunting for clues to the location of an unknown treasure desired simply because it is buried, waiting for a payoff that may never come. Accelerated along by each new revelation and ecstasy. Looking for some kind of truth about our world. Maybe the alternative—"real" life, jagged-toothed and numb—is too wrong to consider. Magic. It's that warm, familiar teleological psychosis. The certainty that there's something that's worth it all, beyond time, beyond space, beyond even self. And the justification for a magical life?

Why even ask?

In the final night, I go ballistic and tear the Jhankri regalia from my body. "Good,"

Mat says, staring on. In wild-eyed trance I charge across the room pounding the drum into frenzy. It doesn't matter. The answers I needed have already come, in dreams and in trance. It feels like everything I've known about the fabric of reality itself has been destroyed. I've made it on my own; well, I've made it somewhere. I understand why I've come here and who these people are.

They want me to stay another year but the rest of the world is calling. Mat tears another chicken apart to seal me back in, to stop the spirits coming when they're not needed.

"You do not have the power. If you stay longer, learn Nepali, maybe then."

As a parting gift, Mat does a rice divination and reveals to me that I have an enemy in America. "One *bokshi*"—a black magician—"trying to make trouble for you. Trying to cause problems. But I will protect you. If he tries to cause more problems, I'll cut my finger and shed blood for you. And then the *bokshi*—he will die. He will be dead."

I've got a flight to Mumbai in the morning. I've got a whole subcontinent to see before I go home. Raj cries when I leave.

Back in Manhattan, six months later, writing this in an all-night café in Union Square, I wonder what I am left with from my stay in Nepal and my training. Though those improbable weeks seemed, at the time, to be a collapsing of years of pouring through occult literature, individual and group magical practice, drug experimentation, consciousness expansion exercises and the stream of my life itself into a single explosive charge, that simple feeling of infinite possibility has become increasingly hard to reconcile with this static, dualist, terrified, dying machine I have come back to. Riding the subway to work each morning, spending each day staring at a computer in a cubicle and returning home to collapse into fitful sleep each night, I think of the Magus in the circle, spinning the symbol system we mistake for the whole of the truth from his four weapons. But there is the Fool as well, jumping blindly into the unknown, and to simply remember that feeling for a second leaves me with hope that Nothing might, in fact, change the world—the realization that the story hasn't all been written, that we don't even have to use the language they've given us.

Across the table from me a group of anarchists is meeting after a day of megaphone ranting in Union Square, discussing the imminent collapse of the Empire over coffee. "Our children won't accept this system forever. They'll be smarter than this." I think of how just an ever-so-fleeting glimpse of a less locked-down view of existence has made that idea of positive change, so readily dismissed before, into a solid, tangible, pressing possibility.

One of the women leading the conversation suddenly, unexpectedly begins to speak of her own magical experiences in hopeful tones. "I'm saying, you know, I live half in the spirit world. Always have, it's just a part of me. I know that this world's just consciousness, just vibration, our thought patterns going out and manifesting in the physical world. Some of the experiences I've had, you just wouldn't believe them, you wouldn't even believe me . . . "

You know, sometimes I wonder what's going on in this world.

In the end, though, it's like my friend Jennie put it to me in an e-mail: "Hey, if you are twenty-two years old and in a position where people are offering to teach you how to FOLD SPACE and you have to DECLINE because it's INCONVENIENT then you are doing very well indeed."

But one must think of the livestock, always the livestock.

I AM NOT
(THAT I AM)

Avenues of Magical Exploration

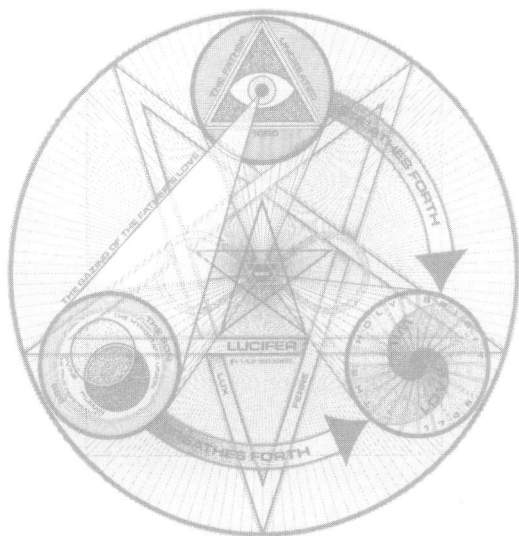

SPOOKY TRICKS

JASON LOUV

They bring you down here into the World from the Outside and then they teach you the Words, and by that time you've already begun to forget magic. Sometimes it tries to come back to you, puts on the mask of an imaginary friend and calls to you from across the schoolyard where they teach you lessons in self and submission. You can see the other place, the one where they know your true name, the place that this is only a reflection of, when you close your eyes. It slides by in strange dreams, sometimes comes out through scribbles in the margins of your schoolwork, but then they teach you the word Imagination. And it is not a real word. And it is not real. Welcome to the World.

You grow up in front of the television, you grow up in front of the blackboard, you grow up wrapped in the black coils of the dragon, dumb, forgetful. *When I grow up I'm going to be a princess. When I grow up I'm going to be a fireman. I'm going to be an astronaut. I'm going to be a ballerina.* Every day of your life they teach you to forget your birthright. Hormones kick in and your body goes haywire with lust, hope, dreams, terrors. *When I grow up I'm going to be on MTV. I'm going to be in the NBA. I'm going to be president of the USA.* On the edge of town you sit on a hill with friends looking down at the twinkling houses, tossing beer cans down into the darkness, heart already grown hard. *When I grow up I'm going to get out of here.* Go walking for hours with your hands in your pockets, staring at the ground, trying to remember something. There was something you forgot. Something you can almost remember, but not quite, just on the periphery, an impossible itch. If you could just remember, everything would be different, you know it . . . The specter of Real Life hangs over you, cleverly named, as if nothing but the forty-hour work week was actually real. All the toys and dreams must be put away now. You didn't *really think* you were special, did you?

When I grow up I'm going to take what I get and learn to fucking like it.

Did we forget something? Best not to think about it, really. Best to get on with life. After all, *everybody knows* that there is no such thing as magic, and what you see is always what you get. And so you become an adult, by sole virtue of the number of years you have lived. You look for a place to glue yourself into the jigsaw, and you have already forgotten how to hear.

And magic crouches in the barren tree outside your locked window and slowly taps all night, saying, play with me, play with me.

Or maybe it doesn't get that far. Maybe you'll find it. Maybe you'll start to take it all seriously, the things that the skewed maladjusted out-caste kids talk about on the fringes of the schoolyard. It starts with that book you find in the back of the public library, the one about magic, *real* magic, that you read secretly under the table in math class. Or it starts with the voices that begin to come. Or with a certain certainty of unknown origin. And one day it makes perfect sense (how long have you been looking for it?), and you try it. Try to do something to reality. And it works. And as your hope grows, you watch the lilting fingers of Hell brush across the people in the school, dragging them down into gray mundanity, addiction, slavery, pregnancy, locked tight into the roles that have been constructed for them, and you realize that if there's any magic in this world that you'll have to work for it harder than anything else you could ever work for, in order to never become like that, gray-eyed, dead to the world's mystery, chained to this waking-nightmare blood-trailing terror we call "real life."

In the back of the class staring at them in disbelief we realize the violence of this planet, that will eat us whole if given half the chance. We come to the Vision of Sorrow and realize that hell exists, it is right beside us always. It waits to swallow us raw.

And in the name of Chaos do you rise against the Beast and declare yourself a crazy little child who disbelieves in it all and you know that this is enough.

We disbelieve in your shadowplay adult world that you create from paper and ink and flashing screens to convince us that we are powerless, saying over and over "this is the way things are, things are, this is the way things are."

And you call yourself a magician because if this is reality then you will make something unreal of yourself, and the more absurd the better. And this is how we begin to discover the true order of things, and how we discover our true elders, and our true names. And how we begin to see how much we truly have to learn.

And cast into the wilderness beyond this fearful culture's walls you wander and explore, mind reeling, chattering to yourself. In the whited-out forests you glance your fear around the edge of a tree. And this hoodoo magic madness is real after all. It chases you, hounds you to the ends. At night they come to you in your dreams and show you the way, and you wander alone and crazy and full of it all, until you begin to find the tracks of others in the sand. As night falls you look for the glow of their fires. And then one day you find them.

And that's where the real magic begins.

The Pure and Violent Mentation of the All

The quest for "magic," which, in the end, may just be a word, has led me into some fairly odd places for a dorky kid from the suburbs to find himself in. The act of declaring myself a "magician" when I was seventeen, just for the sheer what-the-fuckness of it, to see if I could actually become something that wasn't supposed to exist, seemed to prompt such a response from the universe that despite the fact I was thoroughly convinced there was no such thing as magic, I shortly found myself spending hours constructing ornate after-school rituals, speaking to discarnate entities in the woods, hexing reality to get out of detention and entering a bizarre, newly meaningful version of reality lush with symbol, juxtaposition, telepathic impressions, and rhymes and puns of experience itself. In college I pored through tens of thousands of pages of occult literature, trying to suss out the wisdom of the ages, figuring out how everything else stood in relation to it, uncovering a secret history to things; tried my hand at using drugs and sex to provoke occult insight; tracked down and interrogated at length every "magician" I could find, which included most of my heroes. Spent every moment learning to control my mind, to direct my will and imagination. At a certain point it became hard to pretend it was a game any longer, when "real" life seemed like the game now, the simple and plain mask to wear over the endlessly reflecting, recombining, joyous self, each new feint at the mystery opening a new ravine of potential and kinetic experience.

I took myself apart and put myself back together, stripping away every lie I could find, every lie about how things were or how I was supposed to be or what magic was, over and over and over and over again, searching frantically for whatever could possibly be hiding underneath it all, until it felt like there was nothing left. I talked to spirits. I talked to demons. I talked to Gods.

Well. It's an adventure. Might be the last one going. Might be the only one that was ever going. Imagine my surprise when I found out that instead of securing myself a ticket to the little white room where they feed you little yellow pills, I had instead found my entryway to a whole 'nother zone, a golden temple deep in the jungle with only the faintest signs and paths leading to it away from the main roads, inhabited by crowds of people who were wondering what had taken me so long.

So I rode the synchronicities to New York City and the next thing I knew I was editing this book, since the opportunity just up and presented itself, and then ended up in London holed up finishing school and assembling the book and trying to figure out what the fuck had happened to me. Still haven't really pieced that last one together, to be honest.

I found myself gathered with the others in the back of dark pubs plotting out the future.

I found myself dancing all night on the moors with witches on mushrooms and DMT, peering into the realm of the dead and into the "future"; and watching the Aeonic flow begin to turn this world into exactly what it needs to be, and right on time too.

I found myself crunching the numbers, crunching the gematria, scouring the sacred books, rolling up my sleeves and *doing* the magic way more than I ever had before, for hours and hours every day, sometimes all day, scratching around the numinous until it all exploded in the bliss and truth of Ma'at.

I followed it across Europe; to the Roman ruins that only looked like they'd fallen yesterday; to the Vatican where I poured my blood into the fountains of holy water; to the old city of Prague where they made the golem and where Vin Diesel made *XXX*.[1]

I rode the maniacal shark of my desire from the dusty back corners of the library of my childhood all the way to the foothills of Mount Everest, and there, sitting in the dust watching the sun set over the ravines and valleys of Nepal, I sat with a girl reading a book a Tibetan lama had given me, helping her practice her English as she laboriously traced out a line of a Vajra song with her finger and read it right back to my face:

"How can you suppose . . . to have sway . . . over others . . . if you do not . . . have sway . . . over your . . . own . . . mind?"

And so I found myself in India, sunburnt, walking among the oceanside shrines of Mumbai, stepping over the dying fly-covered children carpeting the city streets. I found myself in Goa, wandering the deserted beaches under gray skies, convinced I had found the edge of the world. I found myself sitting in Varanasi, every circuit burnt, watching bodies cremate on the Ganges for a week, staring at the vivid futurism of the skulls turning black, staring at the bloated bodies of sadhus floating down the river. I found myself on the back of a camel in the Great Thar Desert riding into the red sun, convinced I had found the edge of myself, consciousness turned into pure white noise. Camped in the middle of the sands in the middle of the night, staring at the crescent moon in the sky, right above my sleeping camel. It was a tarot card. It was perfect.

(And at this point a giant plastic Tao flies out of a portal and smacks our narrator in the yap, which he promptly shuts. We notice a "$0.99 / Made in Taiwan" sticker on the back.)

Well. Magic. It sure is an adventure. Yes indeedy.

Proposition One

The lowest-common-denominator definition of magic—that sticking pins in a voodoo doll will produce corresponding pains in the person it is a model of—contains the whole doctrine of ritual magic in miniature. Our nervous systems are our models of our universe—therefore, making changes to our nervous systems will produce corresponding changes in the universe, and vice versa.

Proposition Two

Spiders weave webs, beavers build dams and people make magic; they manifest meaning and structure from nothingness. The world is pure magic, it is the image of our DNA writ large in manifestation—it is our sigil and what we have chosen to make with our time. The *stupas* of Lhasa are no more magical than the infernal machinery of New York; it's all what we've chosen to bring forth from ourselves, it's all relative and it's all us.

Hunting Dust

The following is a general theory of magical initiation drawn from my own personal experience, reading and interactions with other magicians. Though magic can never be fully described, as it is by definition beyond definitions, the following model seems to be a good fit for the initial stages.

From first learning to speak until the age of six or seven, children enter what Swiss developmental psychologist Jean Piaget called the preoperational stage, more generally known as "magical thinking." It is in this stage of development that the child believes that the universe is a manifestation of the self.

According to Dr. Benjamin Spock, "In a young child's view, it is very possible that it rains because the sky is sad. If your baby brother gets sick and goes to the hospital, it could be your fault if you were mad at him the day before. If you want something very, very badly and it happens, then your wanting caused it to happen. These are examples of magical thinking. They are also examples of egocentric thinking—not that the young child is selfish. It's just that he cannot take anyone else's perspective, so that everything in the world revolves around him. When he's sad, he cries. So, it must be that the sky does, too."[2]

This state is characterized by the onset of symbolic thought, in which one thing can represent or correspond to another, and marked by the sense that everything, including inanimate objects, is alive and sentient, and capable of emotion and feeling.

Studying this mode of operation in animistic cultures conducting their affairs at the level of magical thinking,[3] early anthropologist Sir James Frazer isolated the basic components of magic as the Law of Similarity—that like produces like, and that an effect resembles its cause (e.g., rehearsing a desired event in ritual will "cause" that event to happen in actuality); and the Law of Contact or Contagion—that anything that has once been in contact will remain in contact, no matter what the physical distance is (e.g., a person may be affected by actions taken towards their hair, nails or blood; or a corporation by its logo). It is on these principles that all sorcery is worked.[4]

The child experiences herself as awash in divinity, and partaking in divinity and the secret connections between things; and because of the limits of both her own cognitive development and those of monotheist cultures, which most developing children are unfortunately liable to find themselves in, she is unable to recognize that everybody else around her may be just as God-like.[5]

This state, of course, cannot be supported in a healthy environment as it prevents empathy or any kind of social ordering. If taken to its limits, magical thinking at this level—of totemic superstition and the presupposition that whatever one does is correct, because one is omnipotent and divine—will quickly end in the career of a serial killer or an American president.

The preoperational stage is quickly replaced by the concrete operational stage, in which the child begins to think logically and in organized patterns about concrete events, and loses the previous intuitive and egocentric focus. The joke is, though, that despite its social limitations, the preoperational stage may provide a much clearer picture of how the universe actually runs than its concrete and abstract operational successors, which are more concerned with how social interaction runs. (Compare, for instance, Frazer's Laws of Similarity and Contagion with Bell's Theorem, which shows that physical reality is non-local.)

It is only through the *loss* of magical thinking that one can fully individuate, and learn to work with other people and come to healthy functioning in modern society. Yet a loss it is, and if one were to find oneself dead-ended behind some anonymous checkout counter, stumbling home every night to find some kind of succor in lite beer and television, the only place left where magic is real, one could hardly be blamed for wondering exactly what it was that went amiss.

Which brings us to magic proper—as in that entertaining, sexy, meaningful, futuristic lifestyle we know and love.

Magicians tend to be people who couldn't quite let go of that childhood wonder, who never quite forgot that feeling of being less separate from their experience. These people often first seek to re-enchant their world, grown gray since childhood, with the tactical use of art, poetry, music, sex, drugs or some other mode of enflaming the imagination before sensing the vast, hidden order of things which lies just beyond the imagination and the possible; the hidden order of which the imagination is a sensory organ for making exploratory forays into.

Magic, then, becomes a disciplined quest to recover the state of magical thinking and claim all of its eccentric treasures, and to break the chains of social conditioning and static personality that have made one less than imminently divine. Armed with the ability to live as a functional adult in "mundane reality," the individual can now make a safe return to the doorstep of magical thinking, and reclaim the spark of divinity within them that, though likely a bit scuffed up by religion, education, media, processed junk food and the daily erosion of life on this planet, will provide no less of a nuclear incident when touched.

The reintegration of this outlook on life, along with the more stable viewpoint, then becomes the initial task of the budding magician—that is, making space for magic itself to manifest, and gaining a foothold in that other place. Reintegration is *not* an easy task. One largely has to go against everything one has been taught about the world; one has to find a way of safely unlearning the neat boundaries that have been placed around the possible. The multitudes of magical training systems that abound in the world represent general, customizable guidelines for doing this.

The crucial difference between the original state of magical thinking and the new one of magical action is that the individual is able to conceive of a universe in which all are God, though some may be forgetful of this;[6] and in which all is One in infinite diversity. The newborn magician has empathy, and as such is able to find the appropriate ends to direct their efforts towards. *And magic works.* The magician has returned to the childhood world of wonder, awe and magic, with all the organizational and emotional skills of the adult. He has gazed upon the face of God and found hir not to be a commanding, authoritarian legislator but instead a constantly growing, learning and exploring androgynous child on an adventure—"I tell you the truth, unless you change and become like little children, you will never enter the kingdom of heaven." (*Matthew 18:3*)

This is the first synthesis; this is where it starts. When one gains access to the magical world, a slipstream which lies just one inch beyond the possible,[7] in a world only a child, crazy person or Artist would so dare to believe in, one will quickly find that the game takes on a life of its own.

I Swear They Had a Shaved Horse Dancing on the Stage With Them

"Casting a magic spell" is easy. The basic mechanism goes like this: You decide what you want (this is often the hardest part)! You make that desire as precise as you possibly can, and make sure that it has a route for manifestation. You then make a *symbolic representation* of that desire occurring—a mantra, a hand movement, a dance, a piece of art or music, or a simple symbol on a piece of paper. Some form of trance state is then entered—through prolonged sex, certain drugs, dancing, meditation, yoga, drinking lots of questionable energy drinks or any other method—and the whole of the self is focused upon this symbolic representation, so that the whole of the universe, for a time, is nothing but that symbol, sent down to the deep levels of manifestation. Ceremonial magic, once taken out of its medieval context, is an incredibly effective (and fun) method for this, the idea being to completely overload all of the senses—sight, smell, taste, hearing and touch—with content directly symbolizing one's intent until complete shutdown of the conscious apparatus. After completing one's working, *you then forget what you have done.* Your desire tends to enter your reality as soon as it leaves your head.

This process works remarkably well. That's really all you need to know about magic. It's motor oil to decrease the friction of life and give you control over how you spend your precious time on this planet.

Of course, there's more. There's always more.

The more you do this, and the more you exteriorize your desire into the world, the more you are, essentially, exteriorizing your own mind. The most visible example of this is the increasingly implausible synchronicities that begin to pile up the more you combine intent and trance. This is the awakening of a faculty of mind that dwells *beneath and beyond* the observed world.

The data registered by our sensory organs is processed and assembled by the brain into the somewhat-cohesive whole that we perceive; our "realities" are therefore *one hundred percent subjective.* They are wholesale fabrications by the brain, which must sort our observations and memory into a personality functional enough to allow our continued survival. That means that there is no difference between *anything* when viewed from a wide enough angle; it is all a product of the brain. Our "self" is no different from its "environment"; it's all the same thing. All is mind. So if the world starts talking to you, don't freak the fuck out or anything. It's just reminding you that it's also a part of you, and not to treat it as separate.

Mysticism is the mastery of the self by interiorization. Magic is the mastery of the self by exteriorization. Magic won't make you lose your mind, but it will relocate it outside of your body. (How could you lose it when it's right in front of your face?)

There's more, of course. There's always more.

How to Take the High Road

It is our will to be enrapt in the divine schematics of the universe, blasted out across the mantle of heaven, burning in ecstasy until the dinner bell rings. Our dreams and our nightmares alike call us home, and it is there that we go. Through our Art do we unify the world of the imaginary and the world of the real until, meeting face-to-face, a third is born in their annihilation.

Our tactics are all encompassing. Mastering the tools of this world—all its tricks of status and aspiration—do we stand above them with our veins coursing with the blood of the Prophets. This is our birthright; our mandate as human beings is nothing less than to swallow the stars. The magician must outsmart the system, that is, the system of creation itself.

I stood on Sunset Boulevard, on the patch of concrete where River Phoenix died, and as I called out to it all, I thought, there will be time enough for all of our dreams.

Our hearts are nothing when weighed against this world.

Between Scylla and Charybdis

The training of the magician begins the moment they wholeheartedly embrace such an irrational and romantic calling. It is not a choice made fully consciously, and often has begun months or even years before the technical processes of the occult have been encountered. Those who will in later life declare themselves to be "magicians" (or whatever you want to call it, it has different names in all times and places) will have often been marked from early childhood by strange qualities, high sensitivity, strange obsessions, an overactive imagination and an inability to fully mix with other children; however, looking to the past for a causal explanation of the present is misleading, as the magician's initiation is conducted by *his or her transcendent Self,* which has very little to do with the lower-case-*s* self we normally experience in four dimensions. This Self is what is responsible for the awakening and dissolution of the individual, and will use anything available—books, music, movies, your environment, people in your life, ambient information, dreams, life experiences—to lead you directly towards it in an ever-tightening synchronic net.

It is the full identification and unity with this entity—your Self Made God—that is the true goal of magic. Research and discernment are a must; false identification or missing the boat altogether would be unfortunate. When one looks around one begins to realize that this experience is universal to all people in all times and places, and that *almost everybody except you is in the process of doing it or has already done it.* (Can you read the shockwaves?)

I AM—THAT—I AM

We seek the numinous through any and all means possible. We find everything to be true, everything to be permitted. To be so jacked up on magic that reality itself bends around you when you enter the room: That is the goal.

We find the following tactics useful.

Initiation

The universe gets as giddy as a schoolgirl with ADHD after eating six bowls of Fruit Loops (with Red Bull substituted for milk) when we respectfully make the leap into magic and offer to play with the cosmos on its own terms. Magic lies between us and the universe, right here, right now, this instant, and always has. (Remember to breathe.)

Love saves the universe every time.

Step the First, Step the Last

Relax, trust, love, silence.

The Sixth Sense

The sixth sense is nothing more than the human imagination, raised to a fever pitch and trained as a scientific organ. The imagination is the sensory array that we use to contact not only our own hopes, aspirations and manifolds of Self, but also the shared dreamtime of our social units and ultimately of our species. There is no such thing as something that is *just* in your head (or *just* anything)—the imaginary is a shared space which everybody accesses all of the time, as the Internet has shown in a metaphorical physical form. Once this is grasped, the phenomena of telepathy, ESP and precognition, as well as the more occult aspects of advertising and the media, suddenly begin to make sense.

The Other World

Accessed through mirrors, trance, ritual, proper living, art and some drugs. The less said the better, as nothing can be verified and in all likelihood it is a territory that cannot be mapped. Often aligns with the mundane world and manifests spontaneously through coincidence and the "feel" of things.

When you were a kid, in the back seat of the car on a long ride, staring out at the landscape flashing by and everything was made strange—but like home, like the best kind of dream—you saw the door.

The land on the other side of the door is inhabited.

Mapping the Psychocosm

Magical or "spiritual" growth is accomplished by going deeper and deeper inside oneself while simultaneously expanding more and more one's agency within the world. The inward turn yearns towards death; the overcoming of the illusory self in the silence of the mind. The outward turn yearns toward love; the overcoming of the illusory self in unity with another.

Chemical Warfare

Drugs are hardly necessary for magic, but can often act like social grease and rocket fuel for its processes. They also have their pitfalls, the finer points of which shouldn't need to be repeated to an educated audience. These are not merely issues of personal safety and comfort, but also political ones. Not only can drug culture be potentially blamed for some of the failures of the movements of the 1960s, but drugs—mainly meaning marijuana, cocaine and heroin—are at this point such a critical component of the web of narcomilitarism and violence that runs this planet that becoming part of the consumption chain is in many cases supporting the wrong people, whether that means Al Qaeda or the Central Intelligence Agency. Unless you know exactly who grew or made what you're consuming, to imbibe any illegal (or, in many cases, legal) drug potentially means imbibing human misery, poverty, slavery, torture and murder.

On the other hand, to claim that the use of consciousness-expanding drugs, especially naturally-occurring psychedelics, has not been a primary driving force in human culture since prehistory, or that they cannot lead to peak experiences of tremendous meaning and lasting benefit, would be lying. To say that any substance is inherently "good" would also be pretty far from the truth. A very large part of the population has at least some experience of consciousness-expanding drugs. Those who use them intelligently, or even who use them for magic, are exceedingly rare. While drugs can be an important catalyst in magic, it should be added, they are certainly not the point or the end state, or even essential to its workings.

Altered states, however, *are* essential, and though drugs may be the easiest way there, they are also the hardest to direct towards productive ends. Peter J. Carroll, one of the originators of chaos magic, made the foundation stone of his approach that "altered states of consciousness are the key to magical power," and it is indeed altered states of all forms that we seek to cultivate. The human nervous system is the best toy in the world, and we are here to explore and innovate with it. This is true on more than just the individual level.

Cultures are largely defined by the types of altered states that they seek to cultivate *en masse*, and also those that they seek to avoid. In the post-industrialized world, that tends to mean the sexual-territorial thrash of alcohol; the frantic, competitive, mechanical acceleration and paranoia of caffeine, refined sugar, cocaine and amphetamines; the flattened-alpha-wave "vegging out" of passively staring at a flickering screen; socially-constricted and -constructed sexual expression; the vicarious mass aggression of sporting events; and the oil-dependent trance of driving an automobile.

The history of magic and Gnosticism can be seen, on one level, as the history of the exploration of new altered states of consciousness. The counter-conspiracy to cultural hegemony has often been to monkey with its bloodstream.

Jazz, rock 'n roll, acid house, hip-hop culture, the Sexual Revolution, the Internet, body modification, the mass popularity of marijuana, LSD and MDMA—all spearheaded by those following the Gnostic impulse of reconnection with something beyond the world of illusion—have all opened suggestive doors of new possibility in the previous century, doors that are now either taxed, policed or closed altogether, though they have all been axles upon which individual consciousnesses, and history, have been revolutionized. The stuff just grows, no matter what they do to clamp down on it.

The forms of altered consciousness that we choose to pioneer and engineer for ourselves and our social groups over the coming decades will determine what doors are opened for us, and how our stories are written. It is through the group-experienced, intent-driven altered state that the magical world is most strongly aligned with the mundane one. Got any ideas?

Sorcery

Remembering by anamnesis, soul-memory, that all is one, one intuits that all may be affected from anywhere, at any time, in any way. It is hardly mystic; you are simply more than you think you are.

Attempting to change your corner of the cosmic game with magic can create *opportunities*, but it's still up to you to take them, even if they're inside you.

Divination

Remembering by anamnesis that all is one, one intuits that any information about the totality may be gained from any fragment anywhere, at any time, in any way (holographic universe principle).

Divination systems tend to be a training system for a psychic faculty that will cease to need props after a certain point. Divine the future in the clouds, the rustling of the wind through the trees, your dreams. Better yet, listen directly to your heart.

Beasties

It is a very "cute" and androcentric contrivance of the "postmodern" (i.e., sarcastic) approach to magic that anything that is not immediately visible is of necessity created and sustained by human belief. This is only feasible from the perspective of the, um, "non-dual experience." Try to stop believing in street-level reality and see where that gets you.

One is at a loss as to what spirits, égregores, demons, angels, gods, Great Old Ones, etheric floaters, lwa, Secret Chiefs and other discarnate intelligences are, but experience has shown them to exist independently of the human mind (not that *anything* can ever be truly proven to exist outside of the human mind). They may appear to be psychological metaphor *up to a point*, but beyond that things start turning all Eerie Indiana. The nature of "praeterhuman intelligences" is perhaps the central riddle of the whole magic game. When venturing into faerie land one is recommended to have one's wits together at all times. Exercise discretion and don't step out of the circle. Invoke to balance, not exaggerate.

And remember that if you invite them in, discarnate intelligences can quickly stop being discarnate.

Sticking It Where It Don't Belong

When performing any magic action whatsoever, be prepared ahead of time to get *exactly what you asked for*, and don't be surprised when things turn out much more literally than you thought they would.

Magusitis

If a black cat crosses your path, it's bad luck; if a dragonfly does, it's good luck—to the superstitious mind, certain events have occult meanings. To the magical mind, *all* events have occult meanings. Under extreme magical consciousness, every street number is immediately broken down and reconstituted through gematria into Qabalistic patterns; every stain in the pavement becomes a rune; every advertisement is trying to reprogram your soul; the fragments of lyrics from the radios of passing cars are talking directly to you; all world events and the intricacies of pop culture are taken to be the signs and portents of Aeonic progression; every movement of the mind is the passing shadow of something huge and luminous.

Literalism, quite dangerously, is often not far behind.

Navigating this is an ongoing part of the magical experience. Laughter is key here—learning to laugh at existence and at oneself. The Neuro-Linguistic Programming concept of the *state break* can also be useful—derailing unwanted trains of thought by some sudden, random and absurd action.

We Float

The primary logical fallacy in magic is the establishment of one-to-one relationships between signifiers and signifieds. Give it a rest. There are never easy answers, as all initiated symbols and texts can be interpreted on several levels and from several angles. Occult symbols and concepts are not "read" with the conscious mind, they are read with the entire entity in all four basic dimensions; they are read with the totality of one's experience and hence none of it "means" anything in and of itself. The "meaning" dwells in the relationship you establish with that symbol in the moment. This applies exponentially more to magical and paranormal experiences. The other world turns to address the easy caress of metaphor rather than the pornography of fact.[8]

Magic exists in and partakes of the character of inbetweenness. It exists in the blank spaces between the sentences, between the personalities, between the "facts" of the matter. In the third mind. Those who can dwell in the blankness between the words and the numbers will be forever free.

Rule Number One of Living in the Twenty-First Century

Whether or not you believe in magic or not, and whether or not magic is viable as a scientific discipline, and whether or not magic is "real" or not is your own opinion, but *It doesn't matter one single bit.* Because politics, pop culture and advertising don't work along any rules *except the rules of magic.*

Conspiracy Theory and Arcane Symbolism

Multiple-choice question: Which is the most powerful magician?

1. The ritualist standing at her altar (altar) conjuring with her four weapons: wand (wand), cup (cup), dagger (dagger) and pentacle (pentacle).
2. The ritualist standing at her altar (her life) conjuring with her four weapons: wand (willpower), cup (intuition), sword (discrimination) and pentacle (material resources).
3. The ritualist standing at her altar (the masses) conjuring with her four weapons: wand (the media), cup (consensus trance), sword (laws and military) and pentacle (the economy).
4. The ritualist standing at her altar (the world) conjuring with her four weapons: wand (active individuals), cup (passive masses), sword (warfare) and pentacle (planetary resources).

5. The ritualist standing at her altar (spirit) conjuring with her four weapons: wand (fire), cup (water), sword (air) and pentacle (earth).

Time

Through magic we reorient ourselves in time, investigate ourselves in our many facets, reach around corners. We ponder the past; seek its secret threads and what it can tell us about who we are. We try to live fully for the moment, be conscious only of this eternal present. And sometimes we make plans for the future, write out our little magic spells, aim high, set goals and it all works out *now*, doesn't it? And in the overlaps and blank spots of our binding of time, in the static, is the real magic made.

In this human condition we try to decipher our sadness, ask our mortality and weakness for its name, and our sorrow is nothing save time itself.

Stumbling through inner London in the rain, alone and crazy from the magic, I came upon something safe. In an abandoned playground in the shadow of the council flats I found a worn stone circle, a hollow carved out in the center, overflowing with rainwater. I had been locked up in my room doing the magic and trying to unravel the puzzles of eternity and here in front me was this offering bowl, the writing carved above it reading simply:

"to catch them
and be filled
again
and again
and again"

And this was magic. And when I looked around me at the empty metal bars of the playground and knew that it was not raindrops but children that would be caught and held safe, I understood that this was real magic. Stark feminine force, a reality as hard and unyielding as the concrete, waiting underneath the wars and the stock market and our rebellion and this playground earth to catch us all. Underneath all the games and the words.

This was surely the work of a Master Builder.

The magic connections we weave underneath the world's seeming. The intelligence that peers in and laughs at our little games.

The Bedside Manner

After the primary initiations one is urged to move the focus away from the self; a watched pot never boils after all and Will is never perfected when it is divided in self-examination. There are infinite masks for a magician to wear but ultimately it is what you add to the lives of those close to you that you will be judged by.

The days of the solitary magician, sitting at home manically charting Qabalistic datum or sitting at the computer discussion "shifting the dominant paradigm" with invisible others, are over. While all magical systems are to be considered fodder for research and fuel for activation, the only thing that will matter in this century is *what you do* with magic. If you want to change reality, then do it. The dominant trait of the new breed is severe professionalism. Those magicians with sufficiently interesting personal style will become the rock stars and fashionistas of this era, as nobody has been before. Most effective of all will be well-funded and visible collectives of individuals.

As they said in *Godfather II*—"This is the business we have chosen."

Affirm the unexplainable with every passing instant. The most frightening moment of all may be the one in which you are taken seriously.

Mythological, Religious and Scientific "Truth"

Use whatever is most effective; they are props. The true goal would be to create your own mythology; your own science; your own religion from the stuff of will, imagination and direct, unprejudiced experience of life. Easier said than done.

Never be afraid to ask the big questions.

High Magic

Turn any television set to the static of any empty channel. The hissing pattern you will see is a 7.3 centimeter radio signal emitted by the Big Bang, cosmic microwave background radiation made up of photons that have spent the last fifteen billion years cooling from that hot instant. The black and white fuzz of the eternal dual principle, split off from that original unity, that first spark, hissing across the screen in endless interplay, like a game of Go, creating trinities, quadrinities; creating all that is through their dance. It is here, the face of creation, in every living room, right there in-between the newscasters and the stars. Turn up the volume and listen to the hiss. In the symbology of the imminent Aeon of Ma'at, of reintegration of spirit into matter, this is the Swan—symbol of firstness, Kether, of regality and purity; who, when approached, chased you from the pond, hissing forth with the viciousness of creation itself.

This is the image of the beginning, unveiled before our furtive gaze.

Since the Copenhagen interpretation of quantum mechanics posits that light is neither wave nor particle until it is observed as either, or that things are neither black or white, one way or another until observed as such, then this shows that by observing our origin we are changing it; that by observing our past we are creating our present. Our gaze, after all, is as concrete of a thing as what it regards.

The Participatory Anthropic Principle, going even further, suggests that the observation of the universe is what is required to make it real. Through staring into that primal chaos are we bringing it order; and so is the Great Work performed, in every instant's gaze. I see that, therefore I am that.

The Final Anthropic Principle, last in this trio of weird sisters, suggests that universes *must* produce intelligence in order for that intelligence to observe the creation of the universe and so make it real. This is an eternal intelligence, an eternal mind, which is the end point of the universe's evolution. Intelligence beyond that of the human. God is not in the machine. We are the machine that will create God.

And this is magic. By observation we create; by investing with meaning do we give form; by physical enactment do we make manifest. And what we observe is the infinite, here for us to create whatever we wish from, the Spirit of God moving over the face of the waters. And with every passing instant do we create eternity. Aum. Hee hee!

Your Point Is

Every man and woman is a star. Every man and woman is God, creating the totality of the universe they perceive in every instant, whether they are aware of it or not. We are all already playing God. And we are all already Gods—we just have to remember how to access that part of us which partakes of that boundless, non-local divinity. And in that non-local space will you find the voices of the light, if you know how to listen.

What the "divine" is isn't the point; the language fails by definition, as it exists of a plane higher than words. It could be DNA. It could be the morphogenetic field. It could be the Holy Guardian Angel. It could be Christ, Krishna, Atman. Ultimately it doesn't matter, because it is the voice of intelligence which guards and guides our progression—an intelligence which knows far, far better than any one of us or any collection of us as a group what is best for us. The voice of love is unmistakable and the entire history of the human quest for truth and meaning can be shaken down to one statement, stamped on the forehead of the entire universe so it has to see it every time it looks in its rusty bathroom mirror, and that is:

LOVE IS THE SECRET OF THE UNIVERSE—END OF FUCKING STORY

. . . end of story. You have now graduated from Consciousness Expansion Class, forever.

Love is the *qiblah* of evolution and of divinity. When adrift in its slipstream, caught in the love-realms of the angelians, we have our purest understanding of things. We have certainty.

The love of the universe.

The love of the future.

The love of each other.

Setting Goals

Create positive change on this planet or shut your mouth.

ENDNOTES

[1] *XXX*, a 2001 action film starring Mr. Vin Diesel, is a parable about Generation Hex and the emergence of the chaos current into the mainstream.

[2] www.drspock.com

[3] What Don Beck and Christopher Cowan's "Spiral Dynamics" model of cultural growth, based on the research of Dr. Clare Graves, refers to as the "purple meme."

[4] Frazer, Sir James G. *The Golden Bough*.

[5] The onset of magical thinking comes at around the same time as that of language; meaning that by this point the child has already been largely *separated* from its innate sense of oneness with the universe, language being a Promethean binding and individuating agent. The very fact that the child believes it can have magical affect on the universe presupposes separation from that universe. Initiates aim to run time in reverse and return to the source of incarnation *while still incarnated*; it is likely for this reason that we so often see people who begin in magic seeking to cause change to the universe quickly dropping this model and instead seeking to wholly merge with the universe. They have remembered an earlier, more "innate" state of withinity. Rather than seeking to become God-like, they seek to become God. Without the realization that being God is really a fairly commonplace experience, this attitude will produce such shady shit as Western civilization.

[6] A classic vocation for the magician then becomes to gently prod others awake; and hopefully through more creative positions than the missionary.

[7] Many thanks to Jack Parsons.

[8] The Yaminahua shamans of the Peruvian Amazon speak of "tsai yoshtoyoshto," or "language-twisting-twisting." According to them, blunt and concrete language frightens spirits away and instead must be constructed in an oblique and open-ended manner. Compare this to the running effort in the Twentieth Century to restructure English around uncertainty and open-endedness, such as Crowley's strictures on "I" and "because" or Dr. David Bourland's "E-Prime."

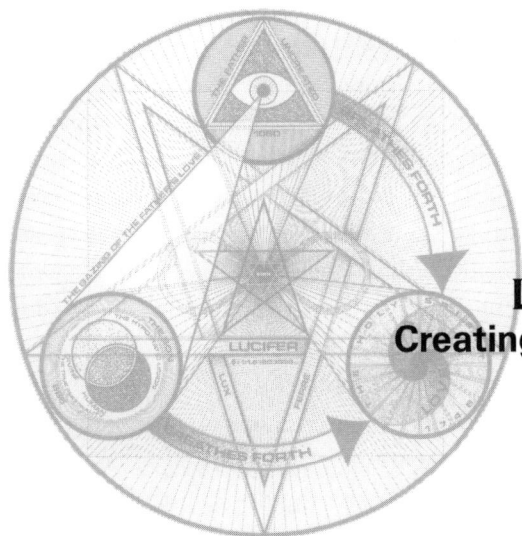

LIVING THE MYTH
Creating Value in a Cultural Void

JAMES CURCIO

Mythology isn't just *Bulfinch's*: it is the living, breathing story of humanity. The stories that really carry through the ages repeat themselves, in different forms, from one generation to the next. Each of our lives is a story, an album, a painting, in which we play the starring role; they weave together into an ever-changing tapestry which we call culture.

The usefulness of a myth must be explored for the sake of creating a ritual that is based on one's own life and life-goals, to focus on the meaning contained within life and amplify it.

On a personal level, a myth is the story of your life. It is the whole, of which your current awareness is but a fragment. There is a cultural dimension of myth as well, which we will deal with; however, the key to creating a living mythology is here, now, in you. We transmit this living mythology to each other through our art, and through the ways we choose to live our lives. Life is a dream you won't remember upon awakening. The tale is what matters. Legends and heroes always lag a generation or two behind the present, and the times we live in are desperately in need of both. *We're living our lives right now.*

Artists are not only those who manage to find a vocation in art. All myth-builders are artists, on the most fundamental level; and art is not just about what different people or cultures find aesthetically pleasing—it is also, and possibly more fundamentally, a process which tells people *what things mean*. A magician is only different from an artist in terms of method. The ultimate intent is identical.

To live our myth we need to first come to terms with our culture, and our history, as individuals. As James Joyce said, history is a nightmare from which we are desperately trying to *awake*. What does it mean to be at this place and this time, and how has it made you who you are? For this we can consult our family trees and personal psychological makeup, but also, and I would say this is more important, the ideological history of our culture.

A history of dates and facts is somewhat irrelevant; all axioms and preconceptions must be evaluated from the vantage point of the task at hand. The value of historic knowledge lies in an analysis of the evolution of ideas, rather than in the necessary validity of "facts." Facts are only useful within a specific context; the methods we use for "investigating" truths in fact create them and, as has been said before, history is written by the victors. Drop it, because everything you know probably isn't true. So it had better be useful, meaningful or, at the least, fun.

The easiest way to *break out* is to psychologically remove yourself temporarily from the culture you were born into. Take a step back. Take ten. Look for everything people assume to be true, and think it through with new eyes. Allow yourself to be the fly on the wall, and start taking notes. Nothing is too small for this deconstruction.

Remember, whether or not we feel estranged from the culture surrounding us, it made us who we are, just as cultural undergrounds, the radicals on both sides of the spectrum, are polarizations of the same ideology.

Deconstructing the Modern Myth

The world that we live in is the result of our ideas and understanding of the universe. Though gravity does not work *because* it obeys Newton's laws, we *did* use Newton to get a man to the moon and back.

While we advance exponentially in technological capability, our spiritual or "biological technology," our maturity as a species, is still two or three thousand years in the past. This is because many of us live according to ideas that were original and groundbreaking . . . in 500 B.C. Most people are unwilling or unable to ask the hard questions—as in, why do we do things the way we do, and what will the end results be?

On the whole, our technology is ecologically and spiritually stupid. The motivating factor in most breakthroughs is nothing other than the urge to destroy or multiply. Modern man is an ape with a rocket launcher.

The basic premises people hold as given, and the realities we each live in, are direct products of archaic behaviors and beliefs that are incongruous with the universe as we currently experience it. Western knowledge has built upon itself without critical analysis of the history of its axioms.

This is the legacy of a simple choice: the artists, priests, scientists and other mythbuilders chose to paint the natural order as something which must be overcome for spiritual advancement to take place. Our current corporate, mass-media culture owes itself, in part, to an ideology that poses itself *against* nature and the natural order. This ideology is present within the religions of Zoroastrianism, Judaism, Manichaeism, Christianity and, to a lesser extent, the works of many of the Greek philosophers. While most people today do not remember Zarathushtra, all of us live in a world fashioned from his models, and by Newton's, Descartes' and so on. A world in which the human dimension is held in tension against nature and where the purpose of the human animal is seen as bringing light to the world, changing a dark, wild chaos into a world of order, is also inevitably a world governed by rationality, with all of its blind spots.

This archaic mentality, when active within the ad-cult of capitalism, engenders a shortsightedness towards the repercussions of our actions that leaves the public mind impoverished.

Breakthroughs in science, philosophy and the arts have all come about through critical analysis of the corpus of available knowledge, in addition to individual creative thought. The lifeblood of artistic and philosophical advancement is struggle: Each new "great" school of art or philosophy comes about as a reaction to the previous, now ossified and static system. Advances happen as a result of people thinking about old problems in new ways. At first, innovators are seen as mavericks; yet a hundred years later, their ideas represent the next tradition that needs to be smashed in the name of progress. If you see the Buddha on the side of the road, squash his cranium with a baseball bat and take his spare dharma.

There is a common misconception, especially within the capitalistic myth, that art and philosophy are useless endeavors—at best mental exercises, at worst, activities for criminals and dilettantes. They forget that all of the great periods in human history have occurred side-by-side with quantum leaps in the arts and philosophy. It is impossible, and irrelevant, to definitively argue which came first. Art and philosophy, without trade, commerce and *application*, are sterile and masturbatory. Similarly, trade and commerce are brutish and myopic when not applied with the sensibility that comes from in-depth philosophical and artistic debate. All are crucial to evolution, but only when applied together.

Starvation, ignorance and poverty aren't biological necessities—they are cultural ones, both cause and effect for the gap between the have and have-nots within society. These problems are unresolved not because they cannot be resolved, but because the systems in place do not require or foster the idea of change. The dynamic of have and have-not in fact polarizes—even empowers—the system. Two parties, one world map. What American doesn't think that they too might one day be rich, or famous? How many Americans would be able to go to their tedious job every day without that dream to keep them going?

The beliefs that root us in this mode of being are too strong for any single "revolutionary" movement to effectively shift them—all that results from such radicals is further polarization. If, on the other hand, people find an alternative that truly works for them, it will likely spread by virtue of its efficacy.

"Dropping out," Timothy Leary style, merely results in obscurity. Many communes have been attempted along these lines. Others have attempted to piggyback on society-at-large, funding Robin Hood schemes with corporate money.

These grow until a certain point. It has been noted in studies of corporations and tribes alike that close-knit familial structures break down around 150-200 members. Interest focuses towards hierarchically determined, individual concerns. Necessary strata of middle management and bureaucracy make the system itself the modus operandi, rather than the best interests of all involved. The original intent is lost as the successful meme graduates into a tradition.

Tribes that grow beyond this "tipping point" must schism as a point of progress, or that schism will merely occur psychologically, as cultural schizophrenia. The binding glue of compassion turns to competition. Greed and competition are biological imperatives for primates; however, so are cooperation and nurturing. We can choose which impulses to act on. This Work is for those who choose the latter.

Study and practice of self-created ritual will invariably provide initiations into your *own* nature. This may also lead you to other kindred, who for whatever reason share a common ideological thread. Whatever way this initiation unfolds will be unique in each and every one of us, as we are all inventing new mythologies, most of which will likely remain untold and die with us.

The method used to bring about this change is simple enough in theory—it is in the practice and application that you will find your trials and rewards. We analyze our maps, our histories and our symbol systems and, through this, continually deepen our experience of our selves. Symbols, religious symbols in particular, are literary devices which, when used properly, refer back to human psychology with a precision that is nearly mathematical, so long as you can decipher the reference. Through unraveling the reality that the symbols point at, and invoking it into the present as it applies to your Will, one may not only understand religious symbols but also live through them. And this, not fanatical belief or faith, is what religion is.

Magic Is a Way of Life—Don't Quit Your Day Job

Magic is a word that has been bandied about occult and counterculture circles for years. Usually it calls to mind dark rituals in graveyards or, to those who associate more closely with the "in-crowds," hierarchical sword-rattling and tedious arguments about copyrights. This word should be cut free from those associations, and reinstated as something *useful*.

In defining his system of "Magick," Aleister Crowley claimed that he wanted to separate magic from its strictly esoteric roots. He proclaimed that "the law is for all." If this was truly his aim, then for all the beneficial tools he did provide to consciousness explorers, he failed.

Yet his definition of "Magick" was a pragmatic one. Magic is either an endeavor which can benefit everyone, or it is nothing at all.

Magic is not what we generally associate with the "occult," either. It does not require you to slaughter chickens or dance in a circle, even if these prove beneficial to some. You don't have to wear a silly cape or carry around massive scepters.

Magic is that which is hidden from the senses. It is metaphysics; it is philosophy. The root question is the same, even if the tools differ: What is *really going on here?* A philosopher uses reason, a shaman may use hallucinogenic roots and drums, and a scientist may use a microscope. Historically, the roots of religion, science and magic are the same.

We can separate people into two ways of looking at the world—those who think that the outside world is "real," and those who don't. But as far as magic is concerned, *it doesn't matter* if the world out there is "real." Not even a little bit. Amusingly enough, it *does* matter that it doesn't matter. The greatest tool used by the magician to ensure freedom is the fact that no matter what discoveries are made in science, psychology or the occult, no one can have the final word on Truth.

This tool is called Doubt. There is no dogma, no grand theory and no overblown ego, that can stand up to this simple tool. With this tool you can avoid ever being taken advantage of by political or religious leaders, by advertisers or gurus: Each of us winds our own path through life, and there are no rules. Authority is an illusion, although hard work is not.

Human existence is a mystery, and all experience is conditioned by relative context. Even the question "is the world out there *real?*" is meaningless without an "I" to ask it. Realizing all of this, magicians take reality into their own hands because they realize that it is truly *their* reality.

Taking this step outside the herd, many would-be magicians immediately fall off a cliff, and never return. They fall into the group that think that there is no "real world" out there. (Hit one of these people on the head with a brick and *then* ask them if it's real.)

An experience I had a couple years ago may help illustrate this point. I was contacted by a woman who was waking up each morning covered in scratches. She asked me if I thought she was "actually" being magically attacked. The following joke from Crowley's *Magick in Theory and Practice* seemed appropriate to relate:

There is the story of the American in the train who saw another American carrying a basket of unusual shape. His curiosity mastered him, and he leant across and said: "Say, stranger, what you got in that bag?"
The other, lantern-jawed and taciturn, replied: "Mongoose."
The first man was rather baffled, as he had never heard of a mongoose. After a pause he pursued, at the risk of a rebuff: "But say, what is a Mongoose?"
"Mongoose eats snakes," replied the other.

This was another poser, but he pursued: "What in hell do you want a Mongoose for?"
"Well, you see," said the second man (in a confidential whisper), "my brother sees snakes."
The first man was more puzzled than ever; but after a long think, he continued rather pathetically:
"But say, them ain't real snakes."
"Sure," said the man with the basket, "but this Mongoose ain't real either."

She didn't get the point of this story, and asked me again if I thought it was *real*. The only thing you can ask at this point is, do *you* think it is real? If so, you can pursue the problem through ritual. Hell, you might even get paid five hundred bucks to perform a ceremony. If you decide to look at it as *not* real, i.e., internal rather than external, it can be pursued through psychotherapy. Either is true. Neither is true.

Magic is a philosophy. It is a way of looking at life. Even a man's ideas of God are just that—ideas.

So let's plumb Crowley's word "Magick" further. Aleister Crowley defined Magick as the "science and art of causing change in conformity with Will." Straightforward enough, except for that tricky word, "Will."

Will is nearly synonymous with Identity—that which one is. However, it is that Identity inflected outwards as action. One is what one does. And if one's doing is equivalent with one's being, then one is practicing magic.

As this all boils down to identity, magic is in many ways a method for performing psychotherapy on oneself. Congruence between one's identity and one's action, even one's vocation, are essential to be-what-one-is.

The magical approach may be pursued alongside more traditional psychotherapy, and according to some rather esteemed in the Western tradition, such as Israel Regardie, it should be.

The magician desires freedom. The first tool towards this, as previously mentioned, is Doubt; the second is Choice. To make wise decisions, based on one's goals rather than social convention or expectation, one must know oneself and be willing to die for the right to make that Choice. It may be for this reason alone that philosophy, psychology and so on aren't just complete wastes of time.

As a philosophy that emphasizes practice, magic provides a way to give meaning to the things that happen to us. It has only been recently, after almost a decade of exploration, that I came to this realization. Many, if not most, of the "tools" on my altar have evolved a deep, personal significance, created through years of working with them. This acquired power has an immediate effect on me when I access it.

Many of the tragedies I have endured in my life have led to leaps of growth and self-knowledge, because I had a tradition—my own! —which allowed me to claim those tragedies and give them meaning as initiations into a new way of being and perceiving the world, regardless of whether or not there is any underlying truth or significance behind what I experience.

The meaning we give to experiences and sensations, even something as simple as a color, is in our hands. For most, this process is primarily automatic, unconscious. However, at some point, and on some level, we have to choose to allow meanings to be given. It is through choosing to accept predetermined meanings that we opt into cultures.

Culture comes about, in part, through an agreement upon certain terms. If a group all choose to give x meaning to object y, they are then entering the same domain together. Some domains are so much more ubiquitous than others, possibly as a result of our biological commonality, that there are some "truth pacts" which are in certain places and times more likely to take hold and last.

Take, for instance, the color yellow. There is the English association of cowardice. Yet Buddhist robes are also yellow, because to Buddhists this is the color of death. We may instead choose to hold a personal association. As a result of a past experience, it may make us feel joy, or despair. Someone may say something to you in a joking manner, but you suddenly feel tears welling to your eyes, because you are reminded of a friend who has died. Getting a handle on someone's "key words," and what they mean to *them*, is coming to learn their language. You learn to not say certain words, or evoke certain images, and to evoke others to make them feel good.

It is this association of meaning, this "naming" of things, which is the root of our ability to build worlds.

The power of this ability must not be understated. Again, the simple choice to consider the base biological drives a hindrance to spiritual life, rather than the path to it, set the predominant historic trend for two millennia of Western history.

It is this ability to choose to create and give meaning, to reconstruct the coal of our experience and turn it into diamonds, for those who have the subtlety to recognize them, which differentiates a magician. This capacity exists within us all. There is not, and should not be, a certain test of capability, though we all strive to exceed ourselves each day.

Of course the traditional magician uses a wand, has an altar, performs invocations, probably practices yoga, uses sexual secretions for magical purposes, defiles virgins, etc. However, all of these "tools of the trade" are symbolic, first and foremost.

The symbolic power of ritual tools is another key of magical practice, which can be analyzed in terms of structuralist and post-structuralist theories on linguistics and anthropology. We construct our reality through mental images and words that we use to represent things in our experience. The references become bounded to that which they refer. In this light, many "primitive" beliefs seem slightly less bizarre—i.e., that a person's true name shouldn't be given away lightly, or that a photograph might steal or trap someone's soul.

Think for a moment about the "magical" power of the word "STOP," or the phrase "I love you." These represent states of mind, and states of being. Even a traditional magician's tools, such as a wand, are symbols. The wand is a symbol for the magician's Will. It is also a symbol for the element of fire, which is then associated with certain tarot cards, gems, metals and drugs. These symbolic connections can form a rich language for constructing and practicing ritual.

Magical practice is one way of coming into accord with the world you live in through direct, conscious use of the associations or "alphabet" we use to interpret our experience. Associations are key to understanding magic. You may have glanced through books on the subject and seen tables of correspondences listing things like the number three, the color greenish-blue, Venus, sandalwood, a dove . . . and wondered to yourself why otherwise sensible people believe that the number three has anything to do with a dove.

There are any number of theories about what these associations "really" mean. Once again, it just doesn't matter. What matters is a consistency that allows for variation within different contexts. An individual letter or word within any given language has no meaning whatsoever without the other letters or words. If someone saw the letter "A" or even the word "CAT" without having seen or heard the English language, it would be a meaningless scribble or utterance. Two plus two only equals four within a specific context, in which it *always* equals four. Meaning is created through relationship and the application of arbitrary but specific rules.

Yet meaning must also be connoted; different people have different associations with "cats," for instance, beyond the literal definition of the term. With a magical alphabet you are building the relationships and associations that construct your reality. To start, it may benefit you to study at least one, if not many, pre-existent "languages." Many turn to the Golden Dawn[5] Qabalah, or similar systems, to "get their wings."

How is this alphabet applied? Take the magical practice of invocation. One steps outside of their normal role, and makes their body and mind a fit receptacle for a particular energy, which is codified in symbols. These symbols are impressed upon the mind as words, but during the ritual, scent, colors, etc., all congruent with the nature of the invocation, strengthen these associations, further exalting the mind to allow this "deity" to indwell within it. Methods may vary highly from mantras, postures, visualizations, the use of "energy" which is activated through concentration, invocations performed through art, chanting, even, to a lesser but more pervasive sense, the stream of consciousness constantly running through your mind. The more you work with specific tools, the more meaningful they will become. A well-used tool becomes an automatic mantra, a passageway into a specific state of consciousness, available at a moment's notice.

The difference between practices is cultural and aesthetic. The ritual garb of a Siberian shaman and the makeup of a performer like Marilyn Manson *can* serve the same function, if the performer approaches the act with this kind of intent, and a rich background in the subject. There is some value in being aware of those who have come before, even if all of our truths differ as individuals. It is a tried and true axiom of art that you cannot break rules that you are not aware of, and all magicians are truly artists-in-training.

So for the time being put aside the useless question of whether magic, energy and spirits are or are not "real," and recognize that what we are working with is our ability to name things, to give them meaning. Just as it is ultimately not the answers but the questions that are the true catalyst of growth, it is not the meaning inherent in things but the meaning that we give to them that holds value.

Art and Ritual

A magician performs rituals. A ritual could be an involved litany proclaimed in an incense-filled room. It could be a massive orgy on satin sheets. Or it could be brushing your teeth. Really, if we get down to brass tacks, a ritual is an intentional action, which has a result. At the most basic level, an effective ritual is an action taken which has a result consistent with its intention.

Furthermore, a ritual is a habit. We even use these two words as synonyms in casual speech. And like any habit, rituals can conflict with each other. As a writer, for instance, I have a number of habits or rituals associated with my writing. I make my coffee. I roll a cigarette. In terms of getting me in the state of mind to sit down and type away for hours on end, these rituals are very effective. However, they conflict in some ways with the rituals I have which get me in the frame of mind to practice yoga.

Every single habit has a cumulative effect on your being. When all are in harmony with internal goals, whatever they may be, you are living your myth, or doing your Will. When every activity is a ritual, you're well on your way to becoming your myth. Though it can result in hours of painful drum-banging for friends and family, fake-it-till-you-make-it is a good rule for green artists.

Some rituals result in greatness. Others do not. A successful ritual is experiential, experimental, rich with symbols and metaphors, scents and movements, all of which have meaning to the participants. When a ritual is pantomimed, it has become dead and must be discarded.

All seemingly effortless, perfected actions depend on a unity of theory and practice, mind and body. You see this with a trained athlete or musician. The distinct muscular actions and thought processes have been streamlined into a simple start-and-stop process. In many ways, experts are less aware of the discrete actions they are taking to perform a task than a beginner.

This holism may in fact be a neurological prerequisite. Experts aren't necessarily smarter than you are; they simply have to think less to perform actions that seem intricate and complex to you. This ease is earned through untold tribulation in private. If you aren't dedicated to earning your title as magician or artist through hard work, you're probably better off leaving it alone. (Or at least dabbling behind closed doors.)

The word "ritual" is usually associated with religion; this has a great deal of historical backing, and may have some linguistic and neurological precedent as well.

The root word of religion, the Latin *religio*, means to yoke or bind together. The *phenomenology* must be tied to *ontology*. Perception and being are brought together, and rituals are the method for bringing about this alchemical marriage. This is also the meaning of the word yoga, as Crowley repeats countless times in his *Eight Lectures on Yoga*: Yoga means union.

Thus, mythology is the embodiment of ritual and religion. Together they serve to tie individuals to a cultural source, or to tie individuals to their own source. There are three primary principles of ritual, which are embodied in myth. These are in essence the same, but the "yoke" applies to the individual, to society and to the natural order. Without ritual, myth would have no way of reproducing itself, or having any effect whatsoever. Without myth, ritual would have no raison d'être.

In whichever case, the function is one of binding or bringing together. You perform ritual to bring the vying aspects of your consciousness into accord with your will. Thus an action that yokes our action and our will together may be considered ritual. Or, a myth teaches individuals within a society how to relate to one another, and how to relate to the cycles of life. Ritual is a process used to connect the individual, the society and the world of nature. Although the process partakes of actions, it can only truly be called "ritual" when all of one's habitual actions have been given mythic resonance.

To be successful, certain prerequisites must be fulfilled. For instance, as all ritual serves to pitch us out of our daily lives in some way, there should be a strong quality of the "otherworldly" in the process. Ritual is "deified" or "spiritualized" activity. Something is called "spiritual" merely as it holds a quality that allows us to distinguish it from regular activity.

Ritual alters states of mind and has the power to create entire cultures. Although it is true that the energies you deal with are just metaphors or projections of your own consciousness, it is also true that they have a mind, will and identity all their own, as much as you do. Be respectful to them. It is incredibly important that the would-be practitioner grasp this before dealing with evocation, possession or conjuration of any kind.

Ritual can put you in touch with any number of different cultural consciousnesses or hive minds. The child of this union is myth, often embodied in art. This common ground is created through the cultural or cultic belief system that is the domain of that mythology. You may, in a sense, consider the whole of a mythology to be the neurological map or domain from which a culture derives itself. The altar, whether it is a physical altar or merely your sanctified place of work or worship, is a crossroads between your individual identity and the energies that inform the universe.

The ritual ground is archetypical ground so that, for instance, in Tantric practice one person embodies the god Shiva and the other the goddess Shakti. By taking on this embodiment, man is doing the work of Gods.

Everything living shares equally in that Divine essence—and embodying oneself within a role sanctioned by the mythology can give it a greater significance and value. For instance, Native American hunters killed animals for food just as we do, but in their case this slaughter was sanctioned by the mythology; it was given a meaning and significance that stood at the very center of everyday life, much as the food itself was necessary for survival. Our cultural preference is to push the "dirty" fact of animal slaughter out of sight. I find it very unlikely that this goes unnoticed in our psychology.

Spoken words, images and sounds all have biological, psychological and electromagnetic effects. Glasses vibrate as a reaction to specific frequencies based on their size or, we could say, based on their character. If you project frequencies, they will create a resonance with congruent vessels, as well as an interference pattern with others. This can be understood in any number of ways.

For instance, in conversation or social interaction, you can behave in a way that creates harmonic congruence, dissonance or both. John Coltrane created a message—some people resonated with it, others didn't.

Ritual creates "frequencies" that resonate the effects we want through sympathetic reaction. If this is done, all you have to do is let the effects come to you. Though we cannot absolutely foresee the effects of our actions, we can count on the universe reflecting back to us a mirror reflection of what we give it, as yin (soft) gives way to yang (hard) and yang gives way to yin. Push, it pulls you. Pull, it pushes back.

These principles can be applied liberally by artists within their work. Eventually, the object itself triggers those associated results without thought or effort. Whether this is the result of psychological suggestion—as Robert Anton Wilson says in *Prometheus Rising*, "what the thinker thinks the prover proves"—or actual energetic sympathy has to be a matter for entertaining coffeehouse discussions because, yet again, it doesn't matter.

Myth is born through the regular practice of ritual. Looking at the myths of different cultures, we see what issues are part of the culture-complex of a particular place and time, and what is really existentially crucial to the human animal in any time and place. Certain themes remain.

Myth intends to provide a connection to our singular source. Art that connects with this source is the same. And sure enough, most of the art that we find in caves and ancient dwellings is religious. Myths only truly have relevance when they have both a cultural and a personal import. For example, the "apocalypse" myth has taken hold of many of our imaginations because on a cultural level, we potentially stand on the brink of a great chaos, which could be the end of this culture and age, if not our species.

Whether or not this becomes part of our history, it *is* part of our psychology, proven by its frequent occurrence within the art of our time. Our myths are symptoms of the state of mind of our culture.

Simultaneously, this image must also reverberate with us on a personal level.

We must be attuned to it. This attunement could be the product of any number of things—fear, fascination, confusion—but I would propose that if the idea of personal apocalypse had no sway over you, the cultural form would be powerless as well.

This is something mythmakers and artists must be aware of, that to be the voice of an age they must speak on these two levels, separate and yet inseparable. It is not an artist's voice that becomes the voice of an age, but rather the voice of an age that speaks through the artist.

Art and Ritual, Practical Fundamentals

Analysis of the history of myth is useless if you don't see how the symbols relate directly and immediately to you. This calls for unusual creative acumen. You must be able to project your life story into a pile of tea leaves, or explore your psyche through painting. The medium doesn't matter. No real evaluation of quality is useful except as it applies to the context and intent of its creation. To simply be what and who we are in the process of creating, and to strive to be more ourselves the next time around—to the magician, this is what holds value.

The four traditional tools of Western magic show us the heart of ritual and creative practice. Ritual is the practice or embodiment of myth, art is the alchemical method of manifestation, and art is informed by dream. It is through a balanced application of the four traditional magical tools that we bring these to life.

These "tools" are the wand, the cup, the sword and the pentacle. Success and balance are encoded within the interplay of these four symbols, when properly understood. On the universal level they represent the creative will, fire, which is given form and tempered by water, the receptive quality. This substrate is honed, analyzed and pared down by the intellectual quality of air, and is finally brought into manifestation in sensations, the element of earth. In the *Zohar*, a Thirteenth Century Qabalistic text considered primary in that tradition next to the *Sefer Yetzirah*, these four elements are represented as the father (fire), the mother (water), the son (air) and the daughter (earth).

We are led to our Will through the constant exploration and exercise of our creative vision. When I say "Will" I actually mean it in two senses. On the one hand I refer to the simple willpower it takes to fuel this creation to life, a verb, the action of creating it. On the other, I refer to the entire process—as a whole—as a single, completed unit. We find ourselves writ large within our creations, and may only come to know ourselves in this complete way after many years of creative experimentation. This is what it is that you have been working on your entire life, without realizing it. Every single action or piece contains the whole within it.

Earth—physical manifestation—is the result of the use of the cup and the wand, and then the sword. In other words, you must be receptive to your intention to create. You may not know exactly what it is that you are going to make, but you must nevertheless be open to it and aware of it in some nonverbal fashion. If the editor comes out too soon, you'll be staring at a blank page.

However, if you give an idea fertile ground to grow in, it *will* grow, even if the seed remains underground for some time. Give it fallow earth and water. When the time is ripe—you will most likely experience this as a psychic pressure that simply *must* be released—you then empty yourself and become a medium for the seed to sprout from.

Finally, once this synthesis has taken place, you can prune it. Many people attempt to start critically and wonder why they are so "naturally uncreative." Creativity is a process many of us need to relearn, though it is second nature to any two-year-old. Criticism and didactics are an integral part of the aesthetic process, but they have no place in the initial fugue of creativity.

In Chi Gung,[7] I was taught that the li (mind) leads the chi. That is to say, it is your intention to create movement that creates movement, before the movement has occurred. The breath follows this, so that eventually there is an integration of the entire system, from intent to action, which flows effortlessly as a whole. This is the intention or "seed" which lies beneath the fault-line of our consciousness. If there is no block to this will on any level, then the action is, in fact, divine. We merely embody it as it manifests.

Theory and abstraction are only useful when they can be applied to even the simplest or most concrete task. This idea itself is tacit within the four-element system. All of the four elemental traits should be developed within an initiate, and it is an application of all four that results in a successful venture. Without pointing fingers, let me say that it has been my experience that many Western traditions, magical and otherwise, emphasize knowledge over intuition, and don't successfully teach techniques for developing creativity, adaptability and receptivity. It is much more difficult to teach creativity than rote devices.

The Bottom Line

All you're really working with is ends and means. Those intelligent and driven enough to practice magic will also recognize that providing benefit to others provides a benefit to oneself as well—and not through some feel-good three-part law nonsense. Society came to be as, without it, most of us would starve.

Myths that resonate with the largest audience survive. Whether or not something is "good art," you aren't even going to hear about the meme unless the resonance pattern it created reaches you, through word of mouth or big advertising budgets.

To summarize: *Ritual is an enactment of a mythology allowing us access to dimensions of our singular and collective being, through the language of symbols with specific connotations, in what is essentially a play-acting process.* The energies and beings dealt with may be thought of as real or projections, but ultimately they are as real or unreal as any other impression that you might have. Every action, word and gesture has symbolic meaning or mythic resonance. This resonance must occur between the myth or ritual and the individual(s) enacting it, in whatever mediums they choose to Work.

Every act that we take has reverberations that we must work with to be aware of, always pushing ourselves to the next level—never looking down at the endless expanse beneath our feet.

Finally, to all of you would-be artists, magicians and myth-builders: Put the book down a while and get to Work.

ENDNOTES

[1] A number of major media groups, including NPR and ABC, have shown that over fifty percent of the American public believes that the world (and, one would assume, the entire universe) was created, exactly as it is, between six and eight thousand years ago. This is, I think, a major case-in-point.

[2] Which we can see in the history of Western thought from 500 B.C. to the present age, as scholasticism and even science merged with the Christian worldview.

[3] We share a heritage that pretends to serve the function of mythology. Santa Claus, the Easter bunny and the Jolly Green Giant—you don't need to skip a beat between them; they're in the same category. However, these "entities" don't help us come into accord with the cycles of life. They coax us into buying things, which is a requisite part of the social order.

[4] Usually movements lose substance either through a shallowing of their core values, until they become an empty, parroted aesthetic, as with most music scenes; or the movement's core values are so emphasized that the meaning within them is lost through literalism, as we can see in the history of the world's major religions.

[5] The archetypal Victorian occult order, which included within its ranks such luminaries as S. L. MacGregor Mathers, W. B. Yeats, Annie Horniman, Florence Farr, Algernon Blackwood, Arthur Machen, A. E. Waite, Dion Fortune and Aleister Crowley. The researches of the Golden Dawn form much of the source material of modern occultism. – Ed.

[6] It may be of interest to those with some familiarity with Qabalah that the magician reverses the process that the universe uses in manifestation, marrying the daughter and the son, to raise them to the throne of the father.

[7] Chi Gung is the cultivation of electro-chemical energy (prana, chi, vril) through the use of certain visualization, breathing, movement and posture practices originating in mainland China. (See asana, pranayama, etc. for similar practices of Indian origin.)

YOUR LUCKY HAND

ANGELINA FABBRO

The consciousness of our world is changing. Previously "fringe" paradigms of science and technology are becoming more and more popular as new research gives us new clues to the nature of the universe. We are pioneering a new era without secrets, where everyone is involved in a holistic model and previous divisions are crumbling under the surplus of information that challenges them. Constantly demanding that more information be mainlined into our minds, we are left with the unspoken mantra of the information age, the steady urging pulse of "faster, faster!" Our progress towards faster communication of information requires new models to support new phenomenon.

Yet we do not have an explanation for why we feel we need to learn so quickly, except the desire to find an end or an absolute truth about the universe, and the broadening of our understanding along the way. There are many means to this end, and the two I want to address are science and magic. It seems as if these two modalities oppose one another—by means of procedure and criteria for what constitutes truth, they differ considerably. However, they are both attempting to find working models they can count on, and they have begun to cross paths with many similar, correlated ideas. Their ultimate goal is the same, and the battle for dominance of human perspective is counterproductive to the realization of the overlap of their respective goals.[1]

Science seeks to explore the nature of our universe by using testable hypotheses that consistently produce tangible and repeatable results. This is used as a basis for the assessment of "truth." It is inherently empirical, often employing reductionism and logic to govern the systems used to define reality. Science does not make claims for anything more than what the empirical data shows.

Spiritual or magical perspectives, on the other hand, have a different set of criteria for what is admissible as empirical data. Information is here integrated from collected personal experience and perceptions. Spiritual perspectives tend to involve the exploration of ideas that are currently untestable by standard scientific procedures, such as intuition, out-of-body experiences and the results that manifest from ritual.

So what *is* existence? Our current model is that everything in the universe is composed of particles—protons, neutrons, electrons, etc. Physicist Arthur Compton discovered that photons behaved like atomic particles, suggesting that light partook of particle properties. He speculated that because light was previously considered to have wave-like properties, perhaps electrons, having been acknowledged as particles, could have wave properties as well. After years of research spun from this hypothesis, the general understanding is that particles bear wave-like qualities in the same way that waves, such as light, bear particle properties. The smallest particles we can trace have a unified, yet dual nature, and they are in constant motion relative to one another.[2]

When it comes down to it, everything on this planet, and probably in this universe, is composed of the same elements. As Masaru Emoto puts it in his book *The Hidden Messages in Water*, the fundamental existence of the universe can be explained in three words: Existence Is Vibration. We are trained to accept that truth is best defined by our immediate, gross senses, yet quantum mechanics generally acknowledges this vibrational principle. When a thing is repeatedly divided into smaller parts, it will inevitably be broken down as far as waves and particles. Now we know that waves and particles are pretty much the same thing. It's an interesting perceptual exercise to pick up two seemingly contrasted objects, like a mobile phone or an apple, and realize that even these are fundamentally composed of the same thing. They fundamentally exist in a state of vibration. If you could shrink yourself small enough, you would discover that atoms are merely a nucleus orbited by electrons, giving each a particular frequency; everything has its own resonance that seems to be correlated to the frequency of its atomic composition. You would discover that nothing is actually static or solid, and that the universe is built upon eternally fluctuating waves.[3]

Warren J. Hamerman, in the March-April 1989 issue of *21st Century Science and Technology*, wrote that the organic matter of human beings resonates at a frequency that can be represented as sound at about forty-two octaves above middle C. The standard for middle C is 262 Hz; therefore the vibration of a human being reaches 570 trillion Hz. Considering Hz means vibrations per second, that means that we are vibrating at 570 trillion times a second.[4]

On the particle-wave level, we can discover the subtlety of our will and imagination. At the synaptic level of the neuron, there are events occurring that involve vibrational shifts and resemble non-local quantum behavior, which can demonstrate the power that the mind seems to have over matter. What I call the Ripple Effect sum-marizes the changing of the fundamental resonance of a thing at the particle-wave level and how it eventually extends beyond "the thing" into "interconnectedness with all things" in the macrocosm. If you are in a sad mood, some influence has affected the particle-waves you would traditionally refer to as a part of yourself, those that support your personalized sense of being. Through the connectedness of the vibration of all particle-waves, a change in vibration and resonance may have possibly manifested as this emotion. This is not to say that emotions are evidence of microscopic particle-wave shifts or vice versa, only that it is plausible that they are correlated, given the holistic model that is developing from our knowledge of particle-waves and how they behave.

Let's say that you had earlier begun to remember a friend who had passed away. The firing neurons of thoughts, memories and nostalgia may have affected some resonant vibration, which would have a cascade effect on the entirety of your brain assuming that the vibration could pass its influences to other particle-waves. This may include several important glands that excrete hormones important to the regulation of mood. In turn, this could affect the whole dynamic and vibration of the brain—and then what? At this point in time, we can only speculate, but given the research we have on quantum phys-ics and altered states of consciousness, we can hypothesize that after reaching the brain the resonance shift will continue on to affect adjoining particles outside the body. In this example, it's easy to see how a room of happy and jovial individuals can be transformed into a melancholy one with the simple addition of a troubled person. The effect happens irrespective of whether verbal communication occurs or not, unless people have made considerations to guard against being "caught up" emotionally.

The innate tendency for the mind to seek new information is blind to "positive" or "negative." The mind automatically attaches itself to a novel vibration if already out-of-balance. This is why mastery of the mind, as many Eastern traditions have em-phasized, contributes to a stable, peaceful attitude and greater awareness of emotional influences. Instead of getting caught up in an emotion, we can allow it simply to pass through us. We broadcast our will, intent and emotional states to each other every day, though most of us are unaware of this.

It is like throwing a stone, a thought or intent into the vastness of the universe. The universe is the ocean where the stone lands; the stone will create the initial change and will continue to cascade the vibration against other vibrations, as the ripples of this effect continue until they hit other ripples from other events, creating an ocean of pos-sibility. The more stones you cast, that is, the more will and imagination you give to a single-minded intent, the better chance you have at making sure that the stone affects the water. It is also possible that more focused intent, for example from a monk expe-rienced in one-pointed meditation, could produce a "bigger stone," in this analogy. Each mind contributing towards an intent helps make the wave bigger and stronger. With several minds vibrating loving and healing intent, as opposed to one malicious bystander vibrating hate, there is a higher probability that the positive intention will outlast the malicious.

It might be noted that love is inclusive—it is generally an idea that promotes the integration of ideas into itself without absolving their identities, just as all exist as individual humans, but are still composed of the same matter. The universe responds well to loving intent because it wants to maximize efficiency; inclusive perspectives allow for more information to be communicated, synthesized and integrated. Hate is exclusive, it seeks to separate and nullify connections and isolate ideas. It might be speculated, then, that love could have an advantage over hate in that it is aligned with what seems to be an emergent property in this model of a holistic system.

It is easy, then, to speculate why magic is effective—why beautiful water crystals form when "love and gratitude" are projected at water in Emoto's research, and why the placebo effect proves itself to be effective in treating patients in study after study just as well as any medication. "Mind over matter" is a saying with more merit than we give it.

Most have had similar experiences to the aforementioned examples, and would claim that when a distraught person enters the room they can tell, even before body language gives it away, that something about the atmosphere of the room has changed, and not for the better. If the melancholic resonance were affecting particles and creating a ripple effect, it is likely that the intuition of the atmosphere shifting could be attributed to the particles of the intercepting individual being affected, following the same line of reasoning. Some would liken this to the "Butterfly Effect" concept in chaos theory, that a butterfly flapping its wings in Vancouver can inadvertently affect the weather in Moscow. The behaviors of all dynamic systems are dependent upon their initial conditions. We most often look at intuition as happening before the event, as a precursor to it. The phenomenon of intuitive knowledge, that is, knowledge that seems to occur spontaneously in awareness, prompting a cognitive interpretation of itself, might possibly be explained this way as well. However, it is probably more true that intuition, if it could be proved by scientific means, is a result of the initial conditions that let us know that there is potential for an event to occur before our mind and the rest of reality catch up to confirm it. This is likely how intuition allows certain situations to be avoided; the intuition is merely a possibility, and acting in accordance with or against the intuition is what will ultimately determine the outcome. With this approach, intuition could still be considered precognitive, given that it occurs before cognitive thought and interpretation, and before there is tangible representation of the shift as a realization of the possibility. Science has disregarded most theories of intuition, as there have been no methods found effective for collecting consistent data.

We're moving on to the idea that information can travel instantaneously, and that itself deserves some explanation with a foray into quantum physics and, specifically, quantum entanglement.

Understanding the phenomenon of quantum entanglement is something physicists are still having trouble with. When a photon, a force-carrying particle, passes through matter, it is absorbed by an electron. The electron, in attempting to return to its original ground state, will emit the proton. Particular crystal structures increase the probability that the photon will decay into two when emitted. Usually, the photons leave the crystal aligned in either a vertically or horizontally polarized light cone contrasting each other. The resulting photon pair is deemed entangled. In experiments passing photons through a vertical polarizing filter, it was discovered that if the photon passed through the filter, then the second would not, as it would clearly be polarized the exact opposite. Measuring one photon's polarization promptly forces the second photon to adopt the opposite polarization. This effect is immediate, even if the two photons are arbitrarily far apart. By affecting one photon, the other entangled or "linked" photon is affected as well. This experiment has even been tried over the course of several miles, and produced consistent results.

These photons, until measured, are in a state similar to that of Schrödinger's cat, the subject of a very popular theoretical experiment that demonstrates why the physics you just read is important in demonstrating that thoughts and the perspective of the observer probably affect reality.

The experiment involves placing a cat in an enclosed box with a small capsule of hydrocyanic acid and a very minute amount of radioactive material. There is a fifty percent chance the radioactive material will decay during the experiment, and if it does, it will trip a mechanism breaking the capsule of acid, and the cat will die. The observer can never know whether or not the substance has decayed and the vial has broken, and there is equal chance for either verdict. The cat, then, is considered to be in both states—dead and alive. Only when we open the box and learn the condition of the cat is this paradox dissolved.

This situation is referred to as quantum indeterminacy, or the observer's paradox: The observation or measurement itself affects the outcome, so that it can never be known what the outcome would have been if it were not observed. The cat is in what is called a "superposition," which is both positions and neither position at the same time. The observer and the measurement are ultimately what shape the reality from the paradoxical possibility. Many skeptics argue against the possibility that magic works, seeking an explanation for incongruence in results. Perhaps outside observers can randomize the process by diluting the intent of the magical working with other perspectives and influences. This would explain why many occult practitioners keep their magical intent out of their general awareness. They feel that avoiding the opportunity to doubt may lead to a higher probability of a desirable outcome occurring. With things kept quiet, there is less chance for interference.

Entanglement and Schrödinger's Cat are examples of the observer determining what will be or is being observed. It might be more appropriate to call the observer the creator at this point. In placing these examples up against claims of ESP, telepathy, telekinesis and magic, somehow such phenomena don't seem as far-fetched as skeptics would like to claim. Whether or not it is ever proved that there is a link between magical notions and quantum quandaries, these discoveries have already inspired the development of new interpretive models.

I recently read an article that discounted much of the current literature that supposes we are creating our reality. Most of it consisted of claims that this notion is pseudoscience and only adopted by mystics seeking to confirm their own detached, disillusioned perspective. The article was well written, but despite the elegant language there was only one real point of argument amidst a heap of personal opinion—that none of this has been proved, and that it is merely speculation. The author is right. What he forgot to add is that it has not been a major focus of scientific study; therefore the possibility of having it proved true or false *hasn't even occurred yet.*

Science and magic are both essentially trying to figure out this complicated thing called "existence," piece by piece. One is doing it by dissecting it; the other is doing it by experiencing it.

Your Bag of Tricks

So you want to make magic. You want to make things happen; you want to make things change. You want to experience it.

Many of us who have come this far were the type of children who would pry open the back of a pocket watch to uncoil the springs and loosen the cogs in an intuitive attempt at understanding the intricacy of the device. Now that we pretend we're grown up, we have a much bigger toy and mystery—our reality and ourselves. And unlike with pocket watches, no one can tell us to Put That Damned Thing Down and Stop Screwing With It.

When you actually "get" the roots of ritual magic, it *can be* simple, and it *can be* harmless—but don't go assuming what it is and isn't until you try it for yourself. Keeping that in mind, this primer should give you a loose framework to begin your adventures with. Much of it is intended to be vague and left open for interpretation. It is malleable; work with what you need.

Certain ideas that recur from tradition to tradition, both in and out of spiritual practice, have been included here along with reasonably neutral terms to illustrate the ideas. Think of this as a kind of theory of universally innate ritual grammar, like Noam Chomsky's universal grammar theory.

If any of the terms fail to make sense to you, keep on reading. They will be explained, if not through what is written, then through your own experiences and continued research on this topic. Most of what you need will be explained as we discuss the ritual composite in detail.

We use ritual because it works. Objective scrutiny is one of the finer strategies for strengthening the framework of a self-designed ritual, though in excess it can be a pitfall, like any perspective taken to fanaticism. If you seek a fundamentally scientific verdict, you're going to be waiting for quite a while. We don't know why it works. Yet we align ourselves with everything, we reveal ourselves as everything; we change ourselves, and thus we change everything.

The purpose of ritual magic is to represent the associative pathways of the magician's Will as symbols that can be used to channel that Will into a receptive vessel for recombination with the universe. For the sake of argument, you can assume that the "magician" I will keep mentioning is one who means to use these techniques to further their aims. It's a fairly androgynous term, and it exists as a constant reminder that we're not just talking about you in the normal, familiar context; we're talking about you in the larger picture of your existence, and your desire to exact changes upon macrocosmic reality by means of microcosmic experimentation. We're talking about magic. Using terms that are specific to magic helps to remind us of this immediateness.

A seasoned magician understands the usefulness of this—as your practice becomes integrated into your everyday actions, terms can maintain definition to bring you back to the awareness of the macrocosm. Magic is like painting a picture in your unconscious. First, you draw the basic outlines, and then paint in objects and ideas that resemble what you want to convey and contribute to the overall work. An artist might paint a grassy knoll, a large red building and a cow. Almost immediately one could conclude upon viewing this picture that the artist meant to convey a country farm. The collection of symbols represents an overall idea. With ritual, an image is built into a prepared, receptive unconscious. Using corresponding colors, elements, objects and ideas to put together a vision of your goal is what ritual is essentially amassed of. Its purpose is to paint the "end result," while simultaneously comprising the means of getting there.

Magic begins with creation, emerges from the unconscious as intent and progresses to action and manifestation shortly thereafter.

It is probably not exactly formed from or within the unconscious, rather, it seems an inherently present force, having been described through the ages as "prana," "energy" or the "life" in all things; waiting as potential to be remembered, unveiled, harnessed. It's also useful to note that "conscious" and "unconscious" are only words. Meditation can reunify these concepts. Young children are often adept at magic because they have not been programmed into a state of awareness where the two are separate.

Without devaluing the importance of self-discipline, it can be noted that mental preparation for spiritual practice is not entirely prerequisite to achieving results. The relative nature of experience must always be considered. Who's to say that my spiritual experience from twenty-two minutes of intense pranayama is less powerful and moving than your five years of dedicated meditative work? It is relative to the person upon whom the experience is exacted. Many magicians fail to realize that conditioning is relative to the mind it is conditioning, and most who spend considerable time on a path forget to pay attention to the path itself rather than the places and goals they are trying to reach. As many have said before: "It's not the place you are going that matters, it's how you get there." Magicians forget that variation and deviation from repetitive measures are what provide consciousness with new avenues to explore. Experimentation is a positive and productive means for encouraging the mind and spirit to develop strong attributes of adaptability. If you always take the same route walking somewhere, how will you learn about the rest of your surroundings; the part of you that extends beyond your routine? How will you learn about the things you have not yet seen? Magicians know that it is foolish to assume that the limits of our universe are within our personal horizon of experience; in fact, many agree that it's foolish to postulate that there are limits at all, and will agree that their reasons for pursuing a spiritual path are really to discover those hidden places around and inside us all.

Now let's look into the other side of the mirror.

There have been so many articles written on the Lesser Banishing Ritual of the Pentagram that I am hesitant to bring it up. Yet, given the amount of collective interest invested in this topic, it has become quite the memetic powerhouse and thus a potent tool that should be researched and used.

The Pentagram Ritual serves to create a clean, clear, yet humble stronghold on the astral plane. An essay by Tim Maroney from 1984 describes "The experience of a proper LBR [as] pleasurable and soothing, yet energizing and empowering. One is made at home in the mystical realm, protected from lurkers and phantasms by strongly imagined wards. This solace from mundane experience is a precondition for more serious works of meditation or ritual, but it can also form a healthy part of the life of the mind by itself."[5]

Self-discipline and mental exercise are also valuable tools; everyone should give meditation a shot and stick to it for an extended period of time to reap the benefits that this kind of experience will bring. Self-disciplined meditation is a wonderful tool and experiment that cannot be experienced through any means other than via its own practice.

Either method of facilitating growth—the disciplined or the spontaneous, or both—is productive and beneficial if the intent of the aspirant is pure. If you have the Will, and you have the goal in sight, then the only thing that matters is how you choose to get there. Use what works best for you!

James Curcio compares the necessity of contemplating ritual theory to that of the actual practice, accusing the way we tend to isolate mind from body, in an archaic, Aristotelean fashion, of getting in the way.

They tricked you. They tricked us all right and proper. You can't have one without the other—how can you begin to establish mastery over a whole system when you fail to acknowledge the synthesis and unity of all of its parts; the obvious correlations and relationships that compose the entirety?

Agreeing with Curcio, I challenge you to find a seamless, perfected system or action that defies the unity of theory and practice. The importance of this unity is evident in the case of trained athletes and accomplished musicians. As he says: "In many ways, experts are less aware of the discrete actions they are taking to perform a task than a beginner. This holism may in fact be a neurological prerequisite. Experts aren't necessarily smarter than you are; they simply have to think less to perform actions that seem intricate and complex to you."

To clarify, this doesn't necessarily mean the task becomes robotic and mindless. I would argue that there is a sense of "mindlessness" that does evolve with mastery—but don't allow your mental lexicon to attribute a negative connotation too quickly. "Mindlessness," in this context, implies mastery over the mind; a sort of "cognitive silencing." The mastered act becomes no more "mindless" than a monk meditating becomes mindless. The awareness is still preserved, even accentuated, without the clutter of mental banter interfering with what would otherwise be a Zen process.

It is generally argued that the actual application and process are more imperative to success than the mental preparation, study and contemplation. I am inclined to disagree, at least partially. Studies have shown that mental recitation and repetition compare significantly to actual practice. An article published in the *Journal of General Psychology* in 1995 cites compelling results from a study on mental practice and musical performance. The study demonstrated that swapping between physical practice and mental rehearsal, or modeled mental rehearsal, can produce musical performances that are synonymous with, and in many cases significantly better than, those weaned on solely continuous physical practice. Participants also had a positive response to the technique, and said that they planned on using mental rehearsal in future practice.[6]

With this in mind, it's easy to see how intellectual theory and abstraction are only worthwhile when applied to the simplest learned tasks. If there is too much thinking involved, our mental clarity, preparation and self are lost to an almost infinite regress of the ego. Our analysis of the situation is not what the situation actually is, it is merely a representation crafted by our own comparative system of analogy, to be stored away and referenced later when useful, usually to compare with another experience that we are ignoring in favor of our mental babble. Repeat *ad nauseum* throughout the whole of daily life.

Our brains are processing all the time. They are compelled to repeat this. Sometimes, they get in the way when we want to do something different. They tend to argue; because being spiritual or magical or whatever you want to call it doesn't fit in with the protocol they have been using to respond to stimulus. Most of us have an experience of Western culture and tradition that places a greater value on knowledge versus intuition and rarely fosters the development of creativity, awareness and plasticity.

Experiencing altered states of consciousness during a ritual is a good sign that you are doing something right. By "right," I mean that you have immersed yourself in a state markedly different from your everyday life in some fashion that allows you to attribute it to magic and associated work. An altered state of consciousness is any state of awareness that you can identify as otherwise different from your normal waking consciousness. When performing a ritual, it is natural that these states develop not only by means of functionality, but symbolic of your intent and the changes you are trying to affect in reality, as well.

Altered states usually function as vessels for productivity not clouded with the normal beta waves that anxiously fight to dominate consciousness. Deep meditation, or triggers such as certain gestures previously linked to the desired state can, through practice, prod the mind into gamma waves.

The University of California at Berkeley and the University of Queensland, Australia have discovered that long-term meditation practice shows significant benefits for focus, at least on visual targets. Monks were able to block out all external stimuli and focus on an image for as long as twelve minutes, steadily and unwaveringly.[7] This one-pointed state of mind coupled with the latest brain imaging technology may give science a snapshot of how the brain focuses. In the future, pharmaceuticals or technological devices could aid the body in shortcuts to meditative states. In the meantime, consider the benefits of a mind focused solely on your desire or goal.

Researchers have only recently begun to acknowledge the psychological and biological significance of meditation and altered states. "Over the past few years, researchers at the University of Wisconsin working with Tibetan monks have been able to translate those mental experiences into the scientific language of high-frequency gamma waves and brain synchrony, or coordination. They have pinpointed the left prefrontal cortex, an area just behind the left forehead, as the place where brain activity associated with meditation is especially intense," according to the *Washington Post*. "The intense gamma waves found in the monks have also been associated with knitting together disparate brain circuits, and so are connected to higher mental activity and heightened awareness, as well."[8]

On top of the heightened awareness allowing you to perceive the subtlety of your interactions with the universe, your brain also receives a supercharge, allowing its neuroplasticity to adapt to the circumstances of ritual—and, later, to return to that state with more ease and concentration. This demonstrates the usefulness of a disciplined spiritual practice, and also the obvious effects of ritual on reality—even on the physical, carbon-based matter that composes your physical being. The altered state of consciousness is preparatory and functional all at once. It is like a car that helps get you to your destination. The ritual is the road; the symbol system is the map. You are the driver, responsible for filling your car with fuel so that you can get where you need to go. The fuel is the fusion reaction of ecstasis[9] and Will that propels the car.

In addition, traditional tools (athames, wands, pentacles, etc.) can be a useful consideration for a few reasons. For one, they are potent physical symbols used for carrying out the Will. Not only is their symbolism imprinted within your mind, but in the hive mind of humanity as well. It is difficult to say where the symbols originated, though the Golden Dawn claims fame for saying that they evolved, through group experience, most of the attributes and associations that were later adopted by many others, such as Aleister Crowley. These tools have enormous reserves of invested belief from ages of consistent acknowledgment and use. Over time these symbols have spread throughout several lineages, establishing a sort of "occult trademark," if you will.

If you asked a stranger on the street what they thought an individual practicing magic would make use of, they would probably suggest a wand or dagger, thanks to the perpetuation of these memes in today's cultural melting pot. It's like any major corporate logo. If someone asks you for something to blow their nose, they will likely ask you for Kleenex, and not facial tissue, as an automatic response just as the stranger in the street is answering automatically. These responses occur without conscious effort, it seems. Considering this, it is easy to see how tapping the unconscious associations of hundreds of thousands of people would be a delightful, useful tactic in any magical effort. Tools can also look really damned cool, which contributes to setting up atmosphere for the ritual—as we know, our environment is very much an extension of ourselves, as are our tools.

The Golden Dawn and most traditions of witchcraft have placed great importance on the creation, consecration, care and sacred nature of these tools. This psychological programming is another simple trigger that can assist in the activation of altered states and reinforce a sense of magical "attitude." Not attitude in the rebellious, adolescent context, but as in a state of mind that serves as a vessel for your Will, safeguarding the intent from perilous doubt. A tangible resource that can serve to strengthen your Will is a magical tool.

There are countless expositions available on the varied and elaborate associations of traditional tools. Generally, they are attributed to the four elements of fire, air, water and earth. From this classic example, it is easy to see how a more complex system of representation can evolve by creating a chain. In *Liber 777*, Aleister Crowley listed Opium and Cedar as correspondent with the Wand. If you were performing a particularly fire-influenced, aggressive rite then you could consider using cedar incenses or perfumes, and quite possibly some opium, either figuratively or literally to provide more symbolic pathways for your consciousness to climb. Think of a dense forest with a treasure at the center. Each time you use another symbol associated with your goal, you forge a path. The more paths you create in the forest, the more likely it is that you will be able to find your goal. Next time you come back to that forest, you will be able to see those paths you made, and reaching the goal will be easier each time you walk them. The treasure is the fulfillment of your intent, the paths your symbols and your unconscious the big piece of paper on which you are sketching this elaborate map. Make a good map, and it will serve you well.

Before designing a ritual or working one upon spontaneous inclination, one should have some idea of what one wishes to obtain or accomplish. For the sake of this primer, we will assume that the ritual to be performed has some basis of direction as opposed to an entirely free-form act. A statement of intent written down beforehand or kept at the forefront of consciousness during your preliminary preparations is very useful. Plenty of creative mages will engage in work without structure and without deciding what it is they want, leaving themselves open to be directed by the cosmos.

Let us proceed, however, with our assumption that the magician wishes to use form in their ritual and that they have a statement of intent prepared.

Phil Hine has stated "The aim of design is to move the boundary of Achievable Reality forwards. To design effectively requires a vision, or end-state." By redefining the limits of "possibility," you can accomplish nearly anything.

A Basic Outline: Timeless Formula Developed in Universal Consciousness

There are several elements to the basic magical equation. They may proceed in any order, and you do not necessarily have to include all of them—some include none of them at all, and still manage to get the job done. Yet these are the bare bones; the skeletal system of many types of ritual or magic consistent throughout occult systems, religions and belief structures all over the world and throughout recorded history. If any of the following portions compel you to generate a more efficient means of accomplishing the task, by all means go ahead and adapt.

1. The Introduction

The introduction is the portion of the working that prepares you for inputting the symbols and actions that will work upon the unconscious to manifest your Will.

The goal here is to prepare the mind, body and subtle levels to receive symbolized desire into the unconscious, sometimes referred to as the "aether" or "void." This can involve calming the mind, grounding the self and ego, and centering focus. Sometimes, it also involves the statement of intent for the working or ritual, and often includes banishing or rites involving protection, such as "calling the quarters" or "invoking the elementals." A small prayer, if not to a deity then for reverence of the working and intent, is usually useful and consecrating enough to get the ball rolling.

The introduction can contain any or all of, but is not limited to, the following: call of the watchtowers, meditation, banishing, casting of circle/square/triangle/multi-faceted polyhedron, consecration, prayer, etc.

2. The Raising of Energies

This is the point where magicians begin to knead their Will into the shape that it will be baked into the void as. This step is goal-oriented at raising energy and calling upon internal power to centralize and focus around the desire of the magician. Ideally, one invests as much vigor and projected force as possible. This step often includes some or all, and is definitely not limited to: invocation, evocation, astral projection, sex, drugs, dancing, singing, chanting/mantras and the induction of trance states.

The magician uses whatever symbols and ideas connect him to his task, using what is necessary to connect himself with his desire prior to subjecting it to the realms of the unconscious. Like the analogy of the treasure in the forest, raising energies charges not only the intent but also the paths leading to it as well as providing a well-rounded attack on desire. The Will of the magician is magnified through the complex web of symbols connected to the intent. This step connects the planes of conscious mind with not-so-conscious mind and reunites the two from their previous division, magnifying the intent as far as the will can stretch. The purpose is to affect changes within the personal microcosm, in the belief that these changes will be, in some capacity, reflected in reality-at-large—commonly referred to as the "macrocosm." Some prefer to keep this step minimal, through the use of brief mantras, sigils or merely projecting their raw will. Others find their workings more effective when an elaborate measure of symbols and ideas are combined with methods of energetic induction, as in the invocation of god-forms or ritualized dancing.

The effectiveness of drumming and dancing, in particular, is interesting. Ritualized drumming has been documented as able to induce EEG waves of the same frequency as that of the drumbeat. Rhythmic dancing is correlated to shifts in body fluids, especially blood, and breathing tends to synchronize with body movements; this combination stimulates what are called baroreceptors. Baroreceptor stimulation results in slowing of the heart rate, reduced arousal and excitability, and increased theta wave activity in the brain, to name a few effects, all of which are notably characteristic of the altered consciousness normally attributed to "shamanic trance states." Both of these examples suggest that rhythm and movement have more prominent physiological implications than we have currently investigated; furthermore, it is quite clear that invoking trance states with these methods is effective enough to manifest results in the physical domain.

3. Ecstasis and Release

Ecstasis, by loose definition, is a lapse in the conscious, rational and discriminatory mind that allows the unconscious or "magical mind" space to function. As this occurs, a form of sadomasochistic bond develops between the two in a very balanced sense of unity and symbiosis. The point where all your efforts and mental crunching come to fruition, ecstasis is the moment where your ritual or rite merges from build-up into climax. Think of it as the orgasm of the whole experience. Of course, orgasm itself has been used extensively by magicians to produce ecstasy, as the orgasmic state of "mindlessness" leaves the unconscious ripe for the plundering.

Whether it is by the use of a few mantras, the angular wave of a symbolic device or wand, or the primal scream of the vessel of the invoked deity, the ecstatic state is reached by pulling a trigger. I have used the final beep of a microwave cycle and destroying an old car with a baseball bat, both on separate occasions, to provoke the ecstatic moment. The creativity of this point is intuitive, pronounced and rich with as much effort as you can feasibly imagine. Let it all in, up and out. Magic words, specific ideas or just the will to enter ecstatic consciousness are all triggers; they are enough to tap into and release your energies into your desire and send your goal off to manifest. As stated, elaboration or simplicity is a personal preference of the magician. This is the climax; this is the moment of truth. Release occurs as the state of ecstasy declines and the Will of the participant(s) surges forward into the unknown depths. This is the make-or-break moment—the more will and force and the less doubt and deviation from your will you produce, the stronger the effects will be overall.

The ecstatic moment and the conjunctive, complimentary release that follows may consist of and include: orgasm, symbolic acting of the desire into manifestation, screaming, bloodletting, collapsing from vigorous dancing, sneezing, emotional out-bursts of extreme expression, magic words or mantras, or a sudden and unprecedented breach into higher reality.

4. The Final Touch

This is the dénouement of the magical act. Most people crave some degree of absolution or completion to validate their actions as final and concrete. Like any state of comfort, this is purely illusion; however, comfort level after a ritual affects personal confidence and determination. If not comfortable, an individual might develop doubt and adversely affect the intended results. Many magicians sum up their working with a few words or ideas to return balance to themselves and their surroundings before continuing on with their comparatively mundane existences. Restoring the balance in the environment and oneself can be appropriate if the rite was particularly taxing on your body and mind, or if you have been working with entities and feel that the influence you contracted from them needs to be put away in order to feel comfortable. Wiccans are compelled to close the circle religiously, ceremonial magicians follow up with a Pentagram Ritual and chaos magicians usu-ally laugh at themselves and their actions.

Aleister Crowley is noted for suggesting that a projection is more likely to manifest when lust of result is avoided. Austin Osman Spare likewise recommended obfuscat-ing one's desires altogether in the vacuity of the mind. It might be worthwhile to write down your ritual and make notes on it, keeping it hidden out of view during times when it is not being written in. Out of sight, out of mind. This way you can compare your results, if any, to your initial anticipation, theories, ideas and feelings about the ritual. Perhaps recording as much as possible before the ritual would be beneficial, so that after the acts in question, one would be able to relax and settle the mind on its new journey towards whatever the heck it was you just forgot. Ritual? What?

It's Time to Reprogram

There can never be enough encouragement for the mind to explore itself and, through itself, the world. Unfortunately, at a young age, along with separating our awareness into varying states of self-awareness or "consciousness," we often give up on the notion that the world is malleable; instead we crumble to the pilgrimage of preordained destiny and of forces of nature beyond our control. We are taught that in order to survive, we must obey.

Yet in order to succeed in magic, there is only one Way: To realize your Way, and then live it.

ENDNOTES

[1] The closer one looks at history, the more that science and magic become completely indistinguishable. – Ed.

[2] Kaftos, Menas and Robert Nadeau. *The Non-Local Universe: The New Physics and Matters of the Mind.* New York: Oxford, 1999.

[3] Emoto, Masaru. *The Hidden Messages in Water.* Hillsboro: Beyond Words, 2004.

[4] Hamerman, W. J. "The Musicality of Living Processes." *21ˢᵗ Century Science & Technology.* Vol. 2, No. 32. 1989.

[5] Maroney, Tim. "On the Lesser Banishing Ritual of the Pentagram." 1984.

[6] Theiler, Anne M. and Louis G. Lippman. "Effects of Mental Practice and Modeling on Guitar and Vocal Performance." *Journal of General Psychology.* Vol. 122, No. 4. October 1, 1995. Also see Driskell, James E., Carolyn Copper, and Aiden Moran. "Does Mental Practice Enhance Performance?" *Journal of Applied Psychology.* Vol. 79, No. 4. August 1, 1994.

[7] "Meditation 'Brain Training' Clues." BBC News, June 13, 2005.

[8] Kaufman, Marc. "Meditation Gives Brain a Charge, Study Finds." *Washington Post,* January 3, 2005.

[9] Any altered state of consciousness suitable for activating unconscious latencies, or what Colin Wilson called "Faculty X," that is, whatever it is within human consciousness that can cause changes within reality "as if by magic." The Greek suggests "stepping aside," in this case from the mundane state. – Ed.

[10] King, Francis and Stephen Skinner. *Techniques of High Magic: A Guide to Self-Empowerment.* Vermont: Destiny Books, 1991.

[11] Crowley, Aleister. *777 and Other Qabalistic Writings of Aleister Crowley.* Boston: Weiser, 1977.

[12] Hine, Phil. *Prime Chaos.* Tempe: New Falcon Publications, 1999.

[13] Vaitl, Dieter, et al. "Psychobiology of Altered States of Consciousness." *Psychological Bulletin*, Vol. 131, No. 1. January 2005.

BENEATH THE PAVEMENT, THE BEAST

Stephen Grasso

Magic is not located in textbooks available on the high street, it does not exist within codified and rehearsed ritual and you can't buy it on your credit card. Magic is a ferocious and mysterious beast, and its secrets and powers must be earned through blood, sweat and tears. It is something that you live, not something that you read about and study. Magic is everywhere and within everything, and the work of a magician is to perceive it and to interact with it. There is magic in the sea at night, in a flight of ravens, in the motion of traffic, in dark alleys, filthy sewers and bright shop doorways. There is magic in abandoned subway stations, riverbanks and public parks. The world is alive with magic. Are you brave enough to step outside and into it?

The term *dérive*, or "drift," was first coined by the Situationist International, who would go for long aimless walks around their towns and cities, reimagining the concrete tower blocks, cenotaphs and public fountains as castles of wisdom, wishing spikes and ponds of eternal youth. The purpose of the drift was to see beauty in the urban landscape and to conquer the tyranny of grim, oppressive town planning through the transformative power of the imagination. Through the technique of the drift, the Situationists could radically change their experience of the city and turn drab stretches of urban decay into a magical landscape of limitless wonder and enchantment. Yet they perhaps stopped short of taking the exercise to its logical conclusion.

Once you have peeled back the dreary concrete mask of the world and uncovered a magical kingdom crawling with spirits, the next stage is to see what you can do within that world, to work out how to speak to those spirits and find out what they might be able to do for you. The technique of the drift does not merely reveal magic, but is a process of engaging with it. It has many different applications and can be used in a variety of contexts. It can be used as a direct method of communication with the spirit or *genus loci* of a particular location or geographical area, or indeed as a means of dialogue with any entity you are working with. It can be used as a method of collecting potent ingredients and materials for sorcery workings, or to seek answers to divinatory questions. The practical applications of the drift are numerous, and the imaginative magician will undoubtedly unlock many more. It can be performed in virtually any location and at a moment's notice; hence it is ideally suited for those situations when you are caught unprepared and need to work some powerful magic on the fly.

The mechanics of the drift are simple. You are attempting to walk between worlds and bring something useful back with you. It is essentially a shamanic journey that takes place physically in real time, as opposed to an internal journey such as the drum-led trances of indigenous tribes like the Jivaro. The drift forces you out of your comfortable centrally heated temple space and puts you on the spot like few other occult practices. It gets your magic out into the world, in a very real and very physical sense.

A drift can begin in several different ways, depending on the situation and the intent. Sometimes drifts can be spontaneous. If you have sufficiently internalized the practice, it's not uncommon to find yourself kicked into a full-on shamanic drift at virtually any moment. Going out to buy a pint of milk, walking home from the pub or visiting the shops can often be transformed into heavy magic without a minute's notice. The spontaneous drift can sharpen up your sensitivity and adaptability to a very high degree, but to get the best from it, you need to be able to receive and filter "information" in an effective manner. The drift is a high-risk occult practice as far as your sanity goes, as it encourages a scary level of openness to spirit communication. Before you know it, you're the mad guy speaking with invisible beings on the high street and going through the bins looking for occult secrets. That kind of thing is pretty much par for the course with this sort of work, so to begin with, it's useful to learn a method of switching it on and off.

It's important to remember that what you are doing is attempting to "walk between worlds"—with an emphasis on the word "between." It's relatively easy to go off into the deep end with this practice and become a paranoid lunatic remarkably quickly, but that's not the point of the exercise. It's your skill as a magician that allows you to safely navigate the wilder areas of consciousness and bring back something useful. To become accomplished at the drift, you have to develop sufficient skill at mediating between your normal day-to-day existence and the hyper-real shamanic experience.

In order to begin the drift, you should look for an appropriate starting place—a physical access point that will allow you to enter into shamanic reality and return again when your business is done. The most immediate and accessible crossover point into shamanic reality is, of course, the crossroads. Every inhabited location will have a crossroads of one form or another within walking distance, and the crossroads is the supreme symbol of intercession between the worlds. However, any work involving the crossroads falls firmly within the territory of the various Gods, Goddesses, Saints, Spirits and Mysteries associated with it. You need to ask their permission before you can go through the gate. This is easier to accomplish if you already have a working relationship with one or more of these entities. The general modus operandi would be to make appropriate offerings to them at their spot and ask if they will open the doorway for you, allowing you to go through and accomplish the intent of your drift. You should seek their blessing for your journey and ask them to ensure your safe return.

The mysteries of the crossroads are essential to the operation of this work. Although it's possible to begin a shamanic drift in a more freeform style, utilizing a physical crossover point such as a gateway, railway arch, narrow alleyway or similar symbolic route, these structures still fall under the domain of the crossroads at an esoteric level. Therefore if the entire operation is performed under the specific auspices of a crossroads entity, with both their permission and their involvement, you are likely to get far more effective results. Once offerings have been made and permission has been granted, you can begin the drift. Depart from your access point, either walking through the gateway/arch or leaving the crossroads in a different direction to which you arrived. You are now entering shamanic reality.

In the early stages of the drift you should begin tuning into your environment. Pay close attention to what's going on around you and try to read the language of the city, or wherever you may be. Look out for any strange graffiti, headlines on discarded newspaper, unusual words or phrases that leap out at you from otherwise innocuous sources, and so on. Pay attention to snatches of overheard conversation, the lyrics of songs echoing from car radios, or announcements from train stations and the like. You are looking for a sign or signal that can be readily interpreted in relation to your intent. Don't try to force it or just make something up to fit. Relax into the drift and wait for something to come through of its own accord. The process of the drift is a two-way dialogue with the spirits. You might have to be patient, but you will know when you're on the right track.

The first piece of information that comes through will either answer your question right off the bat, or else it will lead you on to the next stage in your journey. Sometimes drifts can be resolved very quickly—for example, within minutes of leaving the access point, you see a random piece of street art that answers your question in no uncertain terms. If this happens, then simply return to the crossroads, thank the spirits and ask them to close the door for you. Sometimes it's that simple. Frequently, however, the first signal that you receive will point you somewhere else, or only give you part of the story, leading you further down the road to look for more clues.

You should eventually start to get a sense that you are following a symbolic thread through the city. Each sign you receive brings you a little further towards your eventual destination and the realization of your intent. Sometimes you might lose the plot completely and find yourself clueless as to where you ought to go. If this happens, just relax and tune back in. Try to pick up the thread again and get back on the right track. Occasionally the spirits might throw you a curveball. For example, you might pick up a fragment of map that strongly suggests you need to get on a bus to the other side of town in order to complete the quest. Or you could find yourself going on an elaborate and exhausting journey across the city, only to find what you were looking for outside your own front door. Anything can happen on a drift. You're stepping into a zone of increased potential and should be prepared for any eventual outcome.

One of the biggest obstacles to successful drifting is your own self-consciousness. The message of the drift might clearly dictate that you do something a part of you balks at. You might be required to steal something conspicuous from a public place, or behave in a highly unusual manner at an extremely inappropriate location. Often all that can be done in these circumstances is to go beyond whatever ingrained social conditioning your actions have disturbed and take a leap of faith in the name of magic. It's actually surprising what you can get away with in public without anyone batting an eyelid, particularly in a major city.

The drift can sometimes be hard work, and if you don't come up against the occasional "what the fuck am I doing" moment, then you're not fully engaging with the process. A useful psychological trick for getting beyond any embarrassment or self-consciousness is to put aside the intent of the drift for a moment and just consider the whole thing as an abstract exercise in deconditioning.

If you find yourself hesitating over some fairly inoffensive but extremely peculiar action, for example picking up an old shoe in broad daylight and swapping it with your own, or acquiring an oddly resonant object from the center of a busy roundabout, then you've inadvertently uncovered something very interesting about yourself. You've discovered one of the walls of your personality—something that sets limits on what you personally consider to be acceptable public behavior. What is it doing there? What purpose is it serving? Look closely at the range of emotional responses you've tapped into and see what you can discover about yourself. The process of trying to move beyond one of these tiny barriers in order to acquire a power object could well be considered a powerful shamanic act in its own right.

One of the most difficult and complex aspects of this work is knowing how to strike the right balance between moving with the flow of events and tailoring what happens towards your ultimate goal. It's just as easy to be distracted by tangential phenomena, and forget why you were drifting in the first place, as it is to be so completely focused on your intent that important material is overlooked. Getting the right balance only really comes from experience and practice—so don't be too hard on yourself to begin with. Go where the drift takes you, but always keep in mind your reasons for embarking on the journey. If you feel yourself straying too far from the path, don't be afraid to gently guide yourself back on course. If any odd or tangential material comes through that seems unconnected to your goal, just make a note of it for further investigation at a later date—another separate drift may be required to uncover its mysteries.

To put some of this into context, here are a few practical examples of situations in which the drift can be utilized. The method is ideally suited to divinatory workings, particularly if you need to get a quick answer to an important question but don't have access to paraphernalia such as tarot cards or rune stones. A short divinatory drift can be employed during a lunch break, on the journey home from work, or in any situation where you need to gather information at short notice via non-ordinary means. It requires little in the way of planning or preparation. Simply visit the crossroads, make your offerings, ask the question and see what comes through.

A related information-gathering drift practice is the underworld divination, which can be employed in any city that has an underground tube or metro system. Begin the drift near the subway entrance and literally envision your descent onto the tube system as a shamanic journey to the underworld for hidden knowledge. You are descending to an alien landscape of white-tiled walls, harsh fluorescent lights and metal worms that burrow through the earth carrying semiconscious human cargo. Ride the tube lines until you get the answer you're looking for. Converse with its denizens, read its walls, listen to its voices and try to understand its language. You might want to leave a coin with an underground busker or beggar as payment for any information you receive.

A drift can also be utilized if you need to work some spontaneous sorcery and don't have access to whatever tools or temple space you might normally employ. You would begin the drift in the usual manner and ask to be guided towards ingredients for a gris-gris bag or similar fetish item, which at a push could be constructed from a sheet of paper or small carrier bag tied up with an elastic band or piece of string. You walk the streets until you find a specific number of items for the bag, all of which should at some level correlate to your intent. The ingredients could be anything from curious plants growing between paving stones, to sigils derived from graffiti seen on walls, to just about anything that feels right or manifests itself to you in an odd way. The more often you work with the drift, the better you tend to become at recognizing and acquiring what you need.

After a while you may even find yourself developing a "language" of ingredients to use in work of this nature. As always, resist the temptation to just arbitrarily make up a list of aesthetically pleasing correspondences. Hoodoo ingredients should be revealed to you through the living shamanic process of working the drift. If you want to cobble together a symbol system one afternoon over a cup of tea and some biscuits, then that's fine, but you're only shortchanging yourself and not fully engaging with what you might call shamanic reality. Hoodoo correspondences can't be invented after the fact. They must be revealed to you directly by the spirits, during the drift and in the heat of the moment. That's what invests them with power and meaning. If you skip that section and just casually decide that, say, cigarette ends represent the shell of a human soul, then you're distilling all the magic out of the process. Magic takes place in the wild and unpredictable territories outside of the individual ego, and you can't get anywhere near those areas unless you relax the controls and let the material emerge of its own accord.

Once you've drifted for the ingredients to go in your makeshift sorcery bag, you might then look for an appropriate power spot to construct and charge it. If you're not yet familiar with the psychogeography of an area, let the drift itself guide you to an appropriate place. You could make offerings to the spirits associated with that specific area, or to whatever Gods or Goddesses you may regularly work with, and ask them if they will empower the bag for you. This could involve leaving it concealed at a particular spot, and returning after a set period of time to pick it up. Or it could mean walking counterclockwise around a statue or building seven or nine times with the bag in your hand, or any number of possible formulae. Speak to the spirits, listen to what they have to say, and don't make any deals that you're unwilling to follow through on.

If you plan on working regularly with the drift method, you should gradually start to get a feel for the occult landscape of the city where you live. Try to find out as much as you can about the local history, look at old maps of the area, spend lots of time drifting and get to know the landscape, the environment and its ecosystems inside out. There might be an old crossroads, standing stone, ancient patch of woodland, beautiful river, creepy hospital, wishing well, haunted castle or potent nightclub in your town. Pay attention to what happens in these places. Visit them often, speak to the spirits that dwell there and seek to make allies of them.

Accept responsibility for the patch where you live and operate. Step into the role of local magician in your area. Make friends with the powers that are already there and try to broker mutually beneficial relationships with them. Listen to what they want from you and always keep your end of the bargain. There is always sacrifice, and you get nothing for nothing. If you prove you are willing to address the concerns of your town, it will be more likely to cooperate with you. Discover what arrangements the ghosts and spirits of your city are prepared to make with you and what gifts they may be willing to bestow.

There is no rulebook or step-by-step guide to how this kind of work will play out, as it is all about personal relationships and direct interaction. All that can be given are hints and pointers based on experience. This guide has been written primarily from the perspective of the urban magician, but its principles can just as easily be applied to a rural setting or to whatever environment you find yourself living in. If you live outside of the city, you may find that information emerges via phenomena such as the flight of birds, arrangement of twigs on the earth, cloud formations, shapes made by driftwood on the beach or any number of environmental factors. Try experimenting in different settings and locations to see what comes through.

You could speculate that the series of peculiar omens, superstitions and old wives' tales that have been handed down to us by successive generations are the remnants of codified information derived via methods such as the drift. So by engaging with this process yourself, you are building a direct relationship with both the land you live on, and the environment in which you operate as a magician. You're developing a living shamanism that has nothing to do with the various re-constructionist neo-pagan traditions that flood the occult scene, but grows out of the same methods that shamans have always worked with. Going out into the wilderness, speaking with spirits, and returning with knowledge and power.

THE SCARLET GASH /
LIBER ANON

ELIJAH

The Scarlet Gash

The following excursion of magical curriculum can be of relevance to the advanced initiate for the tracings of the process and evolution of idea, and the transmutation into an ideo-sphere of enhancement.

The general degradation of quality present in any organization is an ever-increasing recourse due to entropic forces—this is the main impetus of natural evolution in which the organism itself is forced to face its own weaknesses and respond accordingly. Any form of imposed hierarchy in this age of Aeonic Syzygy is to be viewed with suspicion, and only those who are truly free can hope to make use of the given structures while present. The Scarlet Gash represents a shifting face of the magical Wyrd, towards the pursuit of a personal evolution in the light of truth.

Nothing is True; Everything is Permitted.

This is a program of study for an individual seeking initiation into the Scarlet Gash. The program itself represents a collective desire to enhance the degree of magical practice present in all aspirants, as well as maintain a certain degree of quality in *the magical current itself*. Every person is different and so is each's way, and so the program designed is adaptable and suitable to the individual. Every study, of course, is subject to alteration and personal tastes. The following is the general procedure for those seeking initiation:

1. The aspirant should already have come to some degree of magical competency.
2. The aspirant is to seek out an initiate of the Scarlet Gash; the *asking*, the *receiving* and

the *solution* to the Riddle of Initiation shall accomplish this.

3. The aspirant shall also create a suitable initiation rite for themselves and may seek fellows to assist as desired.

4. At the end of the appointed period the aspirant shall make some contribution to the public mind of something of the work that they have engaged in.

The following general curriculum shall be engaged in for no less than five months. Experiments and study should be recorded by the individual in whatever desired format.

∀ Indicates a required study, *in addition* to further choice(s).

The Program of Core Study *(Choose two or more)*

– ∀ *Ecstasis/Trance Techniques (Magical-Use Focus)*—Techniques of attaining trance are of paramount importance in the way of magic. So it is that the aspirant shall engage in a variety of experimental procedures of reaching trance. Methods of both inhibition and excitation are common. This is a required study.

– ∀ *Sigilization and Spell-casting*—Learning of the language between worlds, for the enactment and realization of desires. The candidate shall engage in the study of sigil creation and casting using methods of trance above, as well as acts of enchantment. This is a required study.

– *Techniques of Casting a Space*—Wherein the aspirant experiments with a variety of methods of establishing the temple in various spheres.

– *Pranayama (The Science of Breath)*—This simplest of formulas is also one of the most advanced and sets a precedent for usefulness. The aspirant shall establish regular practice and variances of possible use.

– *Banishing(s)*—Wherein the aspirant shall experiment with a variety of banishing procedures.

– *Fetish Creation*—Wherein the aspirant shall engage in a variety of methods for the creation of talismans, amulets, servitors and fetishes.

The Program of Personality Alteration *(Choose one or more)*

– ∀ *Paradigm Study*—Wherein the aspirant shall engage in a study/use of at *least* two different schools of magical thought. Possible schools are Qabalah, Enochian, Atheistic, Monotheistic, Vodou, Shamanism, Witchcraft, Cthulhu Mythos, Thelema. The choices are infinite. This is a required study.

– *Automatic Drawing/Writing*—Wherein the aspirant shall engage in methods of unhinging the conscious mind to allow for free-flow creative egress. All experiments should be duly recorded with external influences.

– *Random Behavior*—Wherein the aspirant shall undergo a variety of behavior modifications randomly and with full implementation.

– *Hate-Fusion*—Wherein the aspirant shall achieve unity with some concept/person/ideology that they find revolting.

– *Working Out/Exercise*—Wherein the aspirant shall engage in an exercise regime. Ideally this shall be a life decision with the obvious benefits to both will and health.

– *Ecstasis/Trance Techniques (Internal Focus)*—Wherein the aspirant shall experiment with a variety of trance methods for the illumination of the soul and modification of personality. Chemognostic[1] techniques are recommended in combination with diverse sexual experimentation.

– *Alternate Sexuality Exploration*—Wherein the aspirant shall engage in experimental sexual behavior to see the effects it has upon the personality. Possibilities can include: men, women, animals, objects, deformed individuals.

The Program of the Public Domain *(Optional)*

– *Poetic Anarchy*—Wherein the aspirant shall engage in some form of public, poetic, anarchistic attack to some ideology or the furtherance of some meme. Examples include random scribbling on walls, graffiti and placing pornography around religious sites.

– *Random Acts of Art*—Wherein the aspirant shall engage in some form of public act of art for some purpose. Anything is possible.

– *Magical Collaboration*—Wherein the aspirant shall engage with fellows in some form of magical collaboration or study.

– *The Scarlet Letter*—Wherein the aspirant shall wear or carry some item that stands out and is unusual upon their person for a set amount of time. This should be worn with some magical intent.

The Program of Celebration *(Optional)*

– *Observance of the Old Holidays*—Wherein the aspirant shall seek to include the traditional Eight Sabbaths of the yearly cycle into their daily life. Magical integration is recommended.

– *New Holiday Creation*—Wherein the aspirant shall seek to create some holiday/spiritual celebration of a meaningful nature. This holiday shall be observed with a great degree of vigilance.

The Program of Advanced Study *(Optional, except where required)*

– ∀ *Divination*—Wherein the aspirant shall engage in the study of one or more systems of divination. A certain degree of proficiency is desired. Possibilities can include: *I Ching*, Tarot, Runes, tea leaves and other methods.

– *Evocation*—Evocation being the summoning of spirits/forces *external* of self. Wherein the individual shall undergo a period of experimentation in the process of summoning and working with entities. Possibilities include Goetic, Enochian and shamanic methods.

– *Invocation*—Invocation being the summoning of spirits/forces *internal* of self. Wherein the individual shall undergo a period of experimentation in the process of summoning spirits and forces and being possessed by them to certain degrees.

– *Sigils*—Wherein the aspirant shall seek out the Alphabet of Desire[2] and engage in advanced work using sigils. This is an extended study and should be continued for years, even after initiation.

– *Astral Magic*—Wherein the aspirant shall engage in a study of various levels of astral magic. Work with the aura, healing, servitor creation, astral spellcasting and communion are examples.

– *Work/Creation of a Weapon*—Wherein the aspirant shall engage with work of one of the traditional elemental tools or other ceremonial gear. The creation of a new type of weapon (tool) as well as resonance is another possibility. Examples can include: athame, pentacle, wand, cup, robe, ring, censor, altar, dice.

– *HGA/Augeoides*—Wherein the aspirant shall seek the Knowledge and Conversation of the Holy Guardian Angel. Being one of the most important operations of an initiate's existence, this Operation cannot be emphasized enough. It should be made of note that there exist multiple forms of the HGA operation, which translate into various systems under different symbolism. Research in this area is required to fully seek this out.

– *The Acquisition of Wealth*—Wherein the aspirant shall seek to the governance of Malkuth and the acquisition of wealth consciousness for the furtherance of the Work.

Closing

As a result of the completion of this schema of initiation, the individual may acquire the *Scarlet Sash* as a magical weapon. The Scarlet Sash will serve as a link and symbol for the aspirant's desire for perfection and the realization of the inner mysteries manifested. The Scarlet Sash may also serve other functions. There is also *an additional program (Liber Anon)* that will be made available to those individuals who wish to explore alternate models and advanced operation. This secondary program, for the initiate, represents new avenues of approach in abstract formation.

Liber Anon

The Works of Flesh (Low Magic)

– The *Alphabet of Desire* is the exploration into the nature of, and ecstasy in, Flesh.

– The *Double* represents the subtle ophidian body of sexual permeation.

– *Sorcery* is a reflection of the perfection manifest in high magic in Malkuth–Yesod and all across the worlds.

– *Random Belief* prevents the restriction of any adopted path unto itself.

–*Ecstasy* is in the nature of itself and is omnipresent.

– *Transmogrification* is the Brotherhood of the Flesh (The Scarlet Brotherhood) to the delight and exploration of Ecstasy.

The Works of Intelligence (High Magic)

– *Invocation* calls forth intelligence of transcendence to surpass the limitation of self.

– *Evocation* calls forth intelligence to the indulgence of transfinite awareness and power of self.

– *Enchantment* is the enactment of intelligence on Mind.

– *Divination* is the pursuit of wisdom through intelligence.

– *Gnosis* and *Liberation* are dual gateways of singularity cascading the spirit towards its reflection and rebirth.

– The *Augoeides* is the personal filter through and of which the magus has determined the horizon of manifestation and becoming.

The works of high magic involve the developing of the inner genius towards recognition of itself. The works of low magic call forth the genius to the enactment and realization of the raison d'être. Both high and low magic converge, as they are dual currents of *movement* in Kia.[3]

So ends *Liber Anon.*

Emanations:

The *Works of Flesh* together comprise the way of Kia in the intercourse of that which is and that which is not. The works are attempts by the shell to maintain its reality by bridging the gap between itself and Absolute Darkness. The goal/effect of traversing either (and both) results in Interface; sporadic leaps through the void to allow for free-form ego manifestation. The works themselves, once the goal has been achieved, must be perfected for the exploration of being. The discovery *of*, acknowledgment *with* and resonance *by* the Word are not the end (as such there never is until ecstasy is quenched by ecstasy), but the enrichment of the Word is to follow. This spectrum is then cast across the worlds for *it* to judge *itself* without resuscitation. The work is never ending and, as such, movement is always a requisite.

Now what of the Qliphoth?

Results of the intercourse of that which is and that which is not. An alternate form of being comprising *it*. When interacted with in our own manifestation, catastrophic results usually follow due to personal imbalance in the magus. The Qliphoth additionally represent the collective substratum of creation (a drop of pre-cum if you will) and so it is that the *Works of Flesh* shall be discussed first.

"The Alphabet of Desire is the exploration into the nature of, and ecstasy in, Flesh."

The sum total of the Alphabet is BABALON, the grand shell of collective refraction.

The personality construct purified of all belief is a complete alphabet, and in so purifying itself the flesh gains the attainment of instantaneous ecstasy. This is also shown in the rising of the Dragon Wyrd and the power of atonement. Retrogressive use of the Alphabet and its perpetual refinement constitute the riding of the Great Whore, lest she master thee…

"The Double represents the subtle ophidian body of sexual permeation."

The Double (also called the ophidian body, "OB") is the emitted being/radiance comprised of astral effluvia. Secreted of the subtle body, the OB is naturally amorphous but can be made hard to anthropomorphic form (or any other vehicle). The OB is of the nature of sex. A burning sun radiating waves of fire for establishment of all contact. The ophidian body can be projected outward to make contact with the shell of another at a sub-awareness level, which then arises into full consciousness. Mental control and influence can be thus enacted through the double. The OB relates to the regions of Mind resonating with Yesod. Forms of witchcraft, and all sexually related magic require development and use of the ophidian body. The fires of Sekhet cause reverberations in Mind (which are sometimes felt as a deep tone of resonance). The OB can also be used to alter the realms of Malkuth from above (and way below).

"Sorcery is a reflection of the perfection manifest in high magic in Malkuth–Yesod and all across the worlds."

It is here that we attain a glimpse of the Way. Its establishment for the manipulation of reality (comprised of Qliphoth at various levels) is constituted by a linkage reverberation of Da'ath (knowledge/death) and Yesod (sex/belief). The reverberation of this linkage impacts the entire tree, shaking the roots/routes of creation with creation (a gateway to Gnosis).[4] The result of successful sorcery comes about by utilization of the Qliphoth. In these cases, the more "pure" (and hence closer to our Lady) the better. The world of the Qliphoth is also Zos[5] in fragmentation. Our predecessor found the inclusion of all bestialities amongst our kind necessary; so it is that the Sabbath is pronounced.

"Random belief prevents the restriction of any adopted path unto itself."

It is in the nature of all creation to come into being, go out and then contain itself (for successful creation, that is). The form of containment for the initial desire offers a nurturing womb for the cultivation of one's refracted ray. Stagnation of this earthen mix is inevitable and the now-grounded fire must be transmuted back to the Flame Itself. The liberation induced of random belief is alchemical transformation of the given shell to clear up the prism of refraction. Dual inversion is the key here to successful utilization and free-belief.

"Ecstasy is in the nature of itself and is omnipresent."

"Transmogrification is the Brotherhood of the Flesh (The Scarlet Brotherhood) to the delight and exploration of Ecstasy."

The shell has been integrated, the body has been purified, restriction is under Will, the initiate is the Way. Transmogrification allows for the ultimate act of sorcery. The casting of the manipulation of Dreamscape. For this is Dreamscape. The boundary of dissolution has been surpassed (as such it is a trial), the transformation of the shell to the pure force of understanding rejoins the many rays of refracted light to become one. The nature of transmogrification is delight in ecstasy. For there is Nothing beyond This, which is another walker's way. The Scarlet Brotherhood is the pronouncement of a Sabbatical Way, Thee Way, as those who know have gained Understanding.

The *Works of Intelligence* together comprise the way of Kia in infinite expansion to move beyond, a furthering of creation. The Works relate the individual light of the inner being through the overcast shell, refracting the Word in myriad ways. The *Works of Intelligence* represent the Dance of the Qliphoth, being a sleight of mind in the transformation of utter horror to effective use and transcendence.

"Invocation calls forth intelligence of transcendence to surpass the limitation of self."

The nature of invocation is to gain a facet on the prism of refraction; to alter the prism/filter by expansion, for every act of invocation brings creation more toward the recognition of unity. The merging of higher resonant shells into lower resonant shells brings forth a spit and polish on the prisms. In other aspects of invocation, sections of the shell lie closer to the inner darkness (*undetected*) and successful invocation dregs these areas forth. Invocation is brought to perfection in evocation (and vice versa). Invocation is the solve of self, whereas Evocation is the coagula of self.

"Evocation calls forth intelligence to the indulgence of transfinite awareness and power of self."

The snipping off and purposeful budding of creation (*in separation*) is one of the grand indulgences. Evocation is exalted, built with the mortar of invocation (ßà). With the purposeful calling of godforms, the self is brought closer to awareness of the infinite. Passage beyond the boundary of the ego boosts the shells' resonance to the transfinite (a region of interface). So by the expansion in/out of invocation/evocation (respectively), a necessary momentum of flux is achieved toward the furtherance of *intelligence.*[6]

"Enchantment is the enactment of intelligence on Mind."

Being a dreamer, we now approach the way of successful dreaming. Of the Mind/of the Logos, there is only one. All forms of division are in the nature of Maya. Enchantment is the implantation of a universal sigil through the preferred route into Mind. The Mind reacts and dreams another dream. Enchantment calls forth the purer forms of Qliphoth due to interaction on the boundaries of Interface.

"Divination is the pursuit of wisdom through intelligence."

The pursuit of wisdom is to be taken as the walking of the Way. The process of divination in its highest aspect is to be considered *"walking through life intelligently."* All other forms of divination (the pursuit of knowledge) are to be considered subsequent to this. Divination allows for attunement with the universal intellect (as well as with the subsequent forms), for the recognition of all ways, as all ways are one way and the one way, many. Divinatory powers increase as one is taken into the fold of the Brotherhood. Prescience, telepathy and all forms of thought sympathy are the proximity measure of shell and Mind.

"Gnosis and Liberation are dual gateways of singularity cascading the spirit towards its reflection and rebirth."

Gnosis is instantaneous revelation due to the shells' intercourse with the universal intellect; this leads to Liberation (glimpses of this are seen through random belief). Liberation is any act of "surpassing" which leads towards Gnosis, such as all forms of Art, Science and expression. Traveling down one's road brings benefits and curses, but the Way yields a new fruition to us as Gnosis arises from within. Liberation is a marvelous word.

"The Augoeides is the personal filter through and of which the magus has determined the horizon of manifestation and becoming."

Much has been said of the Augoeides already in various forms, but the attunement and merging of the boundaries of duality correspond to the horizon of one's universe. The Augoeides/Angel being the silver cord, demarcation Zos-Kia. Intelligence comes in myriad forms, of but one Mind. The emanation of the Greater Countenance sheds forth intelligence in the formless light of rays. These cosmic pools reflect the light of the Sun in various forms upon the ever-mutating surface. The surface of the waters across the face of the deep contains the point of reflection of the greater countenance. This is the Angel.

Here end the emanations of Anon.

ENDNOTES

[1] Use of entheogens for magical purposes. – Ed.

[2] A complete map of the magician's states of being, emanating as complementary opposites from a central unbounded and non-local state (Kia). See Peter Carroll's *Liber Null*. – Ed.

[3] Austin Osman Spare's term for the spark of life. The Qabalistic *Chiah*. – Ed.

[4] Greek for "knowing with certainty." Gnosticism itself is the mainline of the mysteries in the West; the "occult" as it currently stands is in many aspects the faint survival of Gnosticism. Gnostic Christians as well as modern magicians tend to view Christ as a symbol of an inner experience shared by all human beings under different names, rather than a historical person. Gnosis can also mean some form of contact with a higher reality—hence "knowing with certainty," this certainty being akin to heresy within the postmodern era. This term was co-opted by Peter Carroll and the chaos magic movement to mean any altered state of consciousness stark enough to perform acts of sleight-of-mind and sorcery from (this itself being a political choice). The correct term for this, as used in this book, would be *ecstasis*. – Ed.

[5] Spare's term for the "body considered as a whole"—considered in extension, the totality of life on earth. – Ed.

[6] In this aspect *intelligence* is the color of the ray in reflection with the shell.

FUN

THE SUM OF ALL SCENES
Forays Into Group Magical Consciousness

SHAUN FRENTÉ

The fact that I was having a Vision—not just a garden-variety hallucination, but the manifestation of a freestanding icon spelling out all that I promise and all that I must overcome—was enough. The ludicrous fact that it was happening during the pinkest kiss of dawn outside a circus tent in the dewy crotch of the two Kansas Cities, was something I had to accept as undiluted ecstasy. There it was, a tattoo-glyph blazing in my mind's eye as if it had always been there. That was the joke—it had been there as long as *I'd* been alive, as if it was an amalgam of my zodiacal sign (Libra) and my monogram (SMF)—a birthmark in a profound sense. The branding the stars seared upon me at my arrival was duly represented in a set of prosaically inked scales. The triad of names pinned upon me by my parents some time after my conception was worked out in a comic-art rebus: a beefed-out, ornately wounded Christ nailed to the beams of the scales representing "M" (masculine, masochism), and two whip-wielding Betty Page-types, mirthfully swinging in Libra's buckets as if it were recess in a teen gang-deb exploitation film. (These sisters in leather played the dual role of "S and "F," sadism and feminine.)

So there I was, standing mud-caked beside a sleepy stretch of Midwestern Interstate, musing: *How could an overeducated, semantically obsessed gender-bending diva not have seen this all along?* That the strange, turbulent knot I identify as self, bobbing in the tug of so many shifting worldly forces had been lying in wait in a neatly linked set of two oppositions (S/M, M/F)? When I quickly apprehended that the pictorial distribution of dominance and submission across the sexes ran counter to the patriarchal package deal, and germane to my messier view of gender psychology, I was even more impressed by the level of subtlety these transmissions from outside seemed to take on. But again, *how can someone totally miss something so close to them, so out in the open?* As I was having this last thought, a lonely semi buzzed by, leaving the smell of diesel and the afterimage of a profanely huge corporate logo: B&D Trucking. The universe never misses an opportunity to wink, if you're paying attention.

The fact of the matter is that this very deeply felt moment of discovery, bathed in a sense of clarity and harmony, had been prefaced by dancing barefoot in the dirt at a corn-circuit outdoor rave, to sets of godly Detroit and Chicago house music. This connection between a richly cognitive quantum leap and a night of freeform neo-pagan mayhem was neither incidental nor isolated. It's a very concise embodiment of what I cheekily call "disco magic"—a Gnostic leap into the connectedness of things through dance culture, the art and science of a mindbodyspirit hoofing its ass off with the very fabric of our cosmos. It's also an apt capitulation of the most exuberantly turned-on chapter of my life, my passage from being a neurotically cynical student of human sexuality and pop culture to a psychotically positive bodhisattva of the beat, and self-appointed High Priestess of the Church of Disco Discordia.

What follows is an attempt to make sense of a remarkable run of experience, and to amplify the ramifications of this personal journey upon magic and culture at large, and to help script a prescription for a new wave of magical paradigmatics—a process, I would say, already in progress. To such ends, this is also a shot in the dark addressed to anyone else who has found themselves sweating madly in a throng of other bodies no longer distinguishable from their own, ready to talk to God, thinking: *This is more than just the drugs. Am I some kind of crazy born-again raver?* Yes, you are—and you are not alone.

Four years ago, I was so doggedly convinced that "we are not alone," of the acceleration of a new global consciousness through music and dance, that I went so far as to found a fake sect, the Disco Discordians—for the laity, this is the worship of the goddess of chaos, Eris, through club culture. The church may have been phony, but my devotion was real, fomented by weekly—or more than weekly—sessions of total abandon through dancing and whatever consciousness-altering substances were available, if desired. Sometimes it was just an ample supply of Schlitz and Pabst Blue Ribbon, other times, a Chips Ahoy or Sweet Tart doused with the mid-grade LSD that would appear in the unlikely setting of Iowa City, Iowa. But in the end, it was the music that was the binding element, and while I was often the happy recipient of the drugs that would float into town by way of Chicago and Detroit, it was the house music trafficked in from these same two cities that changed my life.

Here is not the place to explain the vicissitudes of electronic music, or to argue for one form of the beat over another as a magical tool in moving the body. However, I personally endorse the overtly spiritual heritage of house music—essentially an evolution beyond the excesses of disco—over the more cold and electronic tendencies of techno. Still, I've always found it interesting that within the techno and trance side of rave culture, so many shibboleths of occultism recur: aliens, angels, the various and sundry "little people" of cutesy raver anime. Do people in large groups consuming large amounts of psychedelics always attract the same archetypes, or have these timeless helper figures of magical passage been co-opted by Sanrio and Nickelodeon? Curiouser and curiouser.

If rave culture at large does seem to be wallpapered with the imagery of a popular notion of "the occult," my experience with house has been more akin to some flavor of Gnosis, or direct experience with "something higher." On top of the numerous anthems that make no bones about decrying that house music "is a spiritual thang," there's a whole sub-genre of gospel-dance wherein wailing plus-size divas celebrate the love and light that came when "He" was found. At first it's easy to simply accept the unnamed He in question as the Jesus of the born-again, given the Baptist revival roots of the form, but often this is ambiguous, as is the nature of the divine love celebrated. During my first immersion into house, I was immediately struck by its unqualified, unapologetic call to capital L love—totally unthinkable in the snarly, jaded "love stinks" despondency of post-rock—as well as by the very carnal rapture that resonates in paeans to the Holy Spirit. As I was throwing my arms up in delirium to the glory of CeCe Peniston's "He Loves Me" I was unsure whether CeCe was getting laid or saved, and with the residual dust of Christian guilt that has clung to me, *that was supposed to make me feel dirty.*

But it didn't. To be sure, I wouldn't be the first to point out that the Rapture of Christian mysticism is at the least very corporeal, despite the faith's frequent forswearing of the flesh, and is at times well-nigh erotic. The classic example of this is Bernini's sculpture "The Ecstasy of St. Teresa," but the same has been said of more fevered Evangelists, among others. Here I was, in bars, basements and rented-out Elks Lodges in a social sphere reserved for drunken pickups, listening to a bass-fueled stream of salvation through love, getting "set free," getting born again—and finding myself seduced by this collapse of bodily *eros* and spiritual *agapé*. In the end, Disco Love is not a case of sublimating the lust of a potential one-night stand through God, any more or less than it is about finding the divine in the random stranger dancing next to you. To use that beloved chestnut of New Age mumbo-jumbo and ancient Californian wisdom, it's both and neither. And the Gnosis of Disco Love is the necessary and sufficient gate into the teachings of Disco Magic—the alchemical transformation of reality through a specially charged libidinalized space.

By my last semester of grad school, the felt promise of such alchemy in such an unlikely place led me to half-jokingly call house music my religion, and I was a ubiquitous fixture in Iowa City's micro-community of house addicts, pill-poppers, hip-hoppers, displaced ravers, urban expatriates, drag queens, tragic alcoholics and compulsive socialites that strangely coagulated around the music. To wit, most of what I'm describing here is not about rave subculture in the strictest sense, although there is no shortage of candy bracelets, teddy bear backpacks or fuzzy fat-pants in my memories. If anything, our strange rural-route facsimile of club-life was a patchwork of so many subcultures, countercultures and pop-cultures that they canceled out into a highly neutral social space, facilitated more or less in a mainstream arena. It was just like some old Buddhist proverb: *The sum of all scenes is no-scene.*

Starting with a cocktail of sundry subjective realities already sets the scene for a charged space of magical shifts. When a sizable percentage of these subjective realities have been heckled by the effects of psychedelics, amphetamines or Jägermeister shots, consensus reality continues to become even more supple. In this splintered social microcosm, beliefs and perceptions begin to buckle from the moorings of daily habit, and in this chaotic state the individual is highly open to suggestion or realignment. This is the perfect time to intervene and start a cult, by the way. As I participated and took notes on this social experiment spontaneously happening week after week, it was the very lack of cultishness around me that was salient. Too often I had learned about experimental groups that quickly descended into varying degrees of guru-worship and streamlining of heterogeneous desires into the canted insistency of manifestos. I was much more interested in a social playground with no teacher, a drunken ocean liner of possibility with no one at the helm—and, indeed, I had found it.

Some might argue that magic is not possible without at least the looming archetype of a grand magus, or the presence of a unified will. I have certainly called many deejays godlike, and there's definitely a kind of unspoken tribal "big man" competition that goes on within all genres of electronic music culture—a kinder, gentler sublimation of the nasty one-upmanship of gangsta rap, let's say. But when a deejay's set sends a crowd into a euphoric frenzy, it's not a case of hero-worship on the part of the crowd or Svengali-like persuasion on the part of the deejay. The person at the turntables is a medium, nothing more—but certainly nothing less, as a masterfully mixed set alone is enough to transport you out-of-body.

I would surrender to the beat, *become* the beat at times. In the Gordian knot of gyrating bodies, broken up into frozen tableaux by strobe light, my normative calibration of space and direction might also turn to vapor. I'd sweat until I thought I'd collapse, but I had no choice but to go on. That was the point that something clicked on, something that I had never even come close to experiencing—it was as if a powerful force were running through me that had nothing to do with ego, yet was still intrinsic to my being. No guru, no master! It had been revealed: *Every man and woman is a Superstar.* The first commandment of Disco Discordia, to be sure.

By the time I'd reached this point, I'd fully dived into my role as platform-heeled acolyte and occasional host-body of the goddess of Chaos. It was in this state that I decided that I could, and would, be whatever the hell I wanted to be—and get away with it. In the shelter of a micro-community as safe and unrestrictive as a flotation tank, I would wriggle up next to all sorts of social boundaries and see how far I could bend them—anything from gender polarities to hardwired mammalian patterns of group formation. Snaking from the anointing vibrations of bass emanating from the speaker stacks, through a crowd of kids with as many dancing styles as is imaginable, past the beautiful high-concept scenesters in stately glam repose by the toilets, I would begin to interact with my environment through a new set of rules that unfolded with each step. And the world would dance with me. Under the influence of psychedelics or not, I sensed a rich vocabulary of nonverbal communication with people I'd never met, developing very profound relationships with people I barely spoke to. Beyond this, a coherence of actions and perceptions would emerge, wherein scraps of overheard conversations would knit together into grand thematics, drunken dancers would spontaneously synchronize against all odds and things I thought about would suddenly appear. (And yes, once I was actually convinced I had become Eris-on-earth. Fake it long enough, and you will, in fact, make it.) To be more prosaic, I was having a conversation with the chaos of the universe through a holistic and intimate relationship with my local surroundings. Not through willed dominance or dutiful submission, but through play.

The skeptical reader might ask why the forces of wild Chaos should be reached through the controlled, steady and, yes, repetitive beat of house music or other electronica. My answer is manifold. One: The rigid grid of space-time coordinates built up in a continuous beat acts as a counterpoint to the randomness generated by two hundred people twisted on E, and through this tension, a mode of acting in harmony with the world is revealed. Two: A simple beat allows for a thoughtless, automatic vocabulary of steps to take over, allowing your consciousness to rise from an awareness of your body's movement alone to *consciousness of your body as an interface with a spontaneously unfolding world.* In other words, you create a hypersensitive micro-model for using chaos as a creative force, rather than a block of opposition. Three: Bluntly, house music makes people move. It can make uptight wallflowers cut loose, and can be so infectious that I've had to bodily remove myself from a room to disturb my groove. As with all magic, Disco Discordianism requires real action, not just contemplation, and the old skool beat passed down from Great Momma Disco is a reliable catalyst for this. Four: The nature of deejay sets makes this movement continuous, yet fractured. Whereas rock is all about single songs, solos and grandiose climaxes, beat culture is all about flow, plateaus and connectedness. Time and bodies become imagined as part of a single continuum of parts, just as the set is in fact an entity comprised of mish-mashed melodies with matched beats, the clash of sampled elements and the cross-faded union of unexpectedly similar songs. And, finally, a corollary: The prolonged intermingling of bodies moving to a pulsating beat without a model of climax does some very interesting things. If you know anything about Tantric sex practices, the key is to prolong coitus for a long enough period that your orgone energies will sufficiently interact with your lover's. When such prolonged contact of orgone is facilitated by hours of dance across countless bodies, the group energy becomes, well, magical.

Such are the pillars of Disco Wisdom, or at least the practical keys to an intense period of initiation. The magic soon contaminated the rest of my life, and as a talking, walking, dancing being in tiny Iowa City I sensed rhythms, musical coincidences and harmonies everywhere—as well as a sense of my influence upon them. My interface with the world wasn't one of aggressively willing other forces to yield, nor was it a case of passive acquiescence. It's more like having a kind of rule book in which the rules change with each turn of the page; and the way things change depends on your actions. In turn, however, the knowledge of the way you *should* act to follow your True Will reverberates from channels beyond yourself. This putative paradox may just be a function of using language to describe such a state of consciousness, whose "meaning" cannot be housed within words alone. It's hardly surprising that a ritual of music, bodily movement and a constant collision of elements in real time can facilitate access to this state of magical consciousness.

Anyway, it worked for me. Strangers I wanted to meet would suddenly introduce themselves to me; friends I was thinking about would suddenly call. Coincidences would rack up to a critical mass of statistically improbable probability. Often these are quite amusing, as my opening story hints at. As some old coffeehouse prophet in Ann Arbor told me years ago, the first thing you notice after enlightenment is that the world gets a lot funnier. I was more fearless, active and intellectually productive than I've ever been—*and* I suddenly looked like Aphrodite incarnate. But whatever I gave to the world, it would give back to me, through objects, bathroom graffiti, random bear hugs, glances and the beautiful wash of filtered French disco-house, wafting around me upon warm brick summer streets.

As this sense of engagement deepened, so did my desire to spread this radiant energy like an Avenging Disco Fairy Godmother. Not surprisingly, I soon found myself enmeshed with a trio of kids on the same trip, and ready to begin a collective work of cultural contagion. We became a highly fecund foursome, whose productive sum was incredibly greater than our parts, working, dancing, thinking together until the membranes of our individual identities became permeable, parts of our selves becoming almost interchangeable. Sometimes we would be mistaken for each other on the street, even though none of us looked alike. And in the process, we started to cocoon ourselves from having any sense of a greater consensus reality. If, as the French psychoanalyst Jacques Lacan put it, "the Big Other" does not exist, then we would build our own cosmology from the bottom up, hammer and tong, and inject it into the mainline of the mainstream.

In the spring of 2000, we unleashed our mass-scale party-as-spell, an effort that consumed months of conception, planning, promoting and playing. Our ambitions were unabashedly huge: to create a "meta-party," a Maryushka-doll model of parties-within-parties-within-the-party, creating a never-ending ripple effect of play, complete with fake museum placards describing sundry subcultural and historical phenomena ("The DJ," "Tupperware Parties," etc.). Called the "NeverNever Party," our experiment was to facilitate a laboratory for interpersonal discovery by bending rules of convention through a complex combination of guerrilla theater, ethnomethodological games, lies, drugs, circus performers, costume changes, installations, collages, pranks and deejays. We leaked out rumors of a made-up drug that was floating around the party (actually dandelion root capsules), and were fed back five different accounts of how it was "heavy stuff." When the police came to raid the affair (we knew they would), we passed out flyers informing the crowd that the cops were a simulation, but that any resistance might meet with a simulated arrest indistinguishable from the real thing. And so on.

While my awakening as a Disco Disciple had been a rush and a push of love and connectivity, our NeverNever dalliance was a simmering of tricksterism, conspiracy and even mild Schadenfreude. Empirical evidence has not yet been gathered to prove if our stated goal of "emitting a perpetual, pulsing party cabal into the dark reaches of infinity" was in fact achieved, but it's certain that our greater mission was accomplished: To draw down and dance with the spirit of Chaos. In the structural blueprint of initiatory processes, it was business as usual. First the boost of that initial euphoric turning on, then the frightening slide into madness that occurs when you tarry in that state for too long. In our case, it was an act of hubris, as we dared to see how much we could play with the seams of our reality according to our caprices. Within a month of our schizoid ritual, one of us had to be temporarily committed, a second almost had a heart attack and fled to convalesce in the pastoral succor of Brooklyn, and my by-then paramour and I slid into the most inert depression we've ever faced. We're still trying to figure out what happened.

Before leaving the Midwest, I managed to pull myself up by my clunky-heeled bootstraps and find a plateau of balance and excitement, but without having psychically processed or empirically assayed my postinitiatory burnout. Magical stagnation inevitably ensued. Moving to New York City in the fatal fall of 2001 did not immediately hot-step the next phase in my evolution. Yet living in America's most densely populated, buzzing, self-involved metropolis—for many people, the avatar of the very idea of City—was certain to reshape my paradigm of the kind of "mass magic" I had dreamed of in Iowa, albeit through channels I never would have foreseen.

As it turned out, the first large-scale social gatherings I attended in Gotham were the massive peace rallies held in the streets during the months that followed the World Trade Center attack—an event that ripped asunder the entire consensus on what was possible for a nation acclimated to the insular Clinton era's "end of history."

The spontaneous urgency with which New Yorkers thronged together was revelatory—it seemed as though, robbed of their accustomed daily reality, people instinctively sought each other out to share a common space, even if not with a clear agenda in tow. For a few weeks, before the scaffolding of political, social and psychological master-narratives scabbed around the traumatic rift to reinstate a refurbished normality, there was a palpable, almost bodily sense that *another world was possible; that the forces of history were up for grabs.* And in those chanting, smiling parades of not protesters, but those bound only in affirmation of life, I saw a glimpse of a human macro-organism beyond the blind, angry mob, reminiscent of my experiments with hive-mind group consciousness.

Given a greater longevity than a few fleeting moments parading down the avenues, could such an organism begin to develop a coherent will, or an intelligence? It is clear that the city-machine, the arm of hegemonic power, did not want to find out, as the police quickly learned how to dissipate rivers of critical masses into consternated rivulets, to divert them into disempowered oxbow lakes, with the chilling efficiency of black science. However, the greater apparatus of "crowd control" in New York extended beyond a reflex-response to potential crisis situations, its grubby tendrils making their way into far more benign avenues: At the time I moved to New York, it was actually *illegal* to dance in the majority of bars and clubs. Why? Dusting off an obscure set of racist city codes from the 1920s used to control black jazz culture, Mayor Giuliani had initiated a crackdown in the name of upholding the "quality of life." Evidently, this meant ensuring life *had* no quality to speak of, and that expressing joy was something to be hidden away, or at least reserved for the elite few who could fit the bill for Rudy's laughable "cabaret license." These laws have since been fought tooth and claw by activists, and ameliorated to some degree, but within a year of this writing I have been personally requested to "stop shaking (my) booty until the cops leave" at a club that had gone to the trouble of booking one of the greatest deejays in the world. As astutely pointed out by the *Village Voice* in consideration of oppression in global politics, New York City was, incredibly, *the only place in the world* with such an absurd proscription, Afghanistan having repealed its own *Footloose*-style fiat the previous year.

The case of New York is exceptional, but is only an acute manifestation of a larger trend. Under the auspices of the "War on Drugs," Congress's RAVE Act furtively slipped past the noses of sleeping Senators as a rider on a child abuse bill, and has helped decimate alternative spaces for dance parties by threatening to harshly prosecute event promoters for the drug possession of *any* attendees. The city government of Detroit has done its best to prevent its annual electronic music conference, despite the fact that its inaugural 2000 edition (a Woodstock for the computer age) brought close to a million bodies to the center of a city in need of life support, without almost any security, without almost any incident. As public space grows more and more policed, our shared landscape becomes limited to high-Roman spectacle straight out of Fellini's *Satyricon*, the steroid-bloated distraction machine of testosterone and death that is the sports industry and concert venues sanctioned by corporate *eminences grises* like Clear Channel. The inherently radical nature of the real-time event becomes limited within monocular perspectives of minimal participation. Concomitant to this is a set of values that venerate the individual above all else, a true cultural manifestation of the bratty upstart god Horus, in which freedom is defined not just by private ownership, but private experience. We are becoming literally unable to face each other.

In short, the preconditions for large-scale group magical workings to happen have become estranged from our behavioral vocabulary. The best way to stop magic from spreading is to keep people isolated, to thwart conditions in which we can evolve modes of consciousness higher than the ego. *It is imperative to the entire human species that we find ways of resisting this kind of subtle, hegemonic control.* Unfortunately, this sort of antisocial solipsism is to be found within today's magical communities (inasmuch as the word "community" even applies). While the mediation of the Internet is important and to some degree necessary for the postmodern magus, and while individual ritual is integral to magic, we need to physically come together. In the shadow of a century of communal ideals turned to totalitarian nightmares, of Haight Street hippies born again as self-serving venture capitalists, the very concept of a collective will has become unsavory, if not inconceivable. Indeed, how can such an organism develop and thrive without domination and coercion? How would it hold together?

A very useful model appears in Ishmael Reed's remarkable novel *Mumbo Jumbo*, the setting of which is precisely the New York City of the 1920s in which black music and dance culture were effectively outlawed. In Reed's conspiratorial fiction, the implementation of cabaret laws is recast as just a recent wave of oppression in a struggle as old as time. Under the rubric of "jes grew" (a term coined by Harlem Renaissance author and activist James Weldon Johnson), Reed knots together jazz, Vodou, funk, dance and pagan mysticism as an irresistible strain of magic—of life, of soul—traced mythically from the Egyptian fertility god Osiris (here a free-loving troubadour of the "Black Mud sound") down to the Cotton Club and the Harlem Renaissance, persecuted all the way by the controlling heirs of the death god Set—the pangenitor of "the Man," the jealous rigid brother who can't feel the funk. (Though *Mumbo Jumbo* predates disco and house, they are the inheritors of jes grew, as well as its suppression.) The tradition of jes grew, as its name suggests, is one that is spontaneous and by its very nature viral and contagious—or, as Reed puts it, an "anti-plague" which enlivens its host. Jes grew, or "the Work," needs no coercion to spread, and as a kind of "super-organism," in the Howard Bloom sense, has a will and direction of its own.

What is truly innovative in Reed's conception of this cultural virus is that, in addition to dance and music, a "Text" is needed for the Work to persist—not a proscriptive Bible, not a rigid set of commandments, but a tradition of accompanying hermetic writings which gives coherence to a shared ecstatic space. The Text (mythologized in the novel as the hermetic writings of Thoth) does not define the magical super-organism of jes grew but speaks to it, guides it along and, in turn, draws from its energy to be renewed and refined. It does not exist outside of the Work in order to explain it as Law, but helps spread its seeds across time and space. It is writing, but in a sense that exceeds the strictures of a rational logos and language.

It is such a Text that my own Disco Magic was wanting. A text yet to be written, save some fragments that have been handed down not on stone tablets but scribbled on cocktail napkins, rambled onto voicemail from a pay phone at three a.m. Without this text, a magical awakening gets stuck in the initial rapture of ecstatic egolessness. For a magical super-consciousness to develop, its participants must have a means of communication, but for that communication to take place outside of the confines of our language-bound egos, *it must take place beyond language as we now know it.* The magical-group text is a multidimensional semantic network combining word, sound, image, symbol and sigil, whose continued "writing forward" uses all of these things to knot individual consciousnesses together. This is precisely why the culture of "the mix," the sample, is crucial and perhaps even necessary to this evolution. In this regard, the infamous "cut-up" novels of William S. Burroughs provide an unexpected paper prototype, wherein film loops, fragments of pop songs, scraps of overheard dialogue and other pieces of libidinally charged words, sounds and images are the matrix for an interdimensional, trans-bodied viral consciousness. (This describes the "plot" of the novels, but it also pertains to the method through which they are written.) We have only just begun to explore the prospect of "cut ups" in real life, in real time, with positive "anti-plagues" instead of Burroughs' thanatos-driven insectoid viruses. Rave culture seems to have stopped short just when things were getting interesting. The live video feeds, the cutting-up of multiple sources from various and sundry cultural strata were a start, but for a full-bodied magical mix-text to happen, the passive audience model must be dispensed with altogether. All host-bodies of the infection must contribute their own signifiers into the shuffle of consciousness. Then various recordings, relics, polaroids and other charged signifiers will be cut in to a subsequent manifestation as the text grows tighter, as the will of the created groupmind unfolds and the beat goes on. (The NeverNever Party was a very rudimentary experimentation with this kind of ontological live mix.)

I have no doubt that such things can happen, or even that they must if magical culture is going to spread—not in spite of, but *because of* the tyranny of the individual that threatens to grind our globe into dust. As the ego is the obstacle of individual magic, it is exponentially so in even conceiving what a group-mind will "look" like. But for such organisms to jus' grow, we first have to come out of our rooms and make the space we want to inhabit. The cynical bubble of a postmodern, post-punk, post-authentic culture can only burst when we get over ourselves, and at the same time, take ourselves more seriously, and spread an elitism that applies to everyone. In the words of the Lady Miss Kier, perhaps the world's truest disco diva: "The world is our clique."

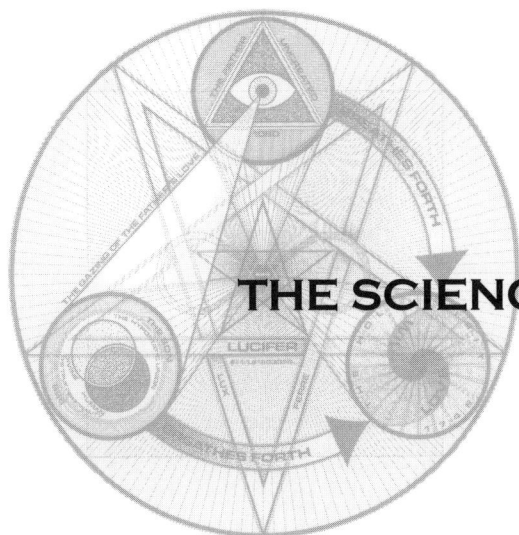

THE SCIENCE OF SUCHNESS

Micki Pellerano

Perhaps it's not the best time to keep a written record. Everything is wraithlike and transient, levels upon levels of visual data from each minuscule thing. The stillness overwhelmed with marble informa-tion. Death gods vomiting stone and fire. Harlots chained to spheres that throb with arcane symbols. Sheets of ether spilling from every surface, like the water that spilled in my bag, but only a little, leaving a path like a snail's, or like the ornamented Japanese lady vomiting entire vegetables until she's sur-rounded by a glistering array of jewels. "She who spits out precious stones." She's palpable.

Only now, where all things are infinitely concentrated—yet expanding and dematerializing into mere probability—can you grasp the elegance and muscular quality of everything. I'm consumed with the desire to make love to precious existence, with its intricate marble curves and beautiful lungs.

The above is an excerpt from my journal, dated January 19, 2002. I had taken psilocybin mushrooms at the Metropolitan Art Museum in New York. I assume the other patrons failed to detect the delicate curves of shadow, the seductive dances of the mineral properties as they mingled with the sunlight from the overhead window.

"This is how one ought to see," said Aldous Huxley, awestruck at the sublimity of the folds in his trousers while under the influence of mescaline.

I have known the origins of many psychedelic visions to be supernatural. Their intricacy and beauty are beyond the creative scope of my mind during ordinary modes of consciousness. The inspiration by which they materialized recalls a phrase employed by the poet Rimbaud, who desired to extend his mental capacities by means of what he called "the derangement of the senses."

What are the senses but a medium through which we interpret reality to suit our understanding? To mistake sensual impressions for actual reality, or to not question the limitations of sensory perception, would both be grave errors.

Scientific research will testify to the existence of very real forces that can be contacted and harnessed, though imperceptible to the senses. What of the forms normally invisible to the eye under ordinary consciousness? Would a shift in our consciousness allow us to perceive larger and more significant realities? By the spiritual and systematic use of psychedelic drugs, is our capacity for truth distorted or expanded? And if psychedelics can be conducive to learning and enlightenment, then why does society regard them with hesitation and fear?

"We all walk in mysteries. We are surrounded by an atmosphere about which we still know nothing at all. We do not know what stirs in it and how it is connected to our intelligence. This much is certain, under particular conditions the antennae of our souls are able to reach out beyond their physical limitations."
  – Goethe

After taking a handful of mushrooms my spine is strong and erect. My hips are poised and confident. Everything meaningless dissolves away and my body pulsates. It's a clearer, more advanced version of myself. My speaking voice resonates with a truth roused from my deepest body tissues. All the feeble preoccupations of daily life seem paltry and extraneous. I am closer to my essence.

I first realized my propensity for experiencing states like these while on LSD when I was in high school. In those days I suffered—as many high school kids do—from all sorts of complications: low self image, poor posture, mood-swings, a discomfort with my body, a desire to be liked by everyone, a paranoia that I might get my ass kicked at any minute, etc.

The first time I tripped on acid, I felt as though my mind had revealed to me all of its hidden secrets. All of nature was playing tricks on me, and truth suddenly rang to Hakim Bey's axiom that "the Universe wants to play." The raindrops were whispering behind the back door. The trees did erotic dances and breathed lasciviously. The grass writhed and bubbled as if stirred by giant worms that raced beneath it. I felt wiser, stronger and enlightened, because I could experience nature in this magical way, and felt as though I could communicate with the energy that inhabits all things. I felt an affinity with this energy. I felt loved by it.

The first time I tripped at school, I was armed and protected by this new wisdom. There was an air of silent confidence to my aura. I walked down the halls with a strong spine, as opposed to my usual adolescent slump. My eyes were focused on what lay before me, rather than shifting around in distraction or anxiety. I gave no thought to the clothes I was wearing, only that my body felt strong and beautiful as it moved inside them. My mind was focused on the inner universe, not the frivolous activity darting about my peripheral vision. I felt in touch with my True Self, a place where self-consciousness vanished. I had discovered something stronger inside me, and I loved myself effortlessly.

"This is how one ought to see," said Aldous Huxley. "Things without pretensions, satisfied to be merely themselves, sufficient in their Suchness."

Huxley often used the Buddhist term for this state of identity, calling it the "Dharma Body." Dharma, in the Buddhist sense, can be defined as the purest truth of things, at their very essence. This state is parallel to clarified states of the spirit-body traditionally referred to by occultists as the Holy Guardian Angel, Higher Self, Augeoides, Purusha or Genius. Many mystery traditions consider the Knowledge and Conversation of the Holy Guardian Angel as the chief objective of magic. The experience has been described as contact with the purest essence of one's psyche; beyond the personality, the conscious mind, the earthly modes of self-identity by which we normally perceive and define ourselves. The Knowledge and Conversation of the Holy Guardian Angel is the supreme level of self-knowledge wherein the conflicts and illusions of the conscious mind are transcended, and the True Self surfaces in the purity of its *Suchness*.

This *suchness* is a state of holiness. In my feeble glimpses of its perfection I have been brought to tears by the sheer beauty of the simplest things, by the overwhelming vastness of the inner universe, by the intoxicating laughter that consumes me because I am possessed by perfect bliss. If metals are transmuted into gold by the displacement of their base qualities, then my experiences with LSD and mushrooms can be described as alchemical.

> *"If it were not for the [Genius], the Philosophic and Experimental would soon be at the ratio of all things & stand still, unable to do other than repeat the same dull round over again . . . He who sees the Infinite in all things sees God. He who sees the ratio sees himself only."*
> – **William Blake**

At the age of six I was introduced to the powers of ritual, and harbored an insurmountable instinct that one day I would develop my latent magical power. In fourth grade, I remember getting impatient with myself because I knew this obsession to be irrational, but somehow I couldn't shake it. I began using the more potent varieties of psychedelics as a tool for mind expansion at fifteen. I began using formal ritual magic at the age of nineteen.

In the years that followed, an involved study and practice of magic and yoga have evolved into central functions in my life. I have discovered that my own magic is an evolutionary process of self-development, an alteration of consciousness. It is a journey in which the aspirant sheds the imperfections that obstruct their latent power and essential nature—the True Will, if you like.

In the search for my personal Dharma, a consistent practice of meditation and ceremonial magic has caused significant shifts in my own outer universe. A positive change in the way in which people react to me, or the way in which events unfold in my favor, has become strangely apparent. My intellect and powers of clairvoyance have become sharper, my capacity to perceive hidden meaning and synchronicity in daily events keener, and my own sense of will and identity have become more clarified. I have developed a broader understanding of the universe and myself. A psychedelic trip, a gateway to contact with the Dharma Body, can be a very intense "shortcut" to these capacities.

Psychedelics have been spiritually useful particularly because I believe the chief objective in magic to be the recovery of one's True Will. Each of our essences have been obscured by conditioning, environment, education, habit and the infinite contradictions that enslave the human ego. Magic is the transmutation of a mundane individual into the realms of sublime genius that dwell beyond the ego. And if used within the right context and in the right mindset, the psychedelic experience can be an invaluable asset in the Great Work.

The impurities of the ego distorting one's Dharma or True Self most commonly manifest themselves as fears, complexes, paranoia, self-restraint, lack of self-love, lack of self-knowledge, lack of self-confidence and the tenacity of infectious belief systems.

Psychedelic drugs can bring the aspirant into two states: Where the ego is dissolved to a degree where these impurities are temporarily transcended, and where the concentrated and often suppressed potency of these impurities become overwhelmingly prominent. The latter is commonly referred to as a "bad trip."

Apart from a fuller experience of contact with the Dharma body, the state of the dissolved ego can invoke all sorts of insight and revelation involving the hidden nature of both the deep mind of the aspirant and his exterior. The universe is a magical place, and psychoactive drugs reveal the mystery in what commonly appears mundane and ordinary. The life breathing inside seemingly inanimate things becomes visible. The energies that surround and permeate the natural world take on visible and tangible from.

The effects of psychedelic drugs are excellent agents in the process of deconditioning, perhaps the most important benefit of my journey in self-transformation. The confining boundaries of my personal reality were obliterated. In light of the expanded possibility brought to light by psychedelia, my existing belief systems vanished, giving way to extraordinary potentials within myself. Timothy Leary believed that the mind could be "reprogrammed" if therapeutically manipulated during a certain point in the acid trip. This theory is analogous to the magical use of symbol and ritual to create impressions on regions of the deep mind accessible during ecstasis, a mental condition where the ego is temporarily deteriorated and contact with the immeasurable unconscious becomes possible.

As I grew older, past the time when I was using psychedelics regularly, I began a passionate study of occult philosophy. I constantly found that I drew retrospectively from my drug experiences to shed light on abstract theories put forth by the books I studied. The malleable nature of matter and thought, the inadequacy of the senses and intellect, metaphysical concepts like the all-pervasive ether and the beings who dwell there, the *kundalini* or serpent power . . . I had already sensed the nature and possibility of these concepts through my examination of the universe in psychedelic trance.

> *"No man is worthy to fight in the cause of freedom unless he has conquered his internal masters . . . He must conquer inordinate vanity and anger, self-deception, fear and inhibition. These are the crude ores of his being."*
> – **John Whiteside Parsons**

A "bad trip" can be as valuable as a good one. Its revelatory powers can serve just as well as an aid in neurological reprogramming to diminish one's restraints and broaden one's scope of potential—provided, of course, that the aspirant is courageous and astute enough to confront and process the information surfacing from his deep mind.

It was, in fact, a bad LSD trip that marked my initiation into a life of magic. I was twenty-two at the time. Just a few hours after the stroke of midnight on the first day of 2002, I dropped some LSD. At the onset of the trip, I began to feel a very intense sensation of pleasure that escalated rather quickly to a point that was pretty overwhelming, and so I retired to the bathtub to be alone.

Something very important was unfolding for me, I was unmistakably certain of it. The intensity caused my body to spasm and my eyes to close involuntarily. Through the darkness, my consciousness seemed to sink deep inside, revealing instructions from what I instinctively knew to be a more advanced part of my own psyche. I found myself in an abyssal landscape scattered with points of light and a gaseous substance. A spiraling nebula appeared before me, and I sensed a voice saying: *This is your will.* Just then, the nebula began to rotate and develop very sharp precise edges, making a formation like a Chinese star. *This is as your will should be.* The nebula, now a sharp-angled formation, accelerated and my head throbbed violently for several minutes with flashes of all the deceit and the complexes I needed to overcome. I was overwhelmed with all my traumas, fears and sicknesses being forced upon me at once from the depths of the repressed corners of my mind. Eventually I regained composure and could understand the symbolic nature of many things around me. These signs were informing me of the required steps in personal and magical development I was to take that year.

I had previously had many potent psychedelic experiences, often of a mystical nature. But that night was the moment in which I became "hardcore" about magic as the central driving force in my life. I knew for certain that there were latent forces within me that *needed* to be nurtured and disciplined.

"The average structure of masses of people has been transformed into a distorted structure marked by impotence and fear of life . . . Man is helpless when he lacks knowledge; helplessness due to ignorance is the fertilizer of dictatorship."
– **Wilhelm Reich**

The psychedelic experience, when entered in a spiritual context, is an *esoteric* religious rite. The other form of religious practice—the *exoteric* form—is meant for the masses, prepared to accept dogma and paralysis in place of knowledge and experience. Spirituality on a global scale has been reduced to the reward/punishment mentality suitable only for dogs and cats. Esoteric religion, however, requires courage and discipline on the part of the aspirant. Its active approach toward spirituality, perpetually renounced by organized religion, is the key to self-discovery and the ecstasies of mysticism and magic.

Psychoactive drugs, like magic, are not for everyone. Particularly since most individuals are so entrenched in their limited concept of reality that a serious shift in consciousness is far too much for them to handle. These people will almost always scapegoat the magnified complexes that become cognoscente during the bad trip onto the drug itself (i.e., "Acid makes me paranoid.") Although the drug did not create these fears, it may have intensified them or created an obsession with a state of mind ordinarily ignored because it is painful or fearful. If a trip serves as an indicator of the very imperfections distorting one's Dharma and impairing self-development in the Great Work, it has provided the aspirant with profound insight into the aspects of his psyche that he must rectify in order to obtain his spiritual objective.

It is important for any developed human being to realize the distinction between "scary" and "bad." So maybe a mystical experience gives you a bit of a scare—or perhaps it makes your brain throb with all the sordid issues that torture your inmost spirit. Yet if you emerge a more developed and enlightened being, that experience can no longer be defined as bad. The evolutionary process of magic demands extreme self-knowledge. If you're going to look inside yourself to the extent that magic requires, you're going to see some twisted shit—but you're better off than the person who's never bothered to look. The man who fears the repressed darkness of his deep mind neglects his fears and complexes, allowing them to torture him subconsciously and ultimately take control of him.

The fact that so many people find psychedelic experiences to be demonic and terrifying comes as no surprise. Western culture thrives on an infectious lack of introspection. In an environment of intellectually and spiritually starved individuals, the absence of spiritual depth and the ignorance of one's true passions instill an urgent desire for conformity and an insatiable hunger to consume as an attempt to "fill the void." These individuals are the ideal specimens for a docile and efficient population: ignorant, frightened, repressed, idealistically distorted and eager to spend money.

Conspiracy theories aside, the machinations of the Agents of Control (government, media, organized religion, etc.) generate the behavioral patterns of society at large. A vicious cycle is created wherein the tenets of society become so regimented that conventional persons—so entranced by popular culture—are profoundly shocked and disturbed at any experience with genuinely potent spiritual value. In addition, citizens are bombarded with propaganda identifying psychedelic drugs as either Satanic or ridiculous, thus predisposing them to fear and anxiety surrounding their effects.

The War on Drugs (or "The War on Some Drugs" as Robert Anton Wilson has astutely called it) is not about altruism. Its chief concerns are battle over an aspect of commerce and culture that the established authorities cannot control, and repression of the expansion of consciousness, which opens doors of possibility and ascertains a wider scope of reality inherently opposed to materialism and conformity.

A society with the benefit of "other-level" experience is not so easily controlled. Experience in magic creates a strong feeling of self-confidence in an individual, because he recognizes himself as a master over his own destiny. Armed with the power to control his fate and realize his true desires, he no longer feels confined and frustrated by the bonds of his culture and all its false idols, because he has found power and holiness inside himself. Dogmatic religion can no longer govern his desires or frighten him with tales of torture and damnation. The tenets of blind faith seem as ignorance when placed beside a wealth of experience. The gadgets and cosmetics of commercial trade, advertising strength and beauty, are seen as meager attempts at imitating the interior splendor of the Dharma Body.

The established authorities must maintain a culture of individuals who are mentally weak and spiritually lazy if they are to keep hold of their dominion. A powerful mind would question and despise its corrupted governing body. A mind accustomed to seeking out its own answers and formulating its beliefs based on experience and observation would be dissatisfied with, and hostile toward, conformity. An experienced spirit might see religion for the ruse that it is.

How few people are, as Huxley said, "satisfied to be merely themselves?" The makers of magic are the seekers of *suchness*. They set out to familiarize themselves with the inner workings of the deep mind and develop the skill set necessary to exert a degree of control over it. Those who choose this path are dedicated to a liberation from the structures imposed by prevailing ideologies; magic and mysticism are the means towards true autonomy. Blaming society is a waste of time—it is already distorted beyond hope. I don't know when, but at some point, amid the sex, the yoga, the acid-trips . . . I realized that the real guru is within.

At times I feel overwhelmed by my incapacity to do anything about the tragic state of affairs spawned by the profound corruption of our species. If the Tantric philosophy is correct, and the universe is interconnected to a degree where each shift in consciousness affects it as a whole, then the efforts a small group place toward personal evolution are working for improvement on a universal scale.

William S. Burroughs wrote: "The Liberal Press and the Press Not So Liberal and the Press Reactionary scream: 'Above all, the myth of Other Level Experience must be eradicated.'"

In our time, the grasp of Darkness over world affairs has been ever increasing. Bloodshed, ignorance and the omnipresent reign of brutality are thickening on the horizon. Like the Gnostics, who sought to escape the infirmities of the world by inner transformation, it is the calling of today's magicians to thwart the prevailing decay by the nurturing of the Interior Light and the exploration of Other Level Experience.

OPENING AND CLOSING THE PSYCHEDELIC TEMPLE

SIMON FORRESTER

The *Sama-Veda* is one of the oldest human religious texts. Six thousand years ago, its authors sang the praises of getting royally high and pondering the secrets of the universe. The Rites of Eleusis, European witchcraft, Chinese alchemy, Siberian mushroom shamanism, Native American peyote traditions, Rastafarianism, South American shamanism and half a hundred other spiritual traditions combined visible rituals with invisible experiences created with the aid of soul-revealing ("psychedelic") substances. People have been doing this all over the world for the whole of recorded human history.

Psychedelic ritual magic works incredibly well, and is often the primary route through which ordinary mortals give birth to themselves as magicians. Combining ritual magic and a psychedelic substance is a way of voyaging into a new world. The altered states produced in this way are often the only altered states that magicians experience until well into their magical practice.

Because our culture has no overarching myths with which a psychedelic magician connects to by birthright, and a dazzling array of available rituals and substances, most possible combinations have never been tried before. Almost the entire territory is uncharted, and you are on your own in making meaning here. If you see God, your brain will not automatically generate the Great Feathered Serpent, or Shiva, or the Horned God, or any other standard, preset cultural form.

This means that performing psychedelic rituals which have power and meaning can require some preparation in the form of programming and educating yourself, preparing and changing your environment, and bracing for results much more powerful than you might expect. There is little to fall back on in our culture, and you have to be prepared for what you are about to do, which is to pry open the gates of heaven.

The Risks of Psychedelic Ritual Magic

The legal status of most common psychedelic substances is crystal clear: They are completely illegal. If you are caught with an illegal substance, you will likely go to jail. However, the law does not apply equally to all people (witness the exceptions made for Native American peyote practitioners), all substances (many lesser-known plant-based psychedelics appear to be legal), or all places (many things which are illegal here are legal in Amsterdam or South America). A clear understanding of the law in your jurisdiction is essential to stay within it and therefore to stay safe. The additional research and work required to stay fully in compliance with the law is vital foundational work.

Psychedelic ritual magic can permanently damage your body and mind. A single disastrous trip can wreck your life. It does not happen very often, but it does happen. You need to know that before you begin. Mitigate the risks, be careful and be prepared. Luck, youth, grace and skill will carry you a long way but, if you rely on them alone, you could be the one to go down and wind up in jail or a mental institution.

Drive a pillar into the ground. Make a strong foundation. Use your intelligence to understand the risks and minimize the dangers. Use the knowledge gathered by countless generations before you to help you flourish and succeed. Read old sources! It is your birthright as a magician to do what your soul must do to manifest fully in this world, and if that means taking some risks, so be it. But if you run those risks foolishly, the world may take your life.

You have been warned.

Be Prepared to Handle the Results of Your Actions

During conventional ritual, if something is not right, the ritual will usually spontaneously abort. Energy will leave, people will get bored, arguments will break out, and not much of anything will happen. The "nothing happened" option immediately disappears once substances are consumed. Once you pop that tab, it's coming, and nothing short of horse doses of Thorazine will stop it. There is no exit. In this respect, psychedelic rituals are particularly potent. You are going to see this through, whether you like it or not, and that in itself is very powerful magic.

Knowing that you are going to be irrevocably participating in your ritual for several hours means preparing for results. Not in the half-assed "well, it might work . . . " way we so often do, but in the complete certainty that you are going somewhere for a long time, and you had best be prepared to like it or hang tough.

Substance, Set and Setting

Tim Leary, the godfather of LSD in America, taught people to watch and change the "substance, set and setting" in order to have good psychedelic experiences. Mastery of these basic skills is important groundwork for psychedelic rituals.

Substance means you should know exactly what you are taking, in what doses and what the effects are likely to be. Experienced practitioners will sometimes take chances, but in general it is essential to know what you are on and what its effects are.

Setting refers to your physical environment. Most rituals pay some regard to physical setting—colored lights appropriate to the work at hand, or running around naked out in the woods. Psychedelic rituals ask for much more from their setting because, in addition to being a good ritual space, the environment has to support a whole group of tripping people. You need comfy chairs, spaces for people to "wig out," and a lot of security and privacy. All substances taken to a trip should be consumed, leaving nothing that anybody could object to other than a lot of people having altogether too much fun. Ritual trips can go badly, badly wrong for hours at a time: Be prepared to have people try and run out of the trip and into the streets, half-naked and tripping balls.

Pick a setting where you can get away with this. Very few urban spaces are suitable without extensive experience and a very, very reliable crew.

Set is the mindset of the people involved in the trip, particularly yourself. Set is where the magic enters the psychedelic space through your intention and your actions. All psychedelic magic involves creating a powerful set and seeing how far it can carry you.

Set also means mental preparation. You, and the people who are tripping with you, should be ready. It is rare that anybody who has not done magical rituals involving psychedelics can really be ready, so for initial outings, pick companions who are solid, and who will break in relatively socially acceptable ways if the energy, intensity or Gnosis grow unbearably intense, as it is likely to. Anybody on "ground control"—non-altered participants—should be completely integrated into the ritual setup. They should absolutely *not* be some random person who does not want to participate that night.

Metaprogramming

"In the province of the mind, what is believed to be true is true, or becomes true within limits to be learned by experience and experiment. These limits are further beliefs to be transcended. In the province of the mind there are no limits."
– **Dr. John Lilly**

While tripping, your energy body or aura becomes expanded and soft. During that open phase, strongly held ideas can cause your energy body to change its characteristics permanently. The most common form of this, widely known to MDMA/Ecstasy users, is emotional catharsis—sudden release of previously long-buried emotions, feelings and ideas, causing a sudden uprush of well-being and happiness once the initial repressed emotions have cleared.

189

"Metaprogramming" was John Lilly's term for the changes in character which focused use of psychedelics causes. In metaprogramming, ideas held consciously or unconsciously before or during a psychedelic experience engrave themselves on reality around the participants long after the trip is done.

If you spend the few days before a psychedelic ritual focusing on how well your life is going, how happy you are at work, at home, in your relationships, then after that experience the ideas you held in your below-thought awareness will become self-evident realities. What was an idea becomes manifest: Magic has been performed!

Banish, banish, banish, banish, banish, banish, banish. BANISH!

Banishing before magical psychedelic use is at least ten times more important than in regular rituals, where it is mandatory.

I believe that a good chunk of the effects we experience from ritual are caused by our aura literally changing size and shape, connecting in new ways to our physical and other vehicles. One extremely common cause of discomfort while tripping is the newly expanded, open, vulnerable aura coming into contact with "yicky."

What constitutes "yicky" varies for different people: nasty street-zombies spouting poison, unpleasant former lovers playing games, horror movies which the local buff just will not take off the screen, nearly all newspapers. Simply pockets of low, dense energy can count as "yicky" too.

Banishing before a ritual really helps in three ways: direct removal of existing yicky, forming an energetic/psychic barrier to the entry of more yicky and creating a safe, pleasant, clean space into which the energy body can grow safely without absorbing new psychic toxins. Remember that a normal ritual will often self-abort through boredom or arguments if there is enough yicky around to be dangerous: People unconsciously detect the problem, and find ways not to participate. The same protection is not present in a psychedelic ritual once it begins, so be aware that you have to use conscious protective practices to safeguard yourself and your crew for the duration of the trip.

The "Lesser Banishing Ritual of the Pentagram" is very effective and superior to many other rituals of similar kinds. Before every psychedelic experience, do the LBRP or something you have personally found to be more effective than that ritual. It is the benchmark for banishing rituals, regardless of how much innovation there has been since it was first used. If your group are not going to do anything that complicated, a simpler but less effective substitute is presented below.

Planning and Executing

It is important to have a plan. You should know long before the ritual starts who is coming, what they are bringing, what they want and what they are going to do during the trip. Because the amounts of energy raised can be so large, extensive coordination often months or occasionally years before the event are necessary to get a smooth liftoff and, more importantly, a safe return.

You can throw something together much faster, but the odds of success plummet rapidly. The complete-commitment aspect of psychedelic ritual cannot be overstated, and giving people lots, and lots, and lots, and lots of chances to back away is important. Nothing is worse than having somebody who should not be there on a psychedelic trip with you, and these problems are compounded many, many times by ritual components.

A typical running order for the pre-trip would be:

1. A month ahead, decide "I will host a six person ritual on the next new moon."

2. Find suitable locations for the ritual. You may want a few choices to discuss with other participants, or you may have a clear idea of where this event should take place. Either way, try to figure out the where-and-when early.

3. Spend a couple of weeks discussing ideas for the ritual. Figure out, early, if anybody is wobbly, or has different goals, or is going through a tough personal patch and therefore liable to lose it completely under strain. If it looks bad, it usually is. If you throw it together at the last minute, and people do not get a chance to back out or think it through, unnecessary meltdowns can result.

4. A week or so before the event, begin to get the physical gear together. Verify the integrity of the location, pack up your tents and bags and the like in a corner of the house, and start stockpiling all related materials there in the "ritual stuff" area. If you are staying at home, start to sequester the room you are going to be working in primarily. Giving the space time to adapt to what is about to happen is really important if it is not going to be horribly over-stretched by the forces generated by the working.

5. Spend the day before the trip with the participants. Meeting for breakfast and doing ritual at night is one common pattern, or camping out together the night before. Get the group groove established and the social level of reality well sated before the magical level kicks in.

6. Make a razor-clear demarcation between the pre-trip fooling around, and the serious getting-down-to-business. Do not segue through this important transition! Before getting started, recheck the plans for eventualities, like being disturbed, or somebody slicing their hand wide open on broken glass. You can't cover everything, but knowing that you've done what you can helps with peace of mind, and keeps fall-back plans

readily available if something goes wrong. Don't stress out, but don't be an idiot.

Ritual Frameworks

1. Restate your intentions. Know why you are there. Verify that you are ready. Make sure everybody else knows these things for themselves, too. A talking stick ritual, where everybody sits in a circle and takes turns speaking, is the best way of doing this that I have seen. Pass the stick until everybody feels that they have cleared their mind, voiced their feelings and are ready to move on. It can take two hours for particularly big events, although fifteen minutes is more usual.

2. Everybody get into their comfy clothes, or fancy robes, or whatever. Begin the transition into ritual state.

3. Opening ritual. Banish, cast a circle. Take a lot of space now, because you are going to need it later.

If you are not going to do the LBRP or some other real banishing ritual, use the *Aum Flower*. Form a circle of all participants, facing inwards. People's arms should be crossed in front of them, right over left. Now join hands. Vibrate *Aum* loudly and clearly for a couple of minutes, making eye contact with all other participants. Simultaneously turn around in place. You do this by raising your folded arms above your head as you rotate your body—with practice, the act becomes like the unfolding of a flower, graceful and easy. Now facing outwards, continue to Aum. On each Aum step forward a little, until the circle is as wide as it can be. Continue to Aum until you feel ready to move on to the next phase. Break hand contact, turn inwards and bow.

This is no substitute for the LBRP or similar rituals, but does offer some protection and is fun enough that most people will take the time to do it. But it is second best, and you should know that.

4. Bless and consecrate any substances to be consumed. Holding them in hand and clearly stating intentions can be enough, or something more ritualistic might be more appropriate. Remember that nothing should be left after this phase, so you can relax more deeply later on.

5. More ritual, and/or simply hanging out in the ritualized psychedelic space.

This space usually lasts about four to eight hours. Take it slowly at first, and remember to be wary of sudden new ideas for group activities of a magical, sexual or more-drugs nature. Weird ideas can take root quickly, which is why we banished so carefully, right?

The psychedelic ritual space is radically unlike that opened up by substances or magic alone, and you may want to open the temple, spend some time seeing how it feels, and close a few times before attempting more focused ritual, like an invocation. Try walking, talking, making art, writing, reading, making and listening to music, meditating or having sex. Learn how the space works before pushing further.

When you are ready to move further in, try invocations, personal change, contact with the divine, worship and general well-being magic. Results-oriented magic is contraindicated because of the difficulty of holding a group on a single goal. Deep healing ritual can rapidly become very scary. Take it slowly and make sure you have plenty of time to fully complete anything you start. Be gentle and careful the first few times.

People with traumatic backgrounds should be very careful exploring those issues in such spaces. It can be incredibly powerful and healing, but it can also mean spending six to eight hours throwing up the guts of your pain all over your ritual space without the resources to integrate, heal and stabilize afterwards: A visit to hell, in other words. Great care and compassion are needed to do that kind of work successfully. Most "blowouts" in psychedelic rituals can be attributed to emotional issues: Look for somebody stressing out about their mother's health or their partner's substance abuse problems or their own traumatic childhood before assuming that the freak out is caused by astral attack or hobgoblins. If somebody does run into serious emotional problems, be aware that other plans for the evening may have to be postponed. Focusing *all* energy on the hurting person can be counterproductive. Wise practice is assigning them one caretaker, and having people take shifts if that person becomes tired or upset.

6. Start to watch for signs of closure—people begin to look bored, get hungry, pair off in corners and talk quietly, stop writhing around on the floor muttering about angels, stuff like that. When you see the beginnings of closure, quickly gather people together again, start a conversation about closing the circle, and when everybody is good and ready, close and banish. Usually people will still be tripping to some degree for hours afterwards—close earlier than you think is necessary if you have any doubts. If people burn out without closing down the space it can be very harsh.

The corresponding closure and banishing to the Aum Flower opening is to form the large circle again, everybody facing outwards. Bow, then join hands, arms extended. Some food or drink is placed in the center of the circle. Vibrate *Hoom* or *Aum* loudly, visualizing all invoked energies being returned to their appropriate places. Once clear, creep back slowly while intoning *Aum* until standing shoulder to shoulder. Raise hands overhead, and turn your body to face inwards while lowering your arms, so that everybody is facing inwards, arms crossed in front of them, right over left, holding hands just as they were at the start of the ritual. Still holding hands, sink to the floor. Let the remaining energy sink into the ground as you lower yourself. Once settled, everybody should eat at least a symbolic bite of the food, and take a sip of water.

Getting Back to Where You Started

A psychedelic ritual can, with very little effort, cause your perception of normal space and time to be completely abolished for hours. Contact with extraplanar entities is the baseline for a DMT experience, and less than that is often considered to be "not really getting off." Furthermore, psychedelics often deposit the tripper in the world of the entities contacted—they do not appear nicely penned in a dark glass mirror, but all around one as the visions boil and wave.

How you get back from these spaces is a critical part of psychedelic ritual.

If you did not banish before the ritual, then most of the energy generated will immediately weld itself to the astral muck of your physical surroundings. Great clouds of psychedelic energy can get caught up in your ordinary, everyday obsessions, resulting in messy trailing finishes where the trip bleeds over into everyday life for weeks in the most unpleasant way.

Did I mention? BANISH!

Picking when to come back down is a key to success. If you begin the magical end of the ritual too early, then the energy of the psychedelics will still be too abundant, and the ritual will continue after you have, in theory, ended it. This is no good.

But if you wait too long, then you won't be able to get into the same spaces you did when the ritual was going fully, and therefore won't be able to banish at all as thoroughly as you would like. The trick seems to be to close and banish as soon as you know, for sure, that you are in a place where the final comedown is going to be rapid and inevitable, but has not yet begun. The banishing should take the dregs of the trip with it, resulting in a flat, even calm that lasts until everyday consciousness is restored.

It is usually fairly apparent when the time is.

The magical circle created during the opening ceremonies usually serves to concentrate and focus the energy liberated in the interaction between the human nervous system, the psychedelics and the divinity which is often so visible during these rituals. Closing rituals should have some predefined place to put the energy generated. Dedicating all remaining energy to planetary healing, and releasing it into the earth, is one solid approach.

While the energy is still fully manifest, the ritual is still going on. It is important that when groups close, they really close, and make a return to normal consciousness over the next few hours possible and appealing. However, if you are beginning to come down, but are still surrounded by bales of shiny, sparkly goodness, putting it all away again can be hard. This tendency to remain ungrounded must be counteracted firmly! At the end of the closing ritual, you should be *grounded*—perhaps still tripping, but tripping in *three* dimensions of space, and *one* of time.

Often the energy liberated can require half an hour or an hour of active grounding. The initial banishing ritual, carefully walking the perimeters of the space, some dance, eating a little, banishing again, tidying up, showering, rebanishing . . . The idea that you close, and that if you closed properly, then that is all you need to do might be true in theory, but is hard to make work in practice with substances in the mix. Keep on grounding until you really know who you are again. If it is just not taking, you may have begun too early—but once you have begun to banish, you really have to finish. Take a shower as part of the process, enjoy it, and try the banishing again afterwards. If it doesn't feel right, keep going. I cannot stress enough how important this is to one's psychic longevity as a psychedelic magician. All that was opened must be closed!

Make the place you are returning to as nice as possible. Good friends, good food, a hot tub. Doing this kind of stuff at Burning Man, where there is no comfortable, quiet place to rest and sleep, and the nearest decent shower is days away, is insane. Do it at home, or in a place from which you can reach home a few hours after you are done, and the grounding process is going to be much, much more pleasant.

If you close, but the energy is still running too hot, close again half an hour later and repeat until *everybody* feels more or less normal. If one person is still going really hard after everybody else is down, that person is probably holding the energy for the entire group. Nobody is really back until everybody is. This is particularly important to remember in cases of meltdown where one person appears to be having a psychotic break and everybody else appears to be fine. It may be an isolated problem, but it could also be a result of a complex group dynamic which projected the entire load onto one sacrificial victim who is expressing the madness of the entire ritual. Be very careful when doing post-meltdown forensics to remain focused on the entire situation rather than putting the entire focus on a single person, even if they are the only person with symptoms.

The space itself can also require extensive work in the days or weeks that follow a good psychedelic ritual, and in the months or years that follow a bad one. Spaces open in many dimensions due to the combined powers, and you are not going to be in the best condition to close them all immediately following the initial ritual. Revisit places you have done this in and tidy up any loose energy you left there. Keep doing it until the space feels normal, and do it again later. If you have any doubts, revisit the space periodically until it is clean, clean, clean. *Leave no trace is a good rule for more than hiking.* Your lingering energy imprint in a place can cause no end of trouble for others, and for yourself.

One tool I like to use is the ritual of unfolding a blanket at the start of the first banishing, and conceptually having the entire event be contained by the blanket. At the end of the night, banish, and fold it up. Nothing gets into the energy field of the local area, because it is contained by the energetic field you created at the start of the event, represented by the blanket. When you close, everything that is not simply banished or grounded is left in the blanket, taken with you, and finally banished in the safety and comfort of your own home or some other location. This is particularly good for "dimensional instability"—weird ripples in space, people looking like mythological versions of themselves, stuff like that. All of that must be completely banished away at the end of the ritual, regardless of how much work it takes. Madness comes rapidly to people who know that they are elves.

Grounding, banishing and reasserting normal reality after rituals is critically important to your long-term welfare. If you do psychedelic ritual, and something goes wrong, you can leave huge chunks of yourself stranded in the astral plane, seeing dreams as realities. You can get sick because your energy body gets punched full of holes. What makes the practice safe is careful preparation, both long and short term planning, and immaculate grounding and clean up. You have to take care of yourself or, eventually, it all catches up to you and you wind up a burnout like those folks you see in the local New Age bookstore with the icky vibes and haunted eyes.

A lot of those people started out like you and me but were careless, overly ambitious and did not pay attention to grounding and banishing. Their life energy leaked out through the holes punched in space around them and, well, you know the rest.

You can do these psychedelic ritual practices safely, but you have to be gentle, careful, slow, delicate and precise. It is not an easy road, but it is old, strong and has a certain grandeur.

Good luck.

FASTFORWARD TO MELTDOWN

ATMAN

From the first sip I knew that nothing would ever be the same. The bitter, green flavors of yerba maté mixing with a solid earthiness, and a strange electric feeling on the tongue. The first swallow caused little shocks and buzzings to ride my spine up and down. I did such breathing as I then knew how, and pulled on the bombilla again, again. Poured over more boiling water. Five grams was starting to feel like a lot.

It was enough to take me quickly. As my spirit rose, a beam of light, like a white laser, burned through my third eye and sent a bolt of pure information into my entire being. I was distracted by a pictorial retelling of the cosmic cycle of birth, as endless starmatter condensed and exploded, while my body was given a thorough purge and overhaul. I was blessed with the knowledge of, and conversation with, a force so much greater than my monkey mind, that I have never been afraid of death again. I was eighteen. I was lucky.

We were all lucky, the first time, the second time. Perhaps if your karma was bad, you'd get a preliminary blowout and never make progress; I knew one girl like that. For the most part, the first trip is free. It works, you get off, and if you took enough you open up to something greater.

Fastforward to meltdown. Sixteen hits of high-test acid, six individuals, two in the morning, 400 square feet of apartment on the fourteenth floor. No one escaped insanity; one of us was hospitalized, briefly. Everyone survived, although not all the relationships did. It was an explosion, not of the spirit eye, but of the snake that lies coiled around the root. I knew madness, and learned the secret pathways between things through color and number. I saw a great eye, with tentacles extending into everything. I still know where to find it.

It was the first meltdown, but not the last. At some point I realized that melting down was a part of the alchemical ritual we were re-enacting, each time purifying a new stratum. This knowledge didn't make things easier, but learning the technology did. Magic is for real when you're this high, and you can't employ the current fad of banishing through ironic distance.

We survived, and learned, and did our sadhana, our spiritual homework. The trail we hacked through the jungle with machetes has fewer vines and roots, strange brambles and poisonous insects; but the jungle teems on either side, new, raw and beautiful. I cannot give you a map of our trail, although I could show you its secret ways.

What I have for you is an outfitter's list: machete and canteen, hammock and scout rifle, bug dope and binoculars. We've found some things to be useful, and we want you to have them, because we don't want to lose any more of you than we have to.

There are a few things you must know how to do, if you want to have any realistic chance of success. The first of these is the ability to concentrate the will, and you achieve this through meditation. The type is relatively unimportant: Vipassana, zazen, raja yoga are all much the same, and to learn any of them suffices. This is a foundational exercise, and while you may not make a lifetime habit of it, you're going to have to do a regular cycle of it until you've actually learned the trick of it. More is better, and doing it every day is crucial.

The second is the basics of pranayama. Panic in psychedelic settings, like panic any time, is largely a function of poor breathing, and employing pranayama will clear out all sorts of ooky weirdness. As basics, you should know how to take full yogic breaths, pot-shaped breaths, and do alternating-nostril breathing. More generally, you will learn to clean your body inside and out, to hydrate and to eat in a way that's right for you. Also, on a pure technology level, pranayama can fight down your nausea when you're still absorbing the drugs, or make it possible to take another hit of salvia or DMT before going under.

Next, you must know how to banish a space. There are a lot of ways to go about this, but the best of them follow a formula of: clearing, consecration, centering, encirclement, quartering and recentering. You may as well learn and employ the Lesser Banishing Ritual of the Pentagram, which is *lingua franca* among ritual magicians and works as well as anything I've encountered, offering a nice launching point into higher reaches of ceremony. This requires actually doing it, a number of times, before it feels smooth and "right." It often cleans up a lot of old psychic bullshit; indeed, if it hasn't, you're not doing it right yet.

Last important category is charging, or enchantment. You must be able to take a vibration from your internal space and project it out into the world as a result. Sigils are an easy approach to this; for a more sophisticated and powerful take, Franz Bardon's hermetic system is unsurpassed. An important skill in this subset is projecting a charge into a cup of water, which can be visibly felt and imbibed by other people. This is the basis of the Eucharist, and any drug work is going to have the Eucharistic element by its very nature.

Assuming a solid base in all that, and assuming a certain amount of experience with psychedelics, and assuming a certain level of initiation . . . where does it all come together? This: Groups of individual magicians coming together to create a ritual space, amplify their intent and consciousness with psychedelics, and merge their strengths to effect spiritual transubstantiation. If you do not instantly grok what to do with such a current after raising it, do not attempt to do any of this! If, on the other hand, you understand that spiritual food is needed to fuel the transformation that our planet and species are undergoing, know that this is the richest source of that spiritual food known to this seeker.

These workings need not involve physical sex, but there is something undeniably sexual about them. They bring the energies of the magicians together and mix them, so that all who leave the circle carry with them a bit of each who entered. Psychedelic ritual sexual magic is the *simplest* form of this kind of working while being among the most powerful. It is "merely" Tantric practice combined with the use of a psychedelic, such as mushrooms, acid or 2C-B, to dilate consciousness and heighten sensation. Usually the sexual congress itself is found at the end of the effects of the drug, not the peak. It is good to have practiced Tantra in a more sober state before trying this, and I can suggest against having sex with someone for the first time while tripping. I can also admit to having broken both of these rules to my great and lasting benefit.

It is at three or larger that things really get interesting. Two magicians getting into one circle to do work together are probably fairly aware of how they relate together, be it as lovers, training partners, brought together by circumstance or what have you. With three adepts, you have three individual dyads to consider, plus the triad. It gets crazier as you add people, becoming totally impossible to keep track of at seven. Beyond that, things break down, and achieving a high level of coherence is unlikely without some sort of additional structure.

Point being, everyone has to get along, at each combination, at a fairly high level. If you've achieved this, thank whatever powers watch over you and strike while the iron is hot! Spend time and energy maintaining your personal bonds, and think hard before damaging any of them. A good working group is the rarest of things.

Groups of three are relatively easy to manage as a sexual working although, again, familiarity is indicated before trying this. Any larger than this and sexual activity is going to perforce break down into smaller clusters, which may or may not be workable (I have no experience here), but which is probably not the clearest path to group unity in any case. A group of three may wish to divide their labor into one person who banishes the space, another who invokes spiritual energy and a third who serves to ground and manifest the current. A study of the three Gunas, and the alchemical principles of Salt, Sulfur and Mercury, will prove rewarding.

Groups of four can be composed in a number of ways, some clearly better than others. Two couples is natural enough and works smoothly. Three of one gender and one of another is not so smooth, especially if men make up the majority. A nonattached dyad working with a sexually functioning dyad are going to find themselves channeling a lot of sexual energy. Elemental symbolism is a natural to employ, and good adepts should be able to randomly choose an Elemental role and fulfill it correctly.

Our experience has suggested certain definite roles that each of these people play. Earth is responsible for things like preparing the sacraments, making sure there are enough blankets, making food, answering the door: Earth will usually take a lower dose if he indulges at all, and ideally will be one of the hosts. Earth is the guy who picks up broken glass, makes sure people aren't freezing, makes tea and won't let people drink it until it cools off, etc. This role is the hardest for me, but I enjoy it a lot when I can do it.

Water is responsible for the water jug. There should always be a large jug of water at a working like this, and it is Water's role to bless and keep that water, and see to it that people drink enough of it, and not too much. In addition, Water is the mood of the group, and should cultivate a joyous and buoyant attitude. He should also be prepared to provide comfort, cheer and distraction to those lost among precepts of order.

Air has the primary responsibility of banishing the space by whatever means she has available to her. We have experimented with group banishings, and have determined that they are, for the most part, less effective. Group invocations work, group banishings don't; you are welcome to test this but we recommend you try it this way first. This banishing can be as simple as a sprinkling with salt water and a censing with frankincense and sandal, or as elaborate as a three- or four-part Golden Dawn-style ceremony. I can confidently recommend, however, that it include sealing and calling the four quarters, drawing a circle around the working area, and invoking above and below. Air thus has the grave responsibility of remaining alert to any damage to the circle and repairing it, and guarding against spirit intrusion. Air handles censing and smudging throughout the working, these things happening at her discretion. In addition, we have occasionally made Air the keeper of the nitrous oxide, although this role has fallen to Spirit also.

Fire performs the all-important invocation over the sacramental substances, and is the keeper of the flame. As such, she is responsible for lighting and extinguishing candles, and is official bowl-packer and dope-blesser. Fire is expected to provide leadership and creative inspiration—not only that, she is expected to know when to provide these things, and when not to. This role is one that many people shy from, because it has a lot of potential for resentment along with it; Fire is the most visible of all the elements when she is overdoing her job. It is critical, however, and any good elemental trip will have a strong and vibrant fire component. Fire is also often given a ceremonial flashlight, for shining on things that need closer inspection.

Groups of four have the dubious honor of being nonprime in a really serious way, and can easily split down into dyads. In general, a four working is going to have a fairly stable character to it. This is not so of the five working, which is quite dynamic and offers many combinations which are viable. I suggest keeping the gender ratio from hitting four of one and one of the other. We have always employed the five Western elements for five-way workings, adding the role of Spirit to the general betterment of the working. If you can get a fifth person, do it.

Spirit is an enigmatic and changeable role, as s/he is the gate between the worlds. Sometimes Spirit takes extra, or smokes some DMT at the peak of the working, or otherwise pushes hirself beyond the veil, or taps into a lake of oceanic calm and just radiates it. Other times Spirit overloads and spazzes out, requiring the elements to support hir and transform the vibration; and sometimes, Spirit passes out completely. This is why the roles should be chosen at "random"; no one should choose this, but everyone should experience it.

The ritual can go something like this: Earth prepares the sacrament and the space, Water fills a jug, Fire lights candles and starts the charcoal for incense and Air banishes the space. Air admits the rest of the elements, starting with Earth, who places the sacrament on the altar, Water, who places the water on the altar, Fire, who places the pipe on the altar and Spirit, who places the nitrous cracker on the altar. Everyone sits within the circle; the altar is outside the circle in whichever direction suits the purpose and the space. There is a moment of meditation, and hands are joined; usually this leads to some auming to get the energies smoothed out.

Water then gets the bowl of water with salt in it (used in banishing the space) and blesses each person in turn with it; he is then blessed by another with the water and returns it to its place. Air blesses each with the censer, as with Water.

Fire then has Earth bring the sacrament into the circle, and Fire performs her invocation over the sacraments, which are then consumed. Next, Water passes the jug around, after blessing it, and each drinks their fill. Fire then gets the bowl, blesses the contents and passes (always to the left, don't you know). At this point the circle is usually abandoned for a change of scene while people go through their ramping-up process. When a solid plateau has been reached, or a strong peak at least, the elements return to the temple and begin the working.

One excellent way to cohere at a high level is to pass nitrous oxide from lung to lung. One person takes a solid lungful, and using a tube or the lips (the tube actually has much to recommend it) passes the lungful to the next person, who passes it on, and so forth. Five people can usually get effects this way. This can be kept up for quite some time.

Another way is for one of the members, or all of the members one at a time, to smoke some DMT or 5-MeO-DMT. Look, this is hardcore behavior and it will change everything for you, so don't do it casually. That said, there's no better way to tear a rip-roaring hole between the worlds of the flesh and spirit.

Simply joining hands and then overtone chanting is perhaps more powerful than either of these methods, if employed by magicians who have done their sadhana. Didgeridoo and drum, cymbal and chant, can all be brought into the space as an avenue of expression. I have done intense work by practicing martial arts in this kind of space, which isn't everyone's bag; certainly dance and movement have their place. All of this brings up a huge current of force, a puissance that acts to further the will and intent established by the opening ritual.

Understand that this takes courage, physical stamina, and not a little finesse and skill. Weird things happen and you have to deal with them, people start freaking out and you don't know why, inexplicable hiccups in the force send hailstones thudding down around you and cause lightning to fork the tree in the front lawn and all you can do is bristle at the back of the neck like a miserable, wet monkey. Maintain sense of humor at all times! Love each other, and trust in your greater power. Sitting cross-legged and auming with a bunch of freaks for an hour is exhausting and all those candles are going to be depleting your precious oxygen. If you are unlucky, or reckless, things may go quite badly: Relationships may come crashing down around your ears, sanity may be deeply rocked and you may bitterly wonder whether it could all possibly be worth it.

Yet I believe that such work is nothing less than service to the planet and universe, and that there is no more rewarding use for a magician's time and effort than this kind of service. It's like tucking enough good karmas into the bank that you can coast on the interest and invest in the future. Our species' long climb to sentience and the stars is a process of alchemical transformation, and these world-moving rituals serve to catalyze that transformation. With every circle, every sip of magic liquor, every shimmering spark in the eye and every moan of pleasure, we are less worm, and more butterfly.

MY LOVEWAR WITH FOX NEWS

CHRIS ARKENBERG

The modern corporation is far more than a building full of people that creates a product or manages resources. It exists in data space and aetheric space as well as physical space. It is an amalgam of will and imagination committed to self-preservation, growth and profit. It wields media to establish its presence and identity in our age of global trade. The corporation is unified in its focus, and manipulates resources in accordance with that intent. It is, in many ways, an individual composed of many cooperative cells that are continuously recycled. The structure persists by its own intent and inertia. It can move, disperse and distribute itself through data networks. It behaves with a single will, informed by the will of the corporate collective, bent towards the same end: maintaining the existence and continued growth of the corporate entity.

As it grows by the energy of those committed to its existence, and by the interactions the corporation engages in with the external world, the corporation begins to take on a life of its own. When the Nike executives go home for the evening, the spirit of the corporation lives on in media, in the minds of consumers and in its product—behind glass windows, walking the streets, sitting in our homes. If successful, it will persist through generations, evolving independently from those who support its existence.

As the corporation expands itself throughout culture, it leaves more and more traces of itself. Logos, ads, product placement, branded wrappers, product carried by consumers, news items, as well as parody and satire of the corporation—all of these can be regarded as its children, tentacles spreading through the noosphere.[1] As such, they are potential points of entry, tunnels back to the source.

Attempting to follow these tunnels back is, of course, dangerous. Putting yourself in a highly suggestive state and then merging into a corporate logo is not recommended (whose existence is more widely believed in, yours or DuPont's?), but the method is there.

The fundamental assumption of the corporation is that "stuff is important," that certain goods and services will always be necessary to human survival and happiness. Conversely, the corporation is impermanent in its mission to fill that perceived need—it is always struggling against market factors, shareholders, fickle customers, employee negligence, corporate watchdogs and bold journalists.

Strike with the inner peace of impermanence. Strike with the relentless change of time, which brings down all attempts at order. Strike with hawk-headed gods and Egyptian queens. Strike with the legends and myths of humanity, rich with depth, meaning and integrity. Amidst the backdrop of history, the corporation is a fleeting moment. Show it this truth.

Considering this, I asked myself: What corporate entity would be accessible, not too powerful and frightening, but still a force against humanity and nature, worthy of receiving a psychic love bomb? Maybe a new player on the international stage, without a large reserve of aetheric mass—one that nevertheless exercises a vast influence on the collective consciousness of our species, hacking away at the human spirit, subjugating our souls to mindless distraction. One that addicts us to lifestyle branding and feeds us factory lies to keep us buying into the hoax of capitalism. Well, why not? The object of my magical assault, I decided, would be the Fox News branch of Rupert Murdoch's News Corporation and, specifically, its Fox News branch.

To this end, I began by temporarily adopting the following belief system for the duration of the working:

1. I believe that information is available everywhere, holographically.
2. I believe that there are other dimensions, or layers, of reality beyond those we normally see and interact with.
3. I believe that there are techniques for accessing these realms.
4. I believe that thoughts and beliefs are tangible aetheric complexes.
5. I believe that all entities, physical and informational, create a psychic aetheric pattern existing across dimensions.
6. I believe that it is possible to influence such entities from a distance by using the appropriate techniques.
7. I believe that the best techniques (and the safest) rely on compassion and love as the central pillars.
8. I believe that belief is the most powerful tool.
9. In short, I believe in magic.

I then outlined the working I would undertake, as an attempt to wage a magical assault on a large multinational corporate égregore[2] of dubious nature and renowned villainy. I would adopt and completely integrate the aforementioned belief system, and *live* the working, which was planned to proceed over the course of thirty-three days, beginning on September 10, 2004. I would reprogram my own local relationship with the spirit of Fox News, magically assault the corporation and inject a love bomb into its memestream, inspiring truthful awareness and rebellion in its acolytes. And I would document the process, and note the apparent effects and perturbations of the working.

And so I began. The following is my record of the war.

September 10, 2004

Initially, I imagined a magical assault as blood and sweat, hitting hard and low, causing as much chaos as possible, Horus ablaze in red war. Yet I had inherent reservations about this approach, from fears that such an aggressive tack would quickly raise alarms in a spirit born under conflict, to a more real concern that I could damage my own fairly even-keeled nature by moving deeply into an extended ritual space with violent and confrontational intentions.

I clearly needed guidance in the matter, so I lit some incense, put on some evocative music, did a bit of yoga while gently breathing and intoning, and started to adjust my head. I then drummed along to the music, chanting with the singers to the end of the song, trying to really throw myself into that frenzied space—magic is, in large part, theatrics and a hearty belief in what you're doing. As the next track started, I packed a bit of herb, a pinch or two of Syrian Rue and a healthy chunk of DMT into a glass bowl and took three large tokes. The kaleidoscopic alien express came barreling down the aetheric superhighway and slammed into my pineal. Even my teeth felt like they were being flattened into dust. I tried to breathe, tried to Aum and intone, but all my pitiful human functions were being laid to ash. I just held on, listening now to seashores and distant spirits lilting through the psychosphere of my timeless moment, chrysanthemummed and electric. It wasn't until I felt our kitten brush against my leg and lie down against me that I received, out of the seemingly chaotic cascade of tryptamine-induced neurometabolism bubbling through my cortex, the spark of insight I was looking for.

It is this feeling of pulsing, flowing liquid—warm life passing through us all. The touch of flesh, the caress of fur and frond, life straining forward against all odds, cycling through creation and destruction, numinous and luminescent. It draws up forms from the milky honey plenum of everything and nothing, weaving a filamentous golden glowing tapestry of atomic flux, accreting into moments of life, form sustained against the steady march of entropy, dissolution, always dissolving to release the building blocks for recombination and regeneration. Life proceeds from death, and death mirrors life. In our eternal moment of incarnation we live and love, smiling, laughing, sharing our dreams and fears, nurturing those around us, hoping to sustain the sacred presence of the absolute. The blood flowing through our hearts, the steady beat of creation. This is the warmth of contact, the unutterable joy of simple touch. This is love, the secret gift packed with amber and powdered diamonds, wrapped in moist fig leaves and palm fronds. I step gently through your doors, glide down your clean halls into the chief executive orifice humming a simple tune of freedom, and set a pulsing love bomb on your desk. I love you.

Look deep inside and feel the beating of your own heart, the starry furnace solar-plexing and struggling to sustain itself, seeking solace, warmth, union, love. Open your heart and let me in. I will help you heal. Let go of your material addictions, your fear of the real and the sacred. You've already let me in. I've always been there. In the blink of an eye, Shiva will destroy your illusion and tear down the hollow edifice of commodity and wealth that holds you caged and insane, as if it were but one more stalk of wheat swaying side to side along the banks of the Nile, shadowed occasionally by the passing of a hawk under the raging heart of Ra high above, burning bright.

September 13

My days begin with fire invocations using the Lesser Ritual of the Pentagram, and end with pranayama and banishings. I'm being drawn towards compassion and Tibetan mysticism, reading Lama Govinda's *Foundations in Tibetan Mysticism* and listening to tapes of the Dalai Lama. After a few days I can feel my mood lightening, my edges softening and my desire to interact with people growing. My notion is that the spirit of Fox simply needs love, and will respond positively to heal itself.

I turn on Fox News to see a few seconds of "Hannity & Colmes" quickly and suddenly warped beyond recognition, like trying to watch HBO when you haven't paid for it, all warped and discolored. I stare somewhat in disbelief for a moment before the cable rights itself to reveal an image of John Kerry at some speech or other. I'm making contact. I watch and soak up the talking heads, the Fox logo and the hypermedia collage of filtered news items, fair and balanced in favor of the corporate multinational edifice looming over us, unaware of the fluttering lashes of a slumbering Shiva.

September 14

I've been listening to the Dalai Lama every day to and from work. I drive more slowly, don't feel particularly stressed about things and feel a bit more drawn to the people I encounter around me.

The spirit of Fox is an aetheric complex living in the minds of all who are touched by it. I look for potential access points, gateways into the beast, doors through which I can access its spirit. The Fox logo—the corporate sigil—offers an easy path in. I remix it into my own sigil, keeping the colors and general form but altering the memetic content to reflect my own intent. Magical rebranding is like changing the locks on the door.

I light candles and incense, turn out the lights and put on an Indian flute raga. Yoga and pranayama breathing for about twenty minutes, with the mantra "I am inhaling into love, I am exhaling into life." I hold a glass of wine and bless it. It is the blood of Fox, which I adore and consume. Next I bless a glass of water as the blood of life, drink it and let the essences mix within my being. I open my Fox sigil and meditate upon it with short, quick breaths, intoning the mantra *Om Mane Padme Fox,* which translates into something like "I am the jewel in the thousand petalled lotus of Fox News."

I continue chanting and breathing more rapidly, allowing spontaneous sexual currents to arise. Suddenly there's a giant black spider standing over me, touching me with its long, thin legs, gently wrapping me in threads, rolling my body from side to side. As my trance grows deeper and deeper, quickening with my breath and the mantra falling off my lips, the giant spider wraps me in its silky web, my flesh dissolves and the amorphous wave of self narrows into a small point until finally, at the peak moment, I open my eyes and stare directly at the sigil, absorbing it completely and projecting it out into the noosphere with all my will. The spider bites and injects its venom into me as I inject mine into it, aiming straight for the heart. It is my will to bring love and compassion to the spirit of Fox News so that it will become an outlet of truth and freedom.

After a few moments of projection and re-absorption, I turn on the Fox newsfeed. Watching the newsdrip is like seeing the mind of the corporate spirit, like the fluid mirror surface of its aetheric body, dynamic and wrapped in hypermedia. Or at least like seeing the most gripping and overt aspect. It is the psychic product of the entire Fox hive, buzzing constantly to provide mental, emotional and physical energy to produce the relentless collage of events, icons, political figures and opinionated analysis, all cleverly crafted and manipulated to tap into viewers' psyches and play to their animal fears and desires, manipulating their thoughts and behaviors with surgical precision. The newsfeed is a dynamic hypersigil,[3] a multimedia spell cast upon millions of lost apes looking for guidance and belonging, naïvely buying the lies sold as truth. Consider the distribution and the number of viewers reached every moment, and it becomes obvious just how powerful the news media has become. Yet I have the ultimate power right here in my monkey hand—all I have to do is press one button to shut it off. Fox News is nothing without us.

The wrinkles on the news anchor's face show me her own suffering, her humanity, reflecting the tragedies and loss encountered in her brief incarnation. I feel closer to her, like we met at a café once and she told me about losing a parent, fighting back tears. She is a pawn in life, a puppet speaking contrived manipulations fed to her by the Fox psychopropaganda team. Her lack of depth as a reporter, her inability to break editorial policy and speak honestly, eats away at her from deep within. She's not free. She's sold out, traded her soul for fame and good pay, flipped that pentagram on its head and chosen a path of materialism. Somewhere way down, nestled between the walls of her very cells, are the vestiges of childhood, the wild hopes and dreams born on playfulness and awe at the miracle of life within and without. It is here that I've passed into and caressed with the warm touch of Pan. Hold my hand and dance with me in golden fields, young again and free. Feel the life beating in your heart and know that the same blood flows through us all, that political and economic theory, consumerism and foreign policy are shallow maps used to apply control and subjugation to the wonder of nature. Know that you are helping the dark Archons of greed and power rise to global dominance. But know that you have the power to bring truth to light, and to fight for the salvation of the human spirit. You are Fox News.

September 15

For forty-five minutes of my morning commute, I chanted *Om Tara Tu Tara Ture Svaha*—"Homage to you, Divine Tara, Radiant Mother of Compassion and Great Protector." Later, wandering around downtown San Jose in a light shamanic trance, I passed the same bumper sticker twice. It read, simply, "Venom."

September 16

I've only been listening to meditative and devotional music. I find myself driving more slowly and generally moving with less hurry. I feel friendlier towards strangers. The pranayama and compassion meditations are beginning to take effect. It feels as if I'm settling into each moment a little bit more. Deep breaths.

I make the standard preparations of setting the candles to flame and getting the incense to send slowly dancing spirals of scented smoke up into the room. I begin pranayama, drawing prana up through the muladhara chakra at the perineum and into the svadhisthani chakra in the solar plexus upon inhalation, then, on exhalation, sending it up my spine like warm amber sap until it globs around my pineal at the ajna chakra. My visualization is improving, and the coursing pranic energy is growing ever more tangible.

After twenty minutes of breathing and yoga, I can feel that the room has shifted into the aether enough to allow contact. I stare at a candle and feel the purity of its flame. The corporate spirit is always present in this space, just as the aetheric signature of all living things abides here. Thoughts and ideas, feelings and emotions—all of these live within the field of dreams surrounding us, the noosphere. I see the Fox anchors poised before us, reduced to mouthpieces shilling for war pigs and corporate pirates. I see the venomous psychopropaganda dripping from the cathode nipple like soporific morphine, digital and brilliant, collaging time in flicker-quick bursts of manufactured reality, blurred and transparent squares of colored meaning pulsing out of the screen at 80 Hz. For all its decadence and profanity, the technology is bleeding right on the edge, ever blurring the fading lines between authentic and simulated. Beyond the power-mad egos hoping to bend the beast to serve their will, the simulacrum grows ever wider, claiming its own territorial stake on reality. It is our alter-reality, dream world of imagination and asylum from flesh.

Everything is both hideous and angelic. The Great Work of all magic is the re-union of opposites to overcome the illusion of duality, the fall from Eden. The physical world brings separation and difference, yet the aetheric field of dreamtime and imagination is not bound to such geometries. There is no distance and no gap, only vibrations. The psychophysical complex of Fox News is right here in the living room with me. It's right inside my head. We're sharing the same brain. TV is a one-way street, but the aether is multidimensional. Here I can caress you gently and whisper sweet everythings into your spirit ear. Here I can see your soul and the hearts of all those beings in your service.

Abstracted and open, I resigilize my first intent. It is my will to bring love and compassion to Fox News, so that it will become an outlet of truth and freedom. Now the sigil has been folded into an anthropomorphic squiggle of sorts, open-eyed and holding a heart in its left hand. This will be the seal for my love letter to the égregore.

Dearest Fox,

Like a warm embrace my love wraps around you. Remember when we held hands and danced together through the dewy meadow morning, cool and alive? I can't stop thinking of you. It's like you're part of me now . . . like we're nestled together sharing our mother's womb, bathed in warm saline love.

Do you still think of me?

Ever yours,
23

September 18

My mid-morning ritual proceeds as usual, with fire invocation, pranayama and yoga. Chanting *Om Mane Padme Fox* I write my love letter and scrawl out the new stylized sigil. I hold the paper over the incense and bathe it in Bangalore smoke, still chanting the mantra, focusing my intent into the dead tree inked with the spell. As I chant, I visualize those who tend the Fox hive, who speak to me through hypermediated images, glowing and radioactive. I love them all. My base chakra glows with prana, and the spark of sexuality ignites. This fire can be very powerful when cultivated and directed. I'm no Tantric master but I know there's a difference between whacking off and drawing out sexual energies wrapped in mantra and deified visualizations. At a certain point it's no longer sexual. It's just energy work, like charging a capacitor. The release is designed, guided towards the moment of greatest compression, when the flesh dissolves and all that stands is the naked Self, resonating with the echoes of mantra and breath, totally open and receptive, hyperaware, everywhere.

As the giant black arachnid visits once again the golden halls of my eternal moment, wrapping itself around me, playing me with its long thin legs, I strike its flesh, cleaving through its shiny and alien exoskeleton, and inject my spell, antidote to the dark poison brewing behind its innumerable eyes. In that instant the spider is gone, my body is gone, my self is razed to the ground and only flames dance in its place. Breathless and taut, I fall into the sigil held before me, absorbing and pouring my will into the channel opened by its image. For a brief moment there is no difference between it and me, no distance between the Fox News Channel and myself. I give my light to the corporation and its servants. I've consecrated and sanctified this statement of my compassion. I place the letter in the envelope and seal it. After banishing and centering I drop my love letter in the mail.

September 19

Rains came early this morning. It feels like the first day of fall, cold and windy. The clouds are moving through the sky quickly, like large gray ships hovering above. I hop on my bike and head off for a ride up into the forest.

I often find visions in the trance induced by rigorous biking, and the wet mountain woods always seem to be heavy with meaning and inspiration. I press on through the brisk air, beginning the ascent. The muscles in my legs strain as my breathing labors to hold its rhythm.

With each strained inhalation I draw upon the strength and persistence of the earth, and on each exhalation I pulse out a sphere of my own power and life, given back to the forest around me. Pushing harder and harder, my veins coursing with battery acid, the energy of life stokes the furnace of my pounding heart, the hairs on my arms standing up with a steady radiance. Water breaks from my flesh like the wetness of the forest. I'm trying to give as much as I take, recycling the life of these woods and impressing my own love upon it, my own deep longing to give strength to the wonder of biology and the miracle of nature.

Finally I reach the peak, and stop to take in the view down the valley, carpeted in pine and redwood, out to the shore and across the sea. Two small clouds shine silver and yellow, catching the afternoon sun. Out across the expanse, small birds arc and turn above the treetops. I'm dripping with sweat. Everything is earthen and deeply present, like I'd eaten a handful of mushrooms. I acknowledge the spirits of these woods, the aetheric denizens moving through the trees like the river winds and the dense fogs born on their passing. The carpet of green covering the mountain across the valley seems to shift, revealing strange faces like giants nestled between the branches. As I stare off, a new mantra rises in my head. I begin to intone it into being, perched on this vista above creation.

Open our hearts to the love of life. Each time I speak it seems more real, leaving my lips to join the spirits on the wind. The land inspires so much love and adoration and wonder in me, as it has in most humans throughout time. The crisis we see today is symptomatic of our painful separation from nature. We suffer from this loss and the deep ecological guilt of having abused the generosity of our mother for so long. Primate instincts drive us to fight and kill for dwindling resources; misguided religions condemn nature as evil, here only to distract and punish us; and lives stripped of meaning seek material compensation, wrapping ourselves in layer upon layer of *stuff*, lost in an empty playground of lifeless toys. There are great powers lost in this game, trapped by it and doing anything they can to keep it running. They've forgotten the beauty of nature, the warmth of mammalian contact, the value of happiness and the limitless joy of compassion. By feeding and nurturing nature we give it the strength to feed and nurture us. Open our hearts to the love of life.

September 22

Today is the autumnal equinox, a magical day of balance, marking our passage into the waning eve of fall. Unfortunately, I've come down with a nasty cold, infecting my entire respiratory tract. I feel like there's about six feet of phlegm packed around my skull, my throat is scratchy and my head hurts. Nobody else I know has this cold. I'm inclined to believe that getting bit by giant aetheric spiders is not particularly good for one's health.

September 23

It's quite difficult to focus much on anything, and pranayama is near impossible. Given that it has been a foundation of this working, it's very disturbing that my respiratory system has been so targeted. It's now clear that the message I received a few days ago—Venom—was a sign of my infection and the nature of this beast.

I've gathered power items from my magical armory—crystals, a raven feather, an old coyote skull, an egg of rainbow obsidian and a plastic Bart Simpson doll I found at a garage sale thirteen years ago and adorned with a third eye and an anarchy symbol. Each of these holds energies from my life and my path into the dream world of my mirror life. I've given them touch, warmth, image and imagination, meaning and history. They are uniquely my children, containers of identity and psychic reflection poured out from my soul like quicksilver. I hold the obsidian as often as possible to absorb the negative energies occupying my aetheric body.

October 1

Tonight I move into the music studio, which is also, conveniently, a ritual space in its own right, decorated with ceremonial masks, crystals and skulls, bookcases full of grimoires and sacred texts, and a loose magical feng-shui coordinating colors and symbols with the cardinal directions. I light some incense and a candle, turn off all the lights except one soft red bulb. I take a few moments to center and arrive at a receptive and creative state, holding the intent of this ritual in my mind. The working will be cast into a fifteen-minute audio track composed of looped percussion, hand drums, chanting, bells and any other accompaniments that might arise in the course of the recording.

I lay down the initial loop at 128 beats per minute and repeat it out to the fifteen minute mark. This will form the backbone of the track and hold the tempo in check. With headphones on and the mic ready, I grab the dumbec and drum out a repetitive pulse for the duration of the track, swaying gently, rocking back and forth as the rhythm takes hold and moves me into a light trance. I rewind and start recording a new track, chanting over and over the mantra from my first contact with the corporate spirit: *Om Mane Padme Fox. Om Mane Padme Fox.* Fifteen minutes later, I repeat this on another track, again chanting and rocking, losing myself in the mantra, breathing fast and short to keep pace with the fiery tempo. Soon I can feel myself begin to incandesce and jump frequencies, my neurons moving into synch with the rhythm. My self-awareness dims as I begin to merge into the music and mantra.

Again, after fifteen minutes I rewind, grab another drum and pound out the next track. This rhythm is faster, in double and triple time to the first. My hands start to feel like water splashing against the skin of the drum, waves rolling on and off. The motion becomes a pattern in time with the sound of the drum, casual but seemingly distant, as if my hands were massaging a surface in response to the percussive beat. The tracks I've already recorded play along in time, the mantra singing out loud as I drum, reflecting itself off the walls inside my skull, projecting out into the aether.

More than an hour has passed, and I continue to descend into the ritual space of my sonic creation, capturing this magic on digital disk. I rewind and grab a temple bell and a Native American worry bag hung with small aluminum cones; I dance wildly, shamanically, in my studio, ringing the temple bell and shaking the worry bag, letting my own voice rise and fall as it may, chanting mantras and making odd guttural vocalizations which seem to spontaneously rise out of the depths of my belly. I am the trance. There is no difference between the music, magic, Fox News and me. We're all the same thing, vibrating in eleven dimensions, being in five, existing in four—but ultimately flat and uniform. Singular. Does this mic pick up the sweat and orgone evaporating from my skin? Does it record the stirring heat of molecular chemistry or the quantum induction of ecstasis? On some subtle, mathematically esoteric level I'm certain it does. The energy of my ecstasy is burned to disk and archived—materialized and hard copied. Every time it's played, the spell will be *re-enacted*. These fifteen minutes encapsulate the last three weeks of my magical life, all devoted to bringing Fox News to a point of greater compassion and connection with the natural world. Electronic media is the new magic. It's the most powerful metaprogramming tool to date and I pray to wield it for the Light.

October 7

I learned that my cousin had been killed in a car crash yesterday, leaving a new wife and child behind. Death is ever hungry. Twice in the last two days I was almost run off the road by commuters with pro-Bush stickers on their cars. In both cases I was chanting the Fox mantra, and it took all my effort to subdue the rising adrenaline and hold to the prayer. I can't help but feel that I'm starting to draw the anger of those who blindly defend the edifice of corporate patriotism that I'm trying to topple. It's like the spider's sending her minions after me to defend the nest.

Fox News is becoming caustic and unbearable. Such intimate contact with the media collective has sensitized me to its sheer darkness. Roger Ailes, Fox News' Chairman of the Board, Chief Executive Officer and president, was the media adviser for Nixon, consultant for Reagan and campaign director for Bush Senior. When he "left politics" he took the helm of the brand-new Fox News Channel to bring us their uniquely unfair and imbalanced reporting. Now he's manipulating the American psyche to put yet another conservative demagogue into office. Roger Ailes is Fox's dark wizard—the man behind the curtain pulling the strings.

October 8

After waking in the morning, I light a candle, play the Fox Chant on my stereo and turn on Fox News, with the volume all the way down. I cringe when the feed dumps into the room, but I've got to persist and press on. Great power exists in the things we dislike. I begin with the Lesser Ritual of the Pentagram and invoke fire. I've started every morning this way for the past month, and banished fire each night. I sit cross-legged on the soft red square, grasp the obsidian egg between my hands and begin fervently chanting the mantra, *Om Mane Padme Fox*. I try to feel the swell of compassion rising within as I stare into the eyes of those I see. Anchors, Republican and Democrat advisors, and pundits grace the live feed, each speculating on tonight's presidential debate, paying homage to the great kaleidoscopic dance of the Spectacle. This is juxtaposed with live scenes of bombing victims a world away in Egypt, home to pharaohs and ibis-headed gods. In the blood-soaked darkness you can almost hear the sounds of scarabs rolling their dung balls across the black sands, the cries of jackals.

As the eyes of all catch me, I reach out to them with deep compassion and grace. I caress the news anchors, hold them and bathe them in love so that they can look at themselves unafraid and honestly. I want them to carry my intent down the halls of Fox News, spreading it to everyone they touch. Simply looking someone in the eyes establishes an unbreakable magical link. I hijack the news feed and turn it into my own broadcast, back into the cable lines and out to the viewers. Magic pirate TV, live and direct. I hold the obsidian up to the égregore and its ghosts, *Om Mane Padme Fox, Om Mane Padme Fox*, staring at the spinning corporate sigil and projecting love into its heart. There are flashes of power and darkness, but they're subdued, kept at bay by the mantra. I place my hands on sacred objects as I chant. The trance envelopes me. I take up the plastic Bart Simpson doll and place my index finger on the third eye drawn on his forehead, tracing his medial outline, pausing at the anarchy symbol I drew on his chest thirteen years ago, circumnavigating his form completely. It is my will to inspire love and rebellion within the halls of the Fox News building. I stand and banish thoroughly.

Destroying Fox News, replacing Bush, legislation and law—all will fail to solve our problems. The root of the human crisis is in each of us, growing in our own ignorance. The only solution lies in the emancipation of love and the embrace of nature and creation.

October 12

A funeral in paradise. My wife and I drove many hours to bury my cousin in the hills northeast of Sacramento. Death walks among the pines, snapping small twigs. Red skies attended our return across the central valley as brush fires filled the air with smoke—the warm winds blowing through the night and filling the car with the smells of ash and ember.

October 13

This morning, which synchronistically happens to be the New Moon in Libra, is the conclusion of the ritual. The total occulting of Luna is traditionally regarded as a time to plant, so it was under this notion that I enter into the ritual, aiming to plant the seed in fallow earth, dampened with fertility.

Upon waking I enter the temple, light a candle and incense, and put on my Fox Chant CD. I burn white sage and, as my own recorded voice resounds around the room, I walk the perimeter of our home holding the smoking sage and intoning the Fox mantra in time with the music. After drawing in several deep breaths, I rise and invoke Earth into the temple.

After the invocation I sit once again and draw out my DMT pipe. Hitting it gently, I burn off some of the resin and inhale a decent-sized hit—just enough to raise my vibration a bit closer to hyperspace. As the light rush comes on, I continue chanting the mantra, *Om Mane Padme Fox, Om Mane Padme Fox*. Still buzzing, I stand and invoke the god-form of Heru-ra-ha, the solar manifestation of Horus, the crowned and conquering child. With burning fires my mask turns to that of a hawk, the wings tattooed on my back sweeping out above me catching the air. "Complete emancipation of the human species."

With my circle squared, the temple purified and banished and my allies on hand, I turn on Fox News, prepared to defend myself against the égregore. Once again, the psychic onslaught of manufactured lies, the carefully crafted simulacrum, surgically shaped and edited, comes streaming out of the cathode ray tube in Luciferian electronic brilliance. Muted, I watch the talking heads, the lost light beings addicted to their own chemical stews of memory and emotion, fear and desire, chattering on and on about the day's Talking Points, force-fed by management to be regurgitated to the captive audience. Breathing deeply, I say prayers for their souls. Tracing the contours of Bart with my right index finger, I pray for greater rebellion and overt agitprop from the writers of "The Simpsons."

I continue chanting the Fox mantra, the track on loop, and begin to feel the animal rise of sexual energies. Sex is, in the end, the greatest weapon I have. My tactical strike, my warp drive and love bomb. Chanting louder and louder I lose myself in the technique of karezza, nearing the edge of orgasm, then backing off, again and again. It gets dizzying as the flesh burns and melts away layer by layer, my hawk wings spreading, the mask flashing between Heru-ra-ha and the face of my avatar, advertising my unconsciously sigilized intention. My eyes focus on the TV, roll back into my head, then vibe the corporate memeplex further. The great spider draws near, tapping at the light shell of my circle, moving from side to side, yet unable to penetrate my defenses. Heru-ra holds firm to my foundation.

Another climb up towards climax and a single ray of sunlight burns through the smoke and falls before me on the red square of my temple. I hold Bart in my left hand, letting the sun fall onto his face. He's my link, my vector, my inside man. As the sun illuminates him from within the semi-opaque hollow plastic of his being, I project my will to inspire love and rebellion within the vast extended entity that is Fox News. Backing off again, I return to the DMT pipe.

Time is standing still except for the steady mantra rising from my lungs. Dust and smoke seem to hang in the air. My temple is a vessel for god, for the Absolute, a vehicle for peace and compassion and conscious evolution towards harmony and unity. I'm vibrating and metaprogramming my being to vibrate more, to up the frequency, to tap into the quantum depths of existence and make the conditions just right to receive and amplify this final spell. Burning, swollen, heart pounding, flames licking at skin, bits of my flesh rising on thermals like fine glowing ash. Everything that was once on the outside of my head is being pushed back in, indistinguishable, undifferentiated, pulsing, contracting into an infinitely dense point existing only in the center of my pineal gland, as if my entire being is but a soft quanta of amber light thrown off by a single molecule of tryptamine sparkling in the aetheric retina of my third eye, momentary and eternal. Winged and masked.

As the star collapses into itself it rebounds with the intensity of a thousand suns, exploding out into supernova, vast and outstretched to the edges of the universe, the outer bounds of the body of Nuit. With it streams my projected will, focused and powerful, into the eddies of quantum flux, the alchemical hologram of creation, swirling and whirling, caressed and cajoled into receptive harmony. I'm a capacitor, fully charged, releasing my voltage in one thunderous burst. I'm the butterfly flapping my wings at just the very right moment in spacetime to dance along and iterate into one bitch of a hurricane. I am, after all, a God. Just like the rest of us. My word is law and I've spoken loudly.

I stand and make my grand proclamation loudly—that we may empower the earth to empower us; that we may throw off the shackles of oppression, greed and power by finding peace and compassion; that we may come together and manifest a new world for the love of life and liberty. I banish Earth in all directions with great intent and focus, then return to each of the four cardinal points to acknowledge them further and give thanks, humbled and gracious. I grab the remote, face the Fox newsdrip and exercise the greatest power I have:

I turn that shit off.

Epilogue:

A few hours after the final rite, news hit the web that arch Fox blowhard Bill O'Reilly was involved in a sexual harassment suit with his former producer Andrea Mackris, the sordid details of which were immediately posted and mirrored across the web. Many elements must coordinate for such an event to come to be, and I take great solace knowing that my work fed those energies and helped inspire rebellion within. Somewhere within the quantum plenum, atoms are vibrating with the sublime will of my intention and the deep, instinctual longing of the species for harmony and freedom. The currents are moving and I've given my love and life to help them along.

Life is so very short, and it's a profound waste of time to get too consumed by matters of the Kingdom. Anger, fear, hatred—these are the real enemies. These are the underlying motivations perpetuating the atrocities and injustices ravaging the planet. Fox News is really only a container of such maladies—a provider, infecting and addicting the masses to pulp fictions and reality simulacrums, carefully washing our brains with lies and distractions. It would be pointless (and dangerous, as I've seen) to charge head-on at such a powerful psychic force. Better to influence individuals, to reach up from the earth and tease out those far distant memories of our days in the trees, connected and alive.

The Fox memeplex provided the hooks into a good chunk of the human unconscious—a hypermedia conduit or vector through which I could contact and influence a very large number of people. It would have been enough to be personally satisfied with having contributed my energies towards a noble end. The O'Reilly suit is just the icing on the cake. I'm certain that the currents flowing through the spirit of Fox News, down its halls, through its employees and into the video feed, have been edged closer to the humanitarian values and dreams held, visible or occulted, in the hearts of all people. In the process, my own magical activism has realized its core value as a compassionate path, not a provocative or confrontational one. And certainly there's been plenty of communication and guidance, from tryptamine realizations and cryptic dreams, trance, ritual, divinations, invocations, meditations; and there have been psychic battles with a giant astral spider, road rage, civil suits and the sudden presence of Death in the lives of loved ones. It's difficult to really understand all that's happened, to decipher the meta-patterns woven through the ritual. It always takes time to integrate novel and transformative experiences.

Addendum
Dear Fox News,

I can't go on like this any longer. I feel like you're only concerned about yourself, obsessively lost in some fabricated illusion. You don't seem to care at all about my happiness, so how can I continue to care for yours? I know that deep down inside there is a kind and gentle person that will blossom some day. But I need to move on with my own life. I really think you should try to get out more often and go for some walks in the country. You really ought to think about some therapy. And not that Freudian shit.

I'll always love you . . . but please don't call anymore.

Sincerely,
23

ENDNOTES

[1] Russian geochemist Vladimir Vernadsky's "sphere of human thought," the third layer of development on the planet after the geosphere (non-living matter) and the biosphere (living matter). – Ed.

[2] Term used by the Weimar Republic-era (and ongoing) German occult order Fraternitas Saturni, as applied to their group-created intelligence GOTOS (who bore an odd resemblance to the vampire in F. W. Murnau's 1922 *Nosferatu*, a film that future FS member Albin Grau was the art director for). The term égregore has become a prominent feature of chaos magic and is often applied to group-created but self-directed discarnate intelligences; i.e., corporations. – Ed.

[3] Grant Morrison's term for a piece of magical art or fiction which, by mirroring the "real" world and then making changes in itself, can cause actual sympathetic change within the world (similar to voodoo doll mechanics.)

HUMAN
GENOME PROJECT

THE SAGE'S GAME
George Holochwost

The Sage of the Falling City felt the pressure of glass on all sides of him, the opening of the cylinder only inches above his skull. Below the rounded bottom, a gold fire stirred. Breathing became painful and icy, while attempts at movement burned with enraged frustration. His reddened eyes shifted in thin pools of mucus, straining to make clear the images of things-once-loved that wrapped like a vista around his smooth prison.

In the days when his head was not so heavy, he walked along the seashore, breathing in the salty wind. Loved by the sun, he would stretch out on the softened sand and push his limbs through it—through the warm surface and into the cool underneath. In those days his cup was emptied by the instincts that made him so simply present.

It was not long after that the terrible ordeal happened. This was the day that the Game was taught to him. Like many games, the rules were plain, and sides were chosen. Thinking himself so very bright, the Sage (who had not yet come to the Falling City and was not yet so wise as to be called a Sage) looked at his Opponent (who wore the Mask of "other-but-was-not") and grinned in a show of self-assurance.

The game had many pieces but there was only one rule—to win. The Sage looked out at his pieces and strangely, his Opponent in the mask chose the exact same ones. The Sage most liked the smiling Fool, in his bright motley that jingled when he rolled and leaped across the worlds while the wonders that were spun from the sky formed the flagstones of his path. The Opponent chose the King who conquered and ruled all that he surveyed, wrapped in the bright jewels of gold, purple, red and black.

The game began.

"Ah, but the Fool has tricks and is so very clever," said the Sage to himself, so very confident in the paradox of his favorite piece and its associates.

The game went on for a very long time, and in that time the Sage began to lose his pieces to the aggressive strategies of the Opponent's King. He lost the Song, the Wind, the Sand, the Twins, the Joy, the Eyes, the Sun.

"Ah, but the Fool has tricks and is so very clever," said the Sage to himself, who now told himself that the pieces didn't matter. He lost the Trees, the Smoke, the Angel, the Devil, the Moon, the Sea, the King.

And still the game went on for a very long time. And in time, all but the Fool had been taken by the Opponent who had played so deftly and with such close attention to his goals and to this strange game as a whole.

"Ah, but the Fool has tricks and is so very clever," said the Sage, who only had one piece remaining. In this way, he became quite terrified, and very cold. The game was not so easy as he once thought. And then the Fool was taken and the game was lost.

The Sage in his shame and anger rose from the table and shook his fist in the face of his Opponent who also rose from the table.

"I will defeat you!" said the Sage. "We shall play again!"

"Oh no, dear Sage. We will not. For you have broken the only rule that this game has. For you have lost!" And with that, the Opponent removed the Mask of Other-But-Was-Not and looked upon his face that was a mirror in which the Sage could gaze into the eyes of his despair.

In terror, the Sage fell back and grabbed his walking stick (which was simple and plain and without pretense) and he turned on his heel to run from the hall that was now flooded with cold shadow.

For days he ran. Days. Nights. Days. Nights. Days. Years. Until the spires and towers of the Falling City rose up around him.

"How will I ever be safe from this Opponent who pursues me?" asked the Sage, who looked desperately for a place to hide. He found secret houses, covered in strange symbols, that one could only enter if they knew the special words and signs. He found powerful tribes where there were warriors who would protect him with their spears and axes if he would be their brother. He found ancient monasteries of stone and silk that would give him sanctuary if he would take their vows. He found hot pools of nectar that steamed with the vapors of transcendence and the bouquets of the one thousand fruits of pleasure that he could eat, and so forget all things for a time. He found great libraries that stretched on beyond the limits of seeing, where he could lower his head into codices, tomes and grimoires in cells deep within their recesses. He found exotic halls of rich lords that writhed with orgies and the talk of power where he could take refuge in the politics of ambition. But none of these would do. For whenever the Sage found comfort in these, the footsteps of his Opponent would shortly find him.

So with this in mind, the Sage wandered . . . and wandered . . . and wandered the streets of the Falling City. And in the darkest corner, off the darkest alley, off the darkest avenues (that wound between the spires and towers of the Fallen City), the Sage found the Hole. And that is where he hid.

But the Hole was very small and very dark and very, very cold. So the Sage dropped a fire coal into the Hole, and he folded himself up, all small and tight, and squeezed his way into the Hole, and although he could not move, and although his breath was staunched by the dust and cold air, the Hole was the safest place he could be. Or so he thought.

For it was but only a moment later that the Sage was looking up into the face of his Opponent who wore the Sage's face and was he.

"Oh Opponent, what shall become of me? I have lost, when I should have won, but you tricked me into losing your terrible game! I will not leave this hole, for although you have found me, you cannot reach me!" said the Sage. Who had no room to tremble.

"Oh? But your hole is not so safe . . . " And with a wave of his hand, the Sage's Opponent made clear the predicament of the arrogant Sage who had lost the game so long ago.

The Sage of the Falling City felt the pressure of glass on all sides of him, the opening of the cylinder only inches above his skull. Below the rounded bottom, a gold fire stirred—breathing became painful and icy while attempts at movement burned like enraged frustration. His reddened eyes shifted in thin pools of mucus, straining to make clear the images of things-once-loved that wrapped a vista of unreachable joy around his smooth prison.

His prison now stood at the top of the highest tower, for all the people of his world to see. And there he stayed for many, many years. Until one day, when he had grown very old and quite sore from his prison, he looked beyond, far to the East, where the great ocean stood, that he had so loved when his head was not so heavy . . .

And thought . . .

"I wish I had never played that game. For against the Opponent that is myself, I cannot win. It was by the sea that I was happy. It was by the great ocean that I felt loved by the sun, and could stretch out on the softened sand and push my limbs through it—through the warm surface into the cool underneath. In those days my cup was emptied and I was happy.

"I will not play this game."

And with that . . .

The voice of his Opponent was carried on the wind. A wind that broke his prison with a mighty gust and carried him far off beyond the Fallen City, back to the Sea, where he removed his Sage's robes and set down his walking stick, and looked out at the sea and smiled as he breathed in his freedom.

And the Sage of the Falling City was no longer, as he had once again become the Child. A child who knew that the only way to beat the Sage's Game was not to play it.

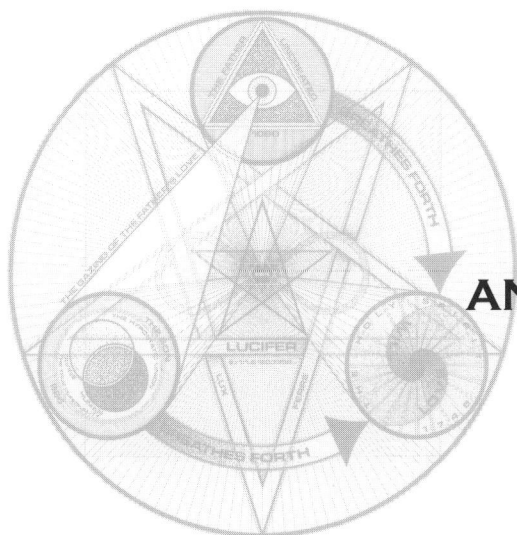

ANGELS OF CHAOS
ELIJAH

"You want the word, that's what you've come for. My advice is, don't ask! Do as I do! Seek out gold—but not my gold—and guard it."
– The Dragon, *Grendel*, **John Gardner**

"Even the gods deserve their pain."
– The Lady's Law

It is my purpose to convey to the reader my experiences as an explorer of the psychocosm of Self. I hope to convey this knowledge with a sense of practical application, and as a possible future arena of exploration for the in-spiring initiate. The techniques and methods used can be adapted to many different formats and aims.

The chaos magical approach is that of the violate. This approach is even subject to its own nature. To achieve the ecstasy of heaven one should violate the violate.

One of the advantages of the chaotic standpoint lies in its practice of paradigm shifting. Note that this perspective is a paradigm in and of itself (other perspectives are possible, of course). How this shifting is viewed is a matter of the magician's personal taste, but I have found that "chaos magic" concerns itself with something that underlies all of the filters of existence. In chaos, all is possible, including nothing. Apparent dualities can be split up and torn apart, fractalized, meshed and fused together in myriad ways. Much as matter and antimatter reactions give rise to liberated energy, reactions of meaning can liberate enormous amounts of free belief. Duality can be expressed as the equation *0=2*, the nominal "truth" of duality manifesting from Nothing. This concept permeates human existence—much in the same way that one sees oneself when standing between two mirrors. It gets clearer as you look slightly askew, with reflections bending hyperbolically to infinity.

Let me present how I have come to glimpse at the madness of truth through chaos magic. Truth can be a very loaded word, of course. Truth and untruth to the mind dealing in the dual are, and can be used as, tools for various forms of manipulation. There is an underlying factor in all of *this* (reality), which is the truth that underlies these tools (beliefs) that we use. This is not true in an absolute sense, but true in probabilities. You shall know truth by its paradox; there are no absolutes (this is false).

There is no limit to desire other than desire's needs.

This will become clear as I approach the concept known as Knowledge and Conversation of the Holy Guardian Angel, from the "chaotic perspective" outlined, above all, in the light (and dark) of truth.

Theory

> *"One thing which I seemed to have lost at first was trust; trust in myself and belief in the vomit of others."*
> – WE, 1999

A long time ago, in a land far far away, there was a magician who sought out God and, more specifically, God's way in the world (magic). He searched the world and found tricksters and black magicians, but none of these satisfied his quest for meaning and truth (*no duh*). In his later years, he ran across a magician living in isolation named Abramelin. This guy seemed to be in contact with some real truth here, and initiated our wandering seeker into secrets of the Qabalah, and a type of "Sacred Magic" for achieving contact with the Holy Guardian Angel through the grace of the most high.

The manuscript of *The Sacred Magic of Abramelin the Mage*, which is composed of instructions passed on from Abramelin for performing the Operation, gives the mindset to adopt as well as prayer-form rituals, which obviously must be personalized by the magician using them. Other magics are also given to poke around with (such as a spell for summoning an army to do your bidding . . . ?) My own version of the Operation is given herein.[1]

The best way for me to illustrate the nature of the Holy Guardian Angel is to tell you of my own form of the Operation and the results thereof. Here's a little theory based upon my Song of Illusion:

- The Holy Guardian Angel is a manifestation from probable time, of the Self (distinguished from the self) in unity and perfection of Will.
- The Angel is a reflection of the perfection of the Magus. Unity is desired to align more fully with the Will. (I shall not touch upon the "black" or "white" brotherhood, and shall talk more fully of something called the Scarlet Brotherhood.) There is another aspect of the Angel that is a reflection across the Tree of Life and into the Tree of Death. This is a "natural" course, as every action includes its inverse.
- The Angel is partly an astral construct towards which energy (prayer-form) is devoted to allow for manifestation.
- The Angel is also an independent being.
- The Angel has access to knowledge (both mundane and magical) that is currently beyond the magician's scope, and can reveal all manner of things.
- There is a Self that underlies self and transcends the temporary ego manifestation of the magician. This ego is a mask of the Self (a.k.a. Kia, shhh). The ego is of the Self and by the Self. Identification is both the key and the cage here.
- The Angel is the thin silver cord of the Horizon, demarcation Zos-Kia. The Angel's unity with Choronzon is an explosion of duality towards a continuous transformation.

Subscribing to all of the above can be of great benefit to the magician because it offers him/her a handle in the formulation/invocation of the Angel, as well as a magnificent channel with which to learn, grow and explore the infinite worlds and beyond. When faced with nothing, one had better well do something!

A side note on dangers. Any invocations and interaction with the outer spaces should not be undertaken until after initial contact with the Angel is established—and *definitely* not in the demonic bindings phase. It seems that the pathways extending through nonexistence, also called the Tunnels of Set, are filled with all manner of energies that can drive an organism completely insane *at best*. The Angel acts as a buffer zone for these experiences, and/or guides the magus in explorations. To those who find Our Lady's order in Scarlet: Blessed art thou among Chaotes.[2]

The Formulation of the Rite of Godhood

"The magician is the ultimate charlatan—for in his games, he fools the very universe."
– Frater Halucifuge, 1999

Let me start with how this all came about . . . It was some time ago that I was involved in a relationship. I had a great deal of emotional attachment. Anyway, something happened in that relationship which was so completely out of the blue, and unexpected, that it shook me to the core of my being (an event which is not out of the range of human potential but was emotionally catastrophic due to a lifetime of programming). My Heart was shredded; my world was shattered. (Flash to a sequence with Elijah Forlorn on the dance floor, the synchronous words ringing out: "I feel like I'm going crazy . . . I feel like I'm going insane . . . " Being the opportunist magician that I am, I decided to try some experiments over the next few days using the great deal of emotional turmoil that I was in. I opted to try the Neither-Neither technique of Austin Osman Spare. I took the images and profundity of Love, my love, in the highest state of adoration and joy and "fused" it with that of its perverted form—the fusion of *apparent* opposites.

In their mutual annihilation, not only did the pain cease, but the liberated free belief (energy) acted as a conduit for something more. Something, which I would realize later, that had been with me my entire existence. I was entranced, and began writing. I wrote out the following, not quite understanding what I had composed:

Grendel's Had an Accident
An X-cursion Into the Land of Liberation
An Invocation of Grendel's Desire

For the initiate to incorporate into a preferred format. The temple is ready, the self is prepared, the trance is induced, the desire stated . . . the summons, the closing, then comes the laughter.

ACT I

Blacker than black, Midnight of Death I summon your bleak Oblivion.
Time again and Illusion seemed drawn up from the heart of Nothing, I call your Bliss.
Take my Pain as an offering to my Self
My hurt is of the Multi-verse, an empty Void in my chest.
Despair, gods of existence, your drama shall reap its wretched sickle on you all.
All shall be undone; the pentagram broken; the pact no more.
An elicitation, an event; something more, a mirror image amongst the swine.
My magic is Death, my death is Life, and my life is Ecstasy.
This is my path, this shall be the cycle, this call to you oh Grendel.
Adoptive son of the Dragon, the Word is upon our shoulders.
Tell of Nothing, let us be destroyed by our Desire so God may die.

ACT II

My soul screams in orgasmic contradictions
—Silxofax Mantadragonia Ziflantamaxia Natasz
Azaximanda Callraptuption Sunta Faxim At Rax Zenfixamaphillaheme—
Grendel, who weeps upon existence, I pray unto myself.
Baphomet, fusion of Being and of Nothing, let us tear Choronzon asunder.
Mighty Set and Lord of Morning let me bear the joy of Liberation.

My Light and my Darkness, this is Nothing, my Self of god, a prophet reborn.
To invoke my being I become—Xephera Xephera Azazas Azathoth—
The Joy of Chaos is my soul. I AM and I AM NOT

ACT III

The Skull is now a silent object, staring mute at me.
The Eye is two-dimensional again, the mage walks alone and
as poor little Grendel has had an accident, so may you all—

I also found that dredging up the memory of that night brought renewed turmoil, which allowed me to nullify it yet again. I was intoxicated for weeks. (This memory was eventually exhausted by this technique.)

At this time, I was also about to undergo initiation into the AutonomatriX,[3] and had to write an initiation ritual. I channeled all of the energy I had into this rite, called the Rite of Godhood. Ever since the composition of "Grendel's Had An Accident," I had noticed a presence about me, something there but not quite there. It did not feel menacing—on the contrary, it felt like home. So I continued. I had some vague notions of what the Holy Guardian Angel was supposed to be, and decided to incorporate something along these lines into the Rite of Godhood. I opted to use the desire of "GodPath" in accordance with one's will.

In addition to "Grendel's Had An Accident," I now present the Rite of Godhood and my exact journal entries of the ensuing Operation, as well as the events transpiring since then.

The Rite of Godhood

Purpose: To call upon the God of Self (Holy Guardian Angel) and "true" purpose. To cause great stirrings in the other consciousness in accordance with one's will. To attune the mind which is not Self with its god path. An advanced initiation to the magical way. Prepare the temple as one sees fit.

Items: Sigils of Set as isolate intoxication. Sigils of Lucifer/Christ as unity and love in shadow light. An ice cube. A sacrament (an immediate intoxicant, in this case, ketamine).

Seal the temple, call Watchtowers to bear witness and protect (also familiars).

I.

Open a Chaos Vortex.

II.

The performance of "Grendel's Had An Accident," Act I (experience a hurt while acting).

III.

a) Perform callings of Set as isolate intoxication and Lucifer/Christ as unity/perfection in shadow light. Summon using spontaneous words (use of constructed sigils).

b) Statement of Intent: "It is my will to manifest that which is potential. It is my will to find the potential lying in wait. It is my will to evolve. It is also my will to ask for a sigil of chaos to call and aid me/us."

c) Declare: "Xiqual Wec!" "Ongo Wec!" "Tomargo Wec!" "Phenomenize dark matter! Do dark matter! Dark matter by whatever means necessary!"[4]

d) Melt the ice cube on your forehead and open the third eye.

e) Perform "Grendel's Had an Accident," Act II.

f) As you say the following words visualize a cosmic chaos-egg around the self. At this point partake of the sacrament. Start spinning around and around, as a dervish. Spin faster and faster while saying the following: *What was hidden has been found, what was silent now is sound, from the darkness to the light, will of god, strength and might. What is mine is mine to keep, send my will, shred the sleep, from the darkness to the light, Binah-Chokmah my will, my might.*

g) The ecstasis part:

From within the dark earth sears
—Visualize a crack in the chaos-egg—
Transmutations, powers and fears
—The crack widens—
From the darkness to the light,
I declare this now by will and by might—KIA!!!
—An explosion as the egg cracks open, Gnosis ensues . . . collapse—

Note: A sigil should manifest during the trance. This is one's own chaos sigil from the universe. Recover.

Banishing

a) Performance of "Grendel's Had an Accident," Act III. As one speaks (slowly) imagine that your voice echoes throughout all of existence. Issuing forth a deep and powerful declaration. (Of war?)

b) Banish as one sees fit. Formalized. Gods (destroy the sigils in fire), watchtowers, other.

Post-Ritual

One must have some form of celebration following the ritual (raves are recommended). Worked sigils to cast should be fired during this celebration as an enactment of Desire.

Final

The rite seems very formalized, but is really not. The only parts that need formality are the intents, but the visualizations and words should flow naturally. The only timing-critical part is, of course, the trance. As per the chaos sigil, who knows what it is/is not. It may be a power, information, spell, calling, banishing. We do not know. A no-mind technique may be of use in divining the sigil's meaning (it has not failed me yet). Also look for "synchronicities." We do not know in what way the sigil will manifest, or in what form.

Welcome to Eternity.

Godhood Results (Journal Entries)
November 1, 1998

The Rite of Godhood was performed. Upon arriving at the site, I realized that I forgot (I think purposefully) my sigils and guidelines for the rite. I performed the rite from memory and constructed the rest. Some very interesting things occurred. The first was that, in arriving at the ritual, I felt sort of hurt/angry because the drummers did not want to partake of any intoxicants with me. I did not know them very well and they did not trust me. I do not blame them as I probably would do the same, but this bothered me. This "bother" seemed to manifest more and more (after the rite) and it seems that similar factors have been brought to the fore, as if the rite induced and called for an analysis and correction of my personality in this arena. This is where I am at now, confronting different "issues." Another interesting thing occurred during the rite: Upon calling Set, I felt a very cynical presence—it felt like, "Oh look, another god aspirant." A sigil manifested during the rite—a sigil whose attribution is the Phoenix.

Its number is 76—it sort of looks like a 7 and 6 combined. Upon being in an "in-between" sleep/awake state on Samhain night, a voice came to me. It sounded like a multitude of robot-like voices in unison, and said something to the effect of, "You were given the first of three. You must plan. You must do this again." I find this all highly unusual (as if yelling at the moon is normal?)—it also seemed as if before I heard the voice, when I closed my eyes, a picture, a formulation of some sort was "mutating." I also noticed that I placed a strong emphasis on the Setian part of the rite, and the calling of the Southern Watchtower was very strong. Ketamine was used as an intoxicant during the rite, and some pot later that night in celebration at a local rave. No personal sigils were fired and again a somber self-reflective feeling saturates me.

This being(s) whose voice(s) I heard, if it is a being at all, frightens and excites me. It feels as if the next part of the rite should be undertaken at the full moon (in a few days). For this part the moon was about sixty-five percent full, and the rite was performed on October 30 between six and eight p.m. (members of the AutonomatriX sent energies my way to be utilized during the rite, from across the U.S.).

November 4

I performed the ritual again last night under the full moon. This vision did not seem as powerful as the first vision, but I was granted another sigil. This one resembles the hand of Eris. It is like the uniting of worlds, the touching of heaven and hell.

November 10

My birthday (Tuesday, sacred to Kali). I'm twenty-four years old. I feel like I'm ninety. I got another tattoo today, on my left shoulder blade—an eye surrounded by a flaming sun, a "symbol" of Kia/Chaos and Self. I channeled all the pain from getting the tattoo into a prayer to amorphous Kia and the Angel.

November 11

A vision of the third sigil of the three. This ritual was performed astrally.
The first sigil is my will in Heaven, the second a gateway/transition and the third my will on earth. The third's letter is J. I do not fully comprehend all of this yet.

November 22

Extreme emotionality last night (due to lack of sleep and life stuff). This emotional unction led me to offer another prayer to my Angel, my Self, my god in the future. I felt the presence moving around me, as if someone was in the room with me. We are moving closer (I can feel it). These prayers and callings must be focused and channeled into one direction to achieve full Gnosis (Knowledge and Conversation).

December 2

I write this now in the last stages of ecstasy. The entire universe is at play. I invoked the gods tonight and was granted a vision of who and what I am. A./As./Grendel—these are WE. The universe was/is/will be a spinning wheel, at the center is/was the Omega Point, the end of all and the beginning. *God?* This was something beautiful and blissful beyond all comprehension. This was the heart of the Chaos star. This Oblivion was a loop in on itself, like a Klein bottle.

It was all "in" the universe; there was something else, but that comes later. This thing that was all, was the culmination of being. The point towards the evolution of all things. There was a hierarchy—not in the stupid human sense, but stages up the ladder towards this oblivion. One could not escape it ("in" this universe) because it is every-where, yet one can be closer to the center. The words fail here—where does a Moebius strip start or stop? It was like an involuted manifold, but the "hole" was part of it also. The gateways and birth canal, this thing was.

The layers came as beings of which I was a part: I am/will be/am not As./A. It seems A. is like the older brother to As. and Grendel is me/We. I was given this meaning and conversation by the three sigils that I received from the Rite of Godhood.

The first sigil, whose number was 76, was heaven.

The second sigil was the vehicle on earth.

The second sigil was a mystery until tonight. This sigil is like a cross section of the god manifold. It revealed itself to me after fusing the other two sigils. This sigil is revelation/transmutation/a unity of heaven and earth. End History.

This was when the being, myself(?) revealed itself/myself to me. It was like it was beckoning me towards Godhood to form my own manifold and, therefore, my own universe. Every person was a part of one of these beings (Holy Guardian Angels?); they were many, and there are more, others, of As. like me, all part of him and he A. This is for all of humanity. The ineffable is; we must reach our own bliss.

Later, after the vision was revealed, I was visited by a goddess. I finished firing the three sigils into the heart of Oblivion on the dance floor. I was placing the third one by this "Dark" dancing woman's feet. She did not see me. She turned around, came up to me, took my hand and said, "Hello. You know who I am, right?"

It was fucking Babalon!!

Now believe me when I say that I have never seen a manifestation "in the flesh" of a deity. This weirded the shit out of me. She swept up my Desire into her being. She took me by the hand, along with a few others, and danced with us. She wanted to play a little also. I felt unworthy, but quickly shrugged this off and played the game.

"I came because you called me, silly," she told me. I told her I was scared, and thought myself unworthy, but she knew and understood me. This was communicated through words and something more. I do not know if Babalon possessed some woman or if this was a physical manifestation, but others saw her, and danced with her also.

There was a form of telepathy (sort of). I think it was A., and he was telling me (sort of) about Babalon and the factions. Babalon was a servant, sort of like a mayor of a city in comparison to a governor of the state. Each of these factions (gods if you will) had their own idea as to how the game should be played. She vanished after this, and I knew she wanted me to partake of her bliss, instead of thinking on it.

Now I speak of the Void. This was terrifying. It was isolated, cold, bleak, black and empty (all in one breath). It was here that things dwelled which were-not and would-not-be. These things were very much like the Chthonic Old Ones. They existed in another universe that touched our manifold at every point. Magic is the ultimate language. There were things in the Void that were *not* magic. This was very, let me repeat, *very* scary, dark, hopeless and dead beyond any words I could use. It seemed that nothing in its "right" mind would want to dwell in the void, as it cracked and dissolved any petty ego associated with it. There is no evil, but the things in the Void came pretty close.

The Holy Guardian Angel Operation is a revelation of one's wholeness. This being is many beings comprised together, "in the future." Kia/Magic/Life/God/Power/Love beyond love and Light.

This message is for all of humanity. This god point is approaching, whatever that means. Maybe a birth of a new universe manifold, "floating" in the Void. Many universes, each with their own being. Perhaps this is Pandaemonaeon.

We are gods, and many people are one of many one and so forth, 'til ecstasy. There is so much more to existence than we might think. I encourage all to try this Rite of Godhood, an attuning with the Holy Guardian Angel, as one of the highest goals of the Great Work. This is the Great Work, to be a universe, to be absolute. It is so much beyond the "human" level now, that words really do not do it at all.

The only thing I can say, and have been saying, is "Oh my god . . . Oh my god." I can't even describe this shit, man.

Let me write a little bit of the background that elicited these un-coverings. This night I invoked many deities.

Moglthox: To steal my corruption and purify me.

Harakhan: To bring me knowledge and wisdom of self.

Babalon: For her ecstasy and love.

Teckno: To transport me to Babalon in his medium.

Tiyet: To purify my dreams and submind, and give me the gift of her silence.

Set: As the dark sun, to show me the majesty and power of self.

Lucifer-Christ: (As LuciferousChristos), to bring Love and Unity. The Triple Goddess of the Moon and Dionysus and others . . . A.

After singing hymns of calling to the deities, but preceding the actual invocations, I read a little bit from the *Book of Revelation* (the part about Babylon and the great Mystery) and a little bit from *Principia Discordia* (concerning Eris and the origin of the universe). It seems now as I write this that my mind is trying to make me forget.

All along (months) I have been offering prayers to my "Guardian Angel" to meet (myself of God). The sigils were received after each ritual was performed. Each rite was performed as instructed by A. (this was written of previously, but I did not know its name). The first two rituals were formalized, but the third was done (astral invocations) on my birthday night with the dance performed astrally. Ketamine was used throughout. MDMA (Babalon's Sacrament) with Ketamine (Old Ones' Sacrament) tonight. I offered prayers and Desire for communication, researched the sigils and found some interesting links.

The second sigil was revealed tonight and is a fusion of heaven and earth. I have not found any "practical" use of these sigils yet, but they have brought me in contact with what I firmly believe to be my Angel, the "perfected" form of me, "in the future" of which I am Grendel/WE and will become As./A. I have never heard of A. before, but it does bear a resemblance to Azathoth. I heard A. somewhere before, a demon maybe, Babylonian? I'll research this.

In final note. Magic is the ultimate communication, and it is right to say that things are playing. All of this is play, a big game. The Void was not. Nice place to visit, but Cthulhu wants to live there (this is supposition on my part—I do not know if "Cthulhu" was there, but there were these things, unwholesome things). This is very much "real," and I exaggerate not. I encourage all magi to undertake the Rite of Godhood, adapting it as one sees fit and picking your own archetype (in my case, Grendel) to align with. With this in mind I hope we can all learn to play a little more effectively.

I love you all.

In Chaos and Bliss, with *Fucking Fuck*,
Elijah.

Summary of Techniques

> "*A certain level of social conformity is present, even among the Chaotes. It is distinctive and yet parallel to format and precision. I emphasize the effect, but the dream sequence is not so easily described.*"
> – WE, 1999

I spent a great deal of time pondering over the ramifications of these rituals, and possible what-if scenarios. Presenting the core ideas of this Operation, we have the following (abstracted to a general form):

• A certain degree of coincidences led me in the direction of the calling to a "higher self" in the formulation of the Rite of Godhood.
• A shocking event happened, which was channeled wholly into feverish desire (prayer/meditation) towards the desired goal.
• This goal was taken to the point of obsession, while learning about the connections of the Holy Guardian Angel.
• Certain alignments with resonant factors of myself were brought into play.
• The Operation was extended over a lengthy duration.
• During the course of the Operation a high degree of social isolation was present in day-to-day affairs. I was left reeling for months after the Babalon incident. I cannot emphasize the great deal of "truth" which was felt at the time of these revelations. Now this is treading dangerous territory, because obsession is sure to follow.

The Rite of Suffering

As one summons the Angel of Light, the reverse impulse is attracted. Mastery and integration of the darkness is necessary for unity. A thorough self-examination and analysis is a must, and identification with all our demonic aspects a key. After initial Knowledge and Conversation with the Angel has taken place, it becomes necessary to make a descent into darkness. The following reflects my own Rite of Suffering. The dictates of the Angel shall guide you in your own form of Mastery of Self (note that this is a never-ending procedure, but at this juncture the reins must be pulled tight). I present this, which can be adopted both within and without pursuit of this subject by the imaginative magician. Angelic contact was established with full Knowledge and Conversation within three months' time; the demonic bindings phase kicked in (under guidance of the Angel) for the remaining time. The total time for my Operation was about a year and two months of intense work. I expect this to vary for each individual.

The bindings represent a conscious attempt to gain control over areas of one's life that have gone unchecked. They are also initiations, all of this happening on an astral level, manifesting physically with synchronicities and a life convergence for each binding. I shall not go into too much of the specifics of each for myself, but attempt to portray a general form that will hopefully be applicable. Each binding was summarized in a sigil form that represented successful completion of the subject. There were four lesser bindings and three greater bindings. The Lesser Bindings are the Binding of the Necessary/Forced, the Binding of the Body, the Binding of the Heart and the Binding of the Mind. The Greater Bindings are the Binding of the Will, the Binding Unto Babalon and the Binding of the *i*.

The Binding of the Necessary/Forced—A sigil was to be designed by myself representing many facets of control over all conditions that are necessary/forced in today's society. This includes direction, bills, career, desire, etc. This initiation/binding coincided with my completion of grad school, and being flung into the world of the mundane. This is actually very difficult, but the decisions and flux caused by the world of discs (money) are as trying to one's mettle as one can get. When the time is right, this section is finished; of this the Angel will instruct you. In order to assist in this area, I adopted a regular practice of money and wealth magic.

The Binding of the Body—This includes a physical regime of exercise and eating "right." I adopted a total overhaul of my physical system. I began working out and practicing yoga (asana, pranayama, mantra-yoga), resulting in a wonderful change of the physical. Of this binding I am the living sigil.

The Binding of the Heart—This was both a recognition of the absolute falsity and the truth of human love in respect to one another, self and divinity. This included the summary of Love under Will, relationships and other issues.

The Binding of the Mind—The binding of the mind was the longest-running initiation, this being a categorization of any, and every, personal demon that the magician has spawned over his life, a monumental if not impossible task. I categorized legions (ha) and sigilized and bound each one with name. This process is as a declaration to the sub-mind for regaining control over demonic factors.

The binding ceremony was the close of this phase after months of intensive labor and self-analysis. This was very tedious, as discovery of one little monster leads to an entire nest of related infections. To this end I used mathematical laws for binding chains of these programs numerically.

The Binding of the Will—The binding of the mind included the complete demonic bindings and oaths of the infernal princes dictated under the traditional Abramelin operation. The Princes of Hell themselves, in recognition of divine right, gave the sigils of this section.

The Binding Unto Babalon—There was more than one facet to this binding. One of these facets took place at a party attended in Austin, Texas. The second aspect took place at a rave in Seattle, Washington. In both circumstances, the events transpiring were of a similar nature. My journal entries can give more insight into the nature of this initiation.

The Binding of the "i"—This is a highly complicated initiation to explain. It is the summary of all the work to date. It represents the ascension of a Master to the Temple in one aspect, as well as "Unity" of the Angel with its inverse in another aspect. The initiation took place across time.

What Are Demons?

> *"Your essence is revealed; Abraxis. Revelation is the Annihilation of Self."*
> **– Law of Addiction**

There are many types and varieties, legion to be exact. In one facet they are base atavisms; some have evolved to incorporate higher integration in order to further their base nature. They have "grown" through repression, neglect and other shadows, and manipulate through secrets and urges. In more extreme cases, when the demon is very powerful, it can possess an individual. This possession occurs in an enrapture of the demon's sphere of influence—like being filled with lust, or as ritualistic possession where the monster is drawn up and takes over. The above exposition deals with the internals of origin, which come from urges. Desires are commanders that suckle and feed the urges. At other times, fear causes these blacker pathways. The gate is opened, the bag of black flesh sewn, the pus of desire fills the sack—and a demon is born.

The identification and civilization of as many demons as possible is necessary to get a grasp on this. Many times these nasty bugs form circuits and feedback loops to enhance and keep their reins of control. Rigid self-analysis and control must endure; sometimes just making a note of a circuit is enough to temporarily defuse it.

The following journal excerpts are examples of the stages in these initiations and notes.

August 1, 1999

Very strange evening and morning. Started out with stupid ego issues, then gave up and everything flowed more naturally. I started the dance for the dance's sake; then ran into a foreign couple from the Netherlands and was treated to a club (Twilo). The energy there was up and I trance-danced into communion with AZ (I was completely sober and on an extreme fatigue ecstasis). I saw a bat-like humanoid creature descending, and then the visage of a sarcophagus-like shape . . .

August 14

I had a dream that the chaosphere tattoo on my leg just went away and I had new flesh covering my leg . . . A black woman with crazy eyes walked by me this morning and said in this deranged voice, "You can't see him . . . but he loves you!"

August 16

This initiation period is pure suffering. Every facet of my life has changed. I see communications all around me all the time and reminders of the cipher of AZ.

August 27

There are so many traps of the magus! It is "safe" to assume that one must never Believe, although belief is useful. Even all of this Old Testament flare that has been called forth from my upbringing is a trap. Every action must be waged against its opposite; I must not falter along this way. Did I forget to mention that everything both inside and outside of existence is insane? Just thought I would clear that up.

October 1

The main occurrence of the Binding of the Necessary was recognized this past Friday, in the early afternoon, which happened as a balanced vision of the direction and path for my life and future. I have to put in the work, of course. To take a perspective and change it for one's benefit is real magic . . . Let me emphasize, that this vision of clarity was *very nice*! To have a clear purpose of Will and focus was quite welcome after the flux I just came from . . .

November 6

The Binding of the Will. Bearing witness to the obsession that is the small fraction of *evil*. The Princes themselves. Humanity's "vilest" parts honed and chiseled into an ingot of fine malevolent intelligence. (Evocation.) Here and now do we bind them, the sublime wellspring of hope. Creation—they bow before its might . . .

Journal Excerpt (Babalon)

There are many faces to the Lady. She comes and "brings" evolution as necessary. She is an alchemical solve et coagula. The Strange Attractor party was an amalgamation of an earthly aspect, although higher forces received the greater interchange. It seemed that any ritual that could have been performed would have been pointless, as the coming of us there was the rite (to what aim, I do not know). Yet I did note that, in us as both physical and spiritual manifestations of the body, there was some "supra" communication going on, other than just words. This was not at all obvious until after the fact. The entire night was fit to one word: Dissonant. It seemed as a cut-up, a temporally deranged Mardi Gras. I ran into many people whom I had never met before (in the flesh), and it all seemed expected. Even the butterfly tattoo that A. has been revealing to me; manifestations of butterfly-like creatures as representatives of its higher Phoenix aspects.

I understand Her. Her rage is subtle and interwoven. She is truly the queen of shells. A perfect slut and whore. She has always been here and is always in myriad forms. She asked me to go home with her. Although she knows that the Will is not to her end, she tries in her ecstasy. She is an exquisite pearl. A potent and powerful guardian. To drink of her cup is the most delicate poison; understanding is a bottomless well. Her burning forms have a hunger. She is to be our mistress and slave, servant and concubine. She is victorious in her inferno, forever amid the brethren . . . How do I write of this? Simply. Ye cannot. I made her swear to be and bind herself to me. A trick? No, her arousal is her nature. She understands the magus and the way. She is to be a tool by us also and a sweet succubus. It is truly frightening how she manifests. She is the queen of the Qliphoth, for we are of her. As our heart swells upward to heaven, the self of "I" comes to understanding in her burning.

The Scarlet Brotherhood

I hate to use the words "I understand," because this is better said in silence, but these writings are one of shared view. I am left to wonder sometimes on the "Grand Illusion" and if, "in fact," this exists separate from deity. Maybe my perspective of "in fact" is at fault here and a more appropriate phrase would be "in mind" . . . As I write this a woman on the bus wants me to move into a corner seat to accommodate her large mass. I do not move, but instead create room for her to walk by and wedge herself in the corner seat, if she desires. She swears—"Jesus!"—and then takes the undesired seat next to me. I am her problem, getting in the way of desire. She probably would have killed me if she could. She exists without. If you have a question, the answers are always there; you just have to open your eyes. The bus has always been a boundless source of wisdom. It is full of solitude (even if it is crowded), the journey is long and there is always enough variety for meaningful divinations. In *its* way of perpetual bliss, *this* always creates. Over the course of its creation, it creates more (to preserve itself in the void?); *all* in all, *it* is a Point. Now, as *this* comes into form, *it* retains itself and we result. Since we are always incident (although ever so lovingly), we are antipodal to the other (as ends of a line segment)—Malkuth in Kether, Kether in Malkuth. The entire process is the becoming, as the unfolding of a lotus. To be cut off from *this* would be impossible to imagine (not that it is impossible, but who would want it), unless . . . one were another One.

This is the distinction between the right- and left-hand paths. The White Brother seeks unity in recognition of *its* being the One. I am *it*, or *it* is I. This is similar to the Black Brother, except in this case the declaration is usually premature and full of pride. This takes us now to the Scarlet Path which, stated simply, is a recognition of both the White and Black Paths, but with the urgency for a new creation. This is the Great Work—a contest, if ye will. The One, in absolute awareness, realized that *it* is (one). So it set about to make love with itself.

Another One? Now this idea is absolutely Satanic in the light of us becoming as it, but this is done (and realized) for the love of its sorrow. Not with the pride of the Black Brother nor the reverence of the White Brother of *its* magnificence (although this is easily understandable). The Scarlet Brotherhood seeks to extend existence, in hopes of becoming another, in the Void, for companionship. I do not grasp the physics. We (the Scarlet Brotherhood) use truth to our ends, neither falling into the vices or virtues of the other extremes (hopefully), but amassing Knowledge and truth through *its* various filters. The path of the Scarlet Brother is one of the highest manifestations of the Chaos Current. A representation of the infinite variety of the One in perpetual flux. She has sought this.

This may sound like a call to arms, but not in the way one may think.

We Are Now Approaching Horizon

> *"Even though a handful of gold dust against a crazy wind is scattered hopelessly, the grains must be fused into a single ingot."*
> – E. E. Rehmus, I'm Over Here.

What is this? Horizon is the boundary of our reality field in the microcosmic and the interface of Universe A and B (existence and nonexistence) in the macrocosmic. The Word of Horizon is aligned with the word Xeper (although there is no affiliation with its sacred trust). Horizon is the Word (without sound, as an infinite wailing) of the Pandaemonaeon. It is here that our Temple is built. An infinite plane extending to infinity. The Scarlet Brother takes leaps toward the Horizon, each time extending *its* ecstasy. This is why we laugh so much. We hold no truth (even this, which does not have to be), another paradigm if ye will.

The Sun Will Rise on the Horizon, and the Sun Will Set on the Horizon. So it is that day and night come about. The conquering son is our keeper. The Will, like a laser, shining through the darkness, guiding us in an interwoven matrix of Black Light.

Our temple is built upon a Scarlet Desert with the Sigil(s) of our Angel burned upon the sands. Anything we will can manifest here. This is the Desert on Horizon (this may take our brethren a little work). *All* is in truth, so thus we accept no truth (but infinite variation). Now this is all fine and dandy, but what have we just presented here? (The bus driver just now intones "last stop in the ride free zone." How appropriate.) Horizon is a paradigm of Unity in extension. An artistic creation. A re-creation. We now have the glittering stars; let us coalesce to become as a blazing sun. The Horizon is also the birth and death of the moon. This is the cup of our Lady (yet to be seen). The Scarlet Brotherhood is the Army of Babalon. She does not accept "membership" on a cosmic scale, but is a coordinator and filter. It is through her that we advance. (Up to a point!) We may choose whatever initiation scheme we desire, but the Angel guides us. (So it is You shall have attained Knowledge and Conversation of the Holy Guardian Angel as a minimum requirement.) This of course is not an excuse for lack of discipline and indiscriminate judgment. On the contrary, to be a Scarlet Angel requires a balance of forces (so we do not collapse or explode, although this can be fun at times). We accept Nothing as Absolute.

So now the Wyrm awakens. A word is issued, a glance back, eyes rush to meet. In desperate sanctity this word is. Its sound is of projection in Silence, and we live on Horizon.

$$\infty$$

Choronzon

"There is no way to anticipate the benediction of that secret arrival. It's not like falling head first into a well of souls; we are already surrounded by those waters."
 – **Linda Kohanov, "Well of Souls"**

Choronzon was the first child of Wisdom and Understanding. It is 333 to cover reflection across all worlds (mind, body, spirit). The base guardian of "Knowledge" in human form to the world without in divinity. Choronzon thus reflects the formation and dissolution gateway of the mind of man. The Beast 666 is the formation of this principle in the Body (Zos). The yet-to-come is 999, which is a fusion of the reflex of body-mind in the real of spirit (or the reverse), thus completing the current and giving rise to the urge for unity. The Beast took on flesh as its necessity in the "realm" of physicality (as this is all necessary for completion). Choronzon's unity comes from unity with the Angel. The Beast gains union with Babalon. The final force is yet to be seen.

The Nature of Babalon

"You're a real whore. Aren'tcha?"
– **Some random porno**

Our life force is beyond our personality. Our personality (ego) is a result of experience, programming, our soul, genetics and other factors in combination. The personality in this reference is called a shell. It is our task to integrate/destroy/align our ego towards Kia. The shell is either destroyed upon death, subsumed or remains as a form of Qliphoth (in whatever part). Complete identification with the personality is the state referred to as "asleep" and "Hell." Babalon is the queen of these shells (egos). She is the embodiment of the ego force, but because she is without "body," she is not false, but being completely empty, she is literally burning in ecstasy. Her want is of continual intoxication of being, which is why she is a whore. She gives to all without restriction. A perfect slut and therefore most holy. She is to be as a succubus for the magus: partner, servant, familiar, tool, temptress. She can (when properly enticed) transmute the very substance of ego. Through her we come to understanding of the nature of consciousness and the fall of man. Her cup can be poison, because if the ego has a shred of itself, this can think itself real and we actually transmute false to false—poison to poison. The magician's consciousness being thrown back into non-awareness allows the Angel to guide one's actions (although guide is an inexact word). It is when this virtue of understanding is gained by the will, that *she* becomes succubus (the Cup). It was then, during this course, that I made her swear unto me. An enrapt state pulsing to and fro, she swore unto her master and servant. She understands all of this, but as is true to her urgency, she attempts to draw the magician into her inferno . . . She is a transmuter. Upon the awakening of the great prophet, when Babalon the great shall fall, this revelation shall become spontaneous among mankind.

"I"

"What has self to do with eye?"
– *Liber CHRNZN*

There are a multitude of mathematical relations for the exploration of shells. Among the most profound are complex numbers (also called imaginary numbers). The set of complex numbers in set theoretic notation:

$$C = \{a + bi \mid a,b \in R \;\&\; i=\sqrt{(-1)}\}$$

This is the set of numbers a (which are wholly real) and the set of b multiplied by the imaginary root i. The graph of a complex value falls on a two-dimensional coordinate system (higher dimensional cases, however, are extremely complex—no pun intended—and require modification into a whole new set of numbers with modified mathematical laws). The horizontal axis is the real axis (consisting only of the a values), and the vertical axis is the imaginary axis. So the graph of the number $(1 + i)$ looks like the following:

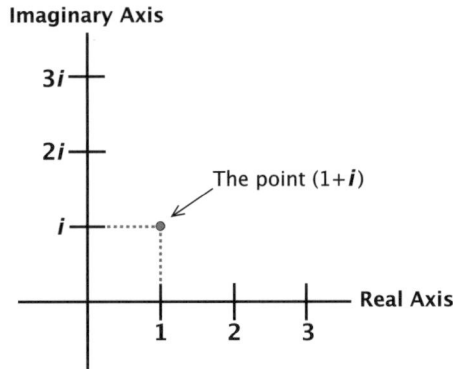

Now let us examine the concept of "i" under various degrees or powers.

Let $i=\sqrt{(-1)}$ be our starting supposition. This is created to assuage our conscious mind that even though "the square root of negative one" does not make sense, we shall assume that there exists something (in this case i) which fills our need. This just *coincidentally* happens to model reality/space-time.

$$i^2 = i * i = \sqrt{(-1)}\sqrt{(-1)} = -1$$

We have a dual degree here that reflects into the negative real axis, that is, the imaginary i reflected to itself brings forth a negative multiplicative identity.

$$i^3 = (i^2)(i) = (-1)\sqrt{(-1)} = -i$$

We have a tri-part power of the imaginary root resulting in a non-real answer that is the negative of our original supposition. A negative value of i.

$$i^4 = (i^3)(i) = (-i)(i) = -i^2 = -(-1) = 1$$

This imaginary root to the fourth degree, four worlds (Tetragrammaton) manifesting in one (the multiplicative identity). The result is Real valued. 1*1=1, 1/1=1.

When contemplating the "i," we see that there is obviously a cyclic nature about complex numbers.

$$i = i^5 = i^9 = i^{13} = i^{17} \rightarrow i^{1+4k} \ (k \in Z)$$
$$i^2 = i^6 = i^{10} = i^{14} = i^{18} \rightarrow i^{2+4k} \ (k \in Z)$$
$$i^3 = i^7 = i^{11} = i^{15} = i^{19} \rightarrow i^{3+4k} \ (k \in Z)$$
$$i^4 = i^8 = i^{12} = i^{16} = i^{20} \rightarrow i^{4+4k} \ (k \in Z)$$

The proof is trivial: For $n \in \{1,2,3,4\}$ and $k \in Z$ given i^{n+4k},
$$i^{n+4k} = (i^n)(i^{4k}) = (i^n)(i^4)^k = i^n(i^{4k}) = i^n$$

Looking at this visually on the graph, we have the "i" rotated about the origin. This is the representation of the fourfold glyph of "eye" of the Binah Exploration.

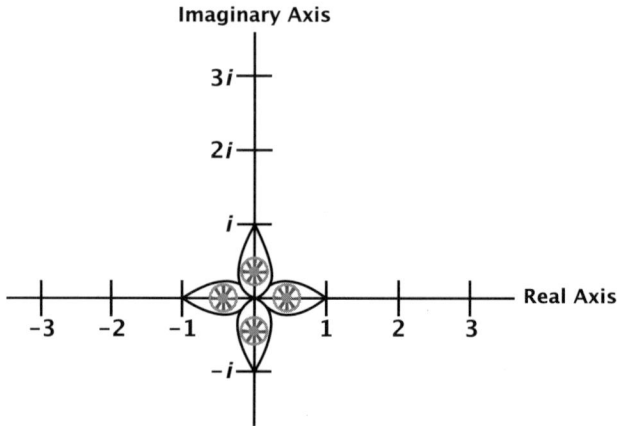

The Binding of the Eye/I

> *"One of these days I'm gonna drag your ass to church and throw some holy water on you!"*
> – **My father**

The following is a modified version of the Mass of Choronzon.[6]

Outline:
- Physical temple prepared;
- Ground and Center;
- Cast the Horizon ***H**;
- Statement of Intent;
- Perform the Invocation of the Angel;

- Perform the Invocation of the First Aethyr;
- Perform the Invocation of Choronzon;
- Explosion;
- Perform the Statement of Office;
- Banish/Collapse the Horizon.

*H—This is a method I created for Opening the Astral Temple on the Horizon of the Scarlet Desert. Any method of creating a sacred space should suffice for the same purpose. The instructions of the Angel shall guide you.

- *Statement of Intent*—It is my will to complete the Binding of the I. Let my total will be done. Angel guide me and aid in this working.

- *Invocation of the Angel*—The angel's sigil is to be drawn astrally while the following calling is read, which is an adapted excerpt from the *Anathema of Zos* by Austin Osman Spare. The prayer should be read with power:

Oh Self my God, foreign is thy name except in blasphemy, for I am thy iconoclast. I cast thy bread upon the waters, for I myself am meat enough. Hidden in the Labyrinth of the Alphabet is my sacred name, the Sigil of all things unknown. On Earth my kingdom is Eternity of Desire. My wish incarnates in the belief and becomes flesh, for I am the Living Truth. Heaven is my ecstasy, my consciousness changing and acquiring association. May I have courage to take from my own superabundance. Let me forget righteousness. Free me of morals. Lead me into the temptation of myself, for I am a tottering kingdom of good and evil. May worth be acquired through those things I have pleasured. May my trespass be worthy. Give me the death of my soul. Intoxicate me with self love. Teach me to sustain its freedom; for I am sufficiently Hell. Let me sin against all beliefs as I call forth the Horizon of Self. Amen.

- *Invocation of the First Aether*—Visualization should be of a void. Call is in the Enochian language.[7]

MADRIAX DS PRAF LIL CHIS MICAOLZ SAANIR CAOSGO OD FISIS BAL-
ZIZRAS IAIDA NONCA GOHULIM MICMA ADOIAN MAD IAOD BLIORB
SOBA OOAONA CHIS LUCIFTIAN PERIPSOL DS ABRAASSA NONCF NE-
TAAIB CAOSGO OD TILB ADPHAHT DAMPLOZ TOOAT NONCF GMI-
CALZ OM LRASD TOFGLO MARB YARRY IDOIGO OD TORZULP IAO-
DAF GOHOL CAOSGI TABAORD SAANIR OD CHRISTEOS YRPOL TIOBL
BUSDIR TILB NOALN PAID ORSBA OD DODRMNI ZYLNA ELZAP TILB
PARMGI PERIPSAX OD TA QURLST BOOAPIS L NIMB OUCHO SYMP OD
CHRISTEOS AG TOTLTON MIRC Q TIOBL LEL TOL PAOMBD DILZMO

ASPIAN OD CHRISTEOS AG L TOLTORN PARACH ASYMP CORDZIZ DODPAL OD FIFALZ L SMNAD OD FARGT BAMS OMAOAS CONISBRA OD AVAVOX TONUG ORSCA TLB NOASMI TABGES LEVITHMONG UNCHI OM TILB ORS BAGLE MOOOAH OL CORDZIZ L CAPIMAO IXOMAXIP OD CA COCASB GOSAA BAGLEN PI I TIANTA ABABALOND OD FAORGT TELOCVOVIM MADRIIAX, ORZU OADRIAX OROCHA ABOAPRI TABAO-RI PRIAZ AR TABAORI ADRPAN CORS TA DOBIX YOLCAM PRIAZI AR COAZIOR OD QUASD QTING RIPIR PAAOXT SAGACOR UML OD PRD-ZAR CACRG AOIVEAE CORMPT TORZU ZACAR OD ZAMRAN ASPT SIBSI BUTMONA DS SURZAS TIA BALTAN ODO CICLE QAA OD OZAZMA PLAP-LI IADNAMAD. IO KIA!!!

(Ye Heavens which dwell [in] the First Aethyr are mighty in the parts of the Earth, and execute the judgment of the Highest! Unto you it is said: Behold the face of your God, the beginning of comfort; whose eyes are the brightness of the Heavens. Which provided you for the government of the Earth and her unspeakable variety, furnishing you a powerful Understanding to dispose all things according to the providence of him that sits on the holy throne, and rose up in the beginning saying: The Earth, let her be governed by her parts, and let there be division in her, that the Glory of her may be always drunken and vexed in itself. The course of her, let it run with the Heavens, and as a handmaid let her serve them. One season let it confound another, and let there be no creatures upon her or in her the same. All her members, let them differ in their qualities and let there be no one creature equal with another. The reasoning creatures of Earth, let them vex and weed out one another, and the dwelling places, let them forget their names. The Work of man and his pomp, let them be defaced. The buildings of him, let them become caves for the beasts of the field. Confound the Understanding of her with Darkness. For why? It repenteth me, I made man. One while let her be known, and another time a stranger. Because she is the bed of an harlot and the dwelling place of him that is fallen. You Heavens, arise! The Lower Heavens underneath you, let them serve you! Govern those that govern; cast down such as fall; bring forth with those that increase, and destroy the rotten! No place let it remain in one number: Add and diminish until the stars be numbered. Arise, move and appear before the covenant of his mouth, which he has sworn unto us in his Justice! Open the mysteries of your creation, and make us partakers of undefiled Knowledge! IO KIA!!!)

- *Invocation of Choronzon*—Visualization should be cases of self in extreme ego attachment.

ANETAB OTHIL LASDI CAOSG ZIRDO LONSHI D-PD ZAR-ZAX SOBRA DOOAIN MADZILODARP TOOAT GMICALZO OMA LRASD TOFGLO POILP L OUCHO ASYMP UNCHI OMA ORS ZACAR GOHUS OADRIAX OROCHA DODPAL CAOSG ABRAMG NETAAB CAOSGO.

(In government I have seated my feet on the Earth—I am the power 333 coursing in the Tenth Aethyr in whose name the God of Stretch-Forth-and-Conquer furnishes Power and Understanding to dispose of all things. Divided: One, let it confound with another. Confound Understanding with Darkness. Move! I say. The Lower Heavens underneath you—let them vex the Earth. I have prepared Government of the Earth.)

• *Explosion*—Visualize a lightening flash descending through the heavens and strike the wand to the floor utilizing (astrally) the Elder Futhark rune Sôwilô ("Sun") and the Sigil for the binding of the Eye which should be received prior to the rite from the Angel. A flashing between both symbols is a good technique—while screaming "IO CHORONZON!"

• *Statement of Office*—The following is an adaptation of a calling given by the Sons of Hermes:

Universe, hear my plea. Earth, open. Let the waters open for me. Trees do not tremble. Let the heavens open and the winds be silent! Let all my faculties celebrate in me the All and the One. The gates of Heaven are Open; The gates of Earth are Open; The way of the current is Open; My Spirit has been heard by all the gods and genii. By the spirit of Heaven, and Earth, the Sea and the currents [experience all in sensation], *the binding of the eye is complete.*

• *Banish/Condense the Horizon.*

The Binding of the Eye—Results

We come here now, unsure and unfit in unfilled and half-managed desires. The shell seeks continual fulfillment of divinity in the act of sex, to proclaim its reality. It seeks to cross the chasm by unity with another shell. This seems false from the start, and it knows this. For the shell is empty. The emptiness is of the ineffable. The most sacred and silent light. The journey inward is the cask cracking open and the shedding of the false ego into empty holiness. This is viewed with stark terror by the shell. I wonder now how this is led astray. The false notion, knowing that it is false, then seeks to realize this by uncovering its falsity (also called the truth of its being). It seeks to unravel itself. This is doomed from the start along this chosen path; doomed because it seeks. Now do not let this seem so daunting—it's not! For along the way, *it* moves to action. The ineffable *nothing* starts to glow with a holy light. The shell notices and continues its efforts. It holds to belief; the light dims. It reaches out with renewed vigor. Belief is nullified. The light is silent. Now what has happened here is creation anew, the light must first be quenched unto the waters. Then, in the blessed blackest of black, does a miracle occur. A moment of utter and complete joy, for the darkness is split asunder and—epiphany! It is! This is absolute chaos, for the light explodes out unto consciousness and the shell glows from within.

It now continues in its light of emptiness and ceases to be dictated by standard confines. Of course, dissonance still occurs, for the shell cannot be cast off (well, almost . . .) until the moment of ultimate initiation. But it now recognizes that it is unreal, and the inner light shines forth from darkness. It now becomes its nature to walk the way it so sought in earnest as a goal. It must express its inner light in a reflection. This is the creation of the Master of the Temple. For the temple is of the Self and it is truly spoken that no life is in this hollow cast. For the Master has now been recreated unto creation. What lies beyond here must surely be folly. It now becomes our task to elaborate on our ways for the instruction of reflected self. She is of us, and here-now-as-always, for we are the Body. The Zos and the Kia, our Outer-Inner structure of being ever-so-distilled from silence. Bearing a glimpse of the future way is like looking back upon one's birth. At the lowest strata we encounter the bestialities of Zos. Always attempting in blind knowledge, rising away from nothing. The attempts become foolhardy until the absolute absurdity called self is reached. Invocation of external illuminations can serve to clear up the intervening miasma as well.

Now what is this Scarlet Path (a view from above)? For Nothing is Absolute; the path of the Scarlet Brother is one of disenfranchisement. What meaneth this? Our brotherhood seeks recreation, thus it is that we are bound beyond time and space into the thrusting disarray of void. To establish a splotch of black amid the white. The inverse spaces bring calamity into their tunnels. The point of crossover is the star of Da'ath. We leap and propel our light (under the guidance of the Angels) into ideospheres and vacuity. A transmutation, ex-nihilo. How this is accomplished is the domain of the given star and is approached quite naturally. The gift of Babalon is that we are of her, and the shells of victory become unraveled. This appears paradoxical at first, for she is Zos complete. But the schizophrenic shards have a new facet about them—many, as a matter of fact. When Babalon the great has fallen, her victory shall be complete. The Body itself shall become cognizant of its inner void/light instantaneously, shredding existence asunder. Our way should not be approached directly, but askance.

The mask called Choronzon is infiltrated by the self, which is its only means of communicating with the light. The quaklephant seeks to merge with the shell and absorb it into his mass. Doing so traps the light in a cage of iron. Consumption on its death follows, where the quaklephant can gibber of its bounty. This victory is neither real, nor false, for the quaklephant is of *us* as well. Its inner light is established as the inverse light of the crossover. It is quite insane; as a matter of fact, it is completely beyond any concept of sanity, even of the lower Qliphoth. When encountering this gibbering soup, silence of both mind and thought is your weapon. The Word of our silence sends the quaklephant scattered.

You are reminded again that our addiction is Mind.

ENDNOTES

[1] For a more detailed account, and the historical manuscripts, please refer to *The Sacred Magic of Abramelin the Mage*, translated by S. L. MacGregor Mathers.

[2] Alternate term for chaos magicians. – Ed.

[3] A group of chaos magicians. – Ed.

[4] This call is in the Ouranian Barbaric language, and is adapted from the "Dark Matter at Hand" rite by Tzimon Yliaster.

[5] This is a chaos magic ritual, composed by Peter Carroll, for opening a rift in reality. – Ed.

[6] Another of Peter Carroll's rituals, designed to invoke the ego or False Holy Guardian Angel and evoke one's total will into reality. All of the rituals referenced in this article are readily available on the Internet. – Ed.

[7] Enochian is a language learned from the Angels by Dr. John Dee and Edward Kelly in the Sixteenth Century; often used by ceremonial magicians in evoking spirits and forces of nature. It might be taken as one manifestation of the "primal language." Terence McKenna demonstrated a similar-sounding glossolalic tongue learned during DMT trips. – Ed.

DREAMS OF A MIDWICH PLANET

STEPHEN GRASSO

A bright, accusing sun rises high over a city scattered delicately with small, budding secrets and mysteries. The dull glow of magic easing up out of the ground, quiet and unnoticed, between concrete tower blocks and red brick houses. Threadbare sorcerers and moth-eaten magicians growing sullenly between the paving stones. Tiny pioneers hiding themselves away in anonymous lodging houses and meager bedsitting rooms. A consortium of small men and dispossessed ladies masturbating tiredly over paper symbols to nudge a promotion at work or a small win on the lottery. Voicing lackluster admonitions to half-remembered powers, shy petitions to gain entry into the hallowed mysteries of the office receptionist's pants. Row upon row of hungry conjurers fever-ishly employing dusty, antique spells to speed the delivery of their hastily scribbled wishes. Is this the shape of our magic? Is this all we can imagine for ourselves? Are these the limits of our expectation?

Black Jacky Johnson, who outwitted the devil and walked with a perpetual limp from the night he spent in hell back in 1862. The terrible shopkeeper of "Blackened Fortunes" that once stood on Grainger Street in Newcastle and sold cures and curses to those brave enough to ask for them. The cruel ex-blacksmith who could speak with dogs and horses, who carried a stick that had its own heartbeat, and who gave a wink and walked out of the world one cold spring morning.

Papa Dynamite, who fought the law and won. Who could heal the sick with his pe-nis and was afraid of no man. Who held court in the upstairs room of "The Ocean" on Portobello Road. Always in full evening dress, sometimes with a boa constrictor draped over his shoulders. Who listened to the problems of the people who came to him and helped where he could. Who put the fear into threepenny gangsters, slum landlords and peers of the realm alike. Who discovered a secret in June 1966 that made him so angry that his fury almost shattered the British Government of the day.

Gypsy Agatha, who could read the future in an old bowler hat filled with strange liquids, her unlikely prophecies all coming true within seven days. Who made amulets out of bone and feathers that could snare any man, potions and perfumes that could lure any woman, brooches and beaded necklaces that could subdue any rival in love. Her body tattooed with a secret map of the doorways, power spots and soft places of Lancashire. Who gave wicked council in matters of the heart to fish wives and wealthy ladies, and continued to savagely deflower the countless heartbroken girls and boys who flocked to her caravan for help, long into her sixties, in return for granting their heart's desire. Who drank neat gin and bragged to sailors that she harvested the lost virginity of her customers in a copper lined jar, but to what end and for what strange purpose?

Tony Cunningham, who lived in a crooked house filled with umbrellas. Who was terrified of the night sky on a midsummer's eve, tended a garden of curious plants and unknown vegetable life, and consorted with pale hopping creatures on the moors at night. Who packed a suitcase one morning and traveled the length and breadth of England on a tandem bicycle, with his invisible benefactor Yellow Morgan in tow, dispensing his sorceries to those in need. Who saved the lives of eighteen miners trapped beneath the earth by striking a hard bargain with oak, ash and elm that he regretted till the end of his days.

Mammy Winter, who smoked cigars and walked barefoot in all seasons. Who claimed she had stopped something terrible from happening to Scotland in 1663 but could never tell a soul, or it would be undone. Who could see through the eyes of jackdaws and magpies, understood the language of cats and kept the people of her village safe from harm when the black plague was raging through Europe. Who lost her beauty in a game of cards, froze up her heart and baked her only daughter into a pie.

I conjure up these spirits to look upon us and despair.

Here are your children. Austere characters in off-the-peg robes intoning barbarous names out of a textbook and imitating the gestures of a bald British heroin addict long dead. Career occultists jostling for a publishing deal, the holy grail of popular magic, empowered by the gods of mediocrity to churn out book after book of the same old, same old. Armchair theorists spitting out rules and boundaries on enchantments they have never touched, secrets they have not earned, Spirits that are unknown to them.

Generations of witchdoctors with their hands tied and their mouths bound, dreaming of gaunt apparitions, clockwork ghosts and a feast of crows. Their impossibly beautiful, fierce passions reduced to empty theory and simple formula. Assailed by postmodern posturing and glib experiment passed off as innovation. Sparks of brilliance few and far between, discouraged and drowned beneath an endless regurgitation of tired ideas, book learning, untested assumptions and secondhand understanding. The carcass of the mysteries picked bare by scavenging pop psychologists, pseudo-scientists and frustrated mathematicians.

It ends tonight. We grew up believing in magic. We made an uneasy alliance with the witch who lived in the cupboard beneath the stairs and befriended the tiny men that lived at the top of the curtains and could come into our dreams. We held lengthy conversations with our own shadows about the myriad flickering worlds only they are privy to. Consulted birdhouses that revealed the future to us in sparrow droppings, feathers and walnut shells. Collected seaweed, stones and pebbles from the beach and made elaborate patterns with them on the sand, secret messages for the ocean that nobody else understood. Planted wishes in the garden and watered them every day with milk and orange juice until they took shape. Kept a box of treasures and knew that each one opened a doorway to a far off land, if we could only figure out how they worked.

One day we were told that none of it was real and were given a box labeled "imagination" in which to bury these things. We grudgingly threw in our friends and allies, our pockets of Halloween soil and handfuls of whispering sand, our ticking chimneys and living telescopes. We slammed the lid, took the box up to the attic and learned how to forget about it all. It wasn't easy. Sometimes we had to stick our fingers in our ears and say "I'm not listening" when the revolving rabbit made of creeping light came out of the skirting board and wanted to play with us again. We didn't listen. We closed the door. Learned how to filter it all out. Put it all away and never looked back.

Some of us. Not everyone could. There were a few of us who kept listening. They brought us a brass key with the slippery and seductive word "grown-up" marked on it, and hinted at the new mysteries it could unlock. We turned the key and nervously shuffled through. Joined furtive circles made of cigarette smoke that curled defiantly in hidden corners of the schoolyard, drank forbidden sacraments of cheap white cider beneath lonely monuments and in the shadow of abandoned bus shelters, and we learned of strange insertions that could connect our hearts and bodies and bring inestimable delight.

We looked upon these things and saw that they were good, but still we remembered a world where orange crayons could be used to speak with spiders, and the gaps between cobbled paving stones were home to an entire kingdom of tiny space faring insect warriors. We looked for magic in a world that shunned the thought of it and mocked the mention of it. Hunted for glimpses of it in neglected places, on an overlooked alcove of the library, in a tattered cardboard box at the secondhand shop, left behind with the dregs of the car boot sale that nobody else wanted. We found some magic and took it home.

It wasn't what we remembered. It gave us hard plastic holes in which to fit the curious misshapen dreams that we'd hung onto, an unfamiliar resting place for all the unnamable things that we had kept hidden in our pockets all this time. It gave us lessons and sums, numbers and words, smells and symbols and it told us to go and learn them. We were uncertain at first, but it told us that this was magic. We had been looking for magic and here it was before us. We had found it, which was more than any of us had expected.

So we learned how to breathe in four/four time. We learned lesser banishings and greater hexagrams. We learned how to turn a sentence into a picture and make modest wishes come true. We learned about the tree of life, the ancient runes and the mysterious tarot. We learned about the chaosphere, the vortex and the death posture. We learned how to invoke and evoke, make changes to our consciousness and reprogram our conditioned behavior. We learned about servitors, égregores and archetypes. We learned about a great many things, and some of us even did them.

We embarrassedly, half-jokingly, took the names "Witch" or "Pagan" or "Magician." Found quiet places in which to practice what we had learned. Behind closed doors we acted out our secret rituals. Hid ourselves away in empty woodlands or hired small private rooms where we could say our incantations and conduct our ceremonies away from the critical gaze of fun-poking onlookers. We met secretly in pubs and bars to talk about what we did. Formed little groups to support each other and share what we knew. We became more confident in our skills and talents, but still, in our irresolute and unguarded moments some of us felt the nagging suspicion that something wasn't quite right about it all. Something was missing.

It kept us awake at night. We couldn't see the shape of the uncertain beast that haunted us. We tried to explain our disquiet to others but got only blank stares and misunderstandings for our trouble. Gradually the source of our apprehensions crept more clearly into view. Magic was not what we had been told it was. Magic was far bigger, wilder, stranger, more beautiful and more mysterious than we had been led to believe. Magic didn't sit at all comfortably within any of the predictable and pedestrian boxes that we had been taught to keep it in. Magic wanted to get out.

Our sorceries are like a wild hawthorn tree that has been forced to grow inside a dank warehouse packed to the brim with boxes of assumption and crates of empty bluster. Twigs and creeping branches have wound themselves tightly around stale ideas and secondhand theory, when it is their nature to stretch out proudly into fierce, undiscovered territory. Leaves of hope and enthusiasm have reddened too soon and fallen on a stark, concrete floor, when it is their nature to blossom into bright, phantasmagoric color and give off dangerous fruit. The bark of our magic has grown dry, cracked and hollow, when it should be strong, vigorous and teeming with life.

Meager pickings for a world eating its own tail. A pitiful breakfast of spells served up to a frightened planet. Something has to change. This world has no need for quiet legions of self-satisfied men mouthing pompous words to their imaginary friends or ranks of complacent women reciting nursery rhymes over a campfire. It needs its magicians to come out of hiding and step up to the challenge of setting their affairs in order.

The time has come for us to stop practicing our magic and start putting it to work.

We treat our sorcery as if it were a parlor game or weekend hobby, forgetting that it is a profession and a role. That there is a reason and a purpose for these things beyond our own amusement. The planet cries out for its magicians to remember their function. The earth groans beneath the burden of a task unfulfilled. The self-regulating system of our reality is at risk because something is not being done. We can't sit on our hands any longer. We are the children of magicians. Our ancestors bequeathed us these things to accomplish a task. Words of power, ways and means, subtle devices, hidden knowledge, skills and wisdom. They were not handed down to us for empty recitation or performance art. There is a job that needs to be done.

It's the role of magicians to get their hands dirty in the places that other people are afraid to go, to speak to the universe and try to understand its nature, to traffic with invisible intelligences on behalf of the wider community, and seek to create meaning for the species we belong to. We have to learn how to use every trick in the book, master all the secrets that our ancestors knew and strive to refine and improve on this body of knowledge. We must become the most potent and effective generation of magicians that this world has ever seen, because when evolution comes, it takes no prisoners. Those are the stakes.

It's all down to us now. There's nobody else left to do this thing. No ancient masters or Secret Chiefs are going to come in and clean up the mess that is all around us. There's just us, and we have to get it done. It's our turn to pick up the torch and run with it. To the finish line if we have to.

It's happening. It's happening now.

Sally Lords has lived by the sea all her life. When she was a little girl her grandmother used to take her for long walks along the promenade. She would eat candyfloss and ice cream, chase seagulls down the road, spend her pocket money in the amusement arcade and then run down to the sands for a story. Her grandmother would fill her head with tales of her own mother and a host of distant aunts and relatives, and the adventures they used to have in the village.

There was Jemima Lords, the Northumbrian sea witch, who brought Charlie Golightly home from a watery grave after he'd been missing at sea for seven nights. Who made old pacts and alliances with mermaids, undines and spirits of the deep. There was Sofia Lords, who could show unmarried girls the face of their future husband in the dank waters of rock pools in return for a penny. Who could return lost things and missing possessions for her clients, which she claimed she had found washed up on the shore at midnight. Sarah Lords, the midwife, who never lost a child. Howard Lords, who married a mermaid princess and disappeared beneath the waters. Lisa Lords, whose good manners and bargaining provided safe passage and full shoals for the village's fishermen during the bitter winter of 1784.

Sally treasured her grandmother's stories and would sometimes pretend to be brave

Jemima or wicked Anna Lords, who had cursed the village for seven years. She would have tea parties with sand and seaweed, hold made-up conversations with starfish and hermit crabs, and constantly worry her parents by always swimming much too far out into the water by herself. The tall tales of her ancestors thrilled her heart, and she knew that when she grew up she wanted to be just like them.

At school she was bright, but prone to daydreaming and flights of fancy. Her teachers labeled her an underachiever and complained that she would frequently stare out of the window during lessons, and then be furious when chastised for it, as if the billowing waves were more worthy of her time and attention than the classroom. She left at sixteen and went to work on the checkouts at the local supermarket, slept with a boy and gave birth to a baby called Rosie.

On New Year's Eve, just after her twenty-first birthday, she first started having the dreams. It was the same thing every night. A terrifying, almost hallucinogenic vision of the raging sea. Her tiny body awash and at the mercy of vast, unnatural waves. A deafening rush of water pounding her skull. Her senses addled by endless, violent waters. Her heart chilled with the primal fear of something terrible moving quickly beneath her in the deep.

When Sally's grandmother died in the spring, her uncertainty was suddenly gone. She woke up early one morning, put on the silver locket that had been left to her, and went down to the shore. She lit a white candle before the sea, and prayed to her ancestors—all of the great ladies and subtle gentlemen of her bedtime stories—and she asked them what it was that she must do.

They had been waiting for her all along. Slowly, ever slowly, Sally began to learn. She listened to the sea and it furnished her with songs. She went for long walks along the beach at dawn and received many treasures washed up on the lonely sand. Signs and portents, a message in a bottle, driftwood sticks and seashell oracles, all the tools of her trade. She visited her ancestors with offerings every Sunday, spent many long hours in conversation with the dead, and a nascent grasp of her role began to blossom intuitively within her.

She asked for introductions and they were granted to her. She rekindled all the old alliances with the Mother of Fishes, the Beautiful Siren, the Captain of the Seven Seas and the Prince of Pirates. She learned how to call undine daughters from the waters and charm them to perform spirit work for her. She learned how to sing songs that could calm the storm or stir the seas into motion. Steadily, a rich knowledge and understanding of the Mysteries rose like sunken debris from the dark ocean bed of her being into the light of consciousness.

Sally turned her space on the supermarket tills into an elaborate shrine to the ocean spirits, decorated with shells and seaweed, blue beads and photographs, cockles and mussels, starfish, sand paintings and the fruits of the deep. Nobody dared question her. She sat at the heart of her town and began to serve the mysteries by caring for the desperate people who passed her way. Lonely ladies would come to her with their groceries and furtively ask for their fortunes to be read in the shells. Battered wives would seek her counsel and protection. Despondent girls and pitiful boys would visit her in tears and leave with something extra and enchanted surreptitiously slipped into their shopping bags. They came to her with their troubles and their heartache, their fears and their failures, and Sally was always there.

Then the drums began to sound again on the beach at night. Sally waited and soon enough they came. The curious and the brave, the lost and the needful. They heard the drum patterns on the wind and something in their hearts responded, nervously compelling them to put aside worldly things for a while and go down to the shore to celebrate their mother, the ocean. The infinite, rolling womb from which all life was born, and the source of the watery mysteries that flow within us.

In time, the numbers started to grow. More and more people from the village and surrounding areas appeared on the beach each month, and Sally would always be there to lead them in simple, beautiful celebration of the ocean's mysteries. A raft filled with offerings would be pushed out into the sea for the Mother of Fishes, the rhythms would start to pound, and the night would come alive with music and dancing beneath a fat moon and a sky filled with stars.

Sally's midnight ceremonies fulfilled a need that had long been neglected. Her services addressed areas of the spirit that priests and doctors had forgotten how to administer to. The dances she held gave shopkeepers and bankers, plumbers and sex workers, builders and criminals a chance for open communion with the mysteries and a window into the numinous. No one was turned away and nobody left without a taste of direct contact with the spirits. Those who came to her ceremonies always returned.

Magic stretched out from Sally and reached into the lives of everyone around her. It gave hope, support and meaning where there had been emptiness, confusion and sorrow. It fixed unsolvable problems, took away fear and cured chronic despondency. It conjured strength and empowerment and put it into the hands of those who needed it. It picked up the thread of evolution and tied it to the ankle of the species, a beautiful great ape shambling roughly into tomorrow.

It's happening. It's happening now. In broad daylight, just around the corner, at the end of your road. Generation Hex wipes the dirt from its brow, bites through its umbilical chord and walks abroad in the world for the first time.

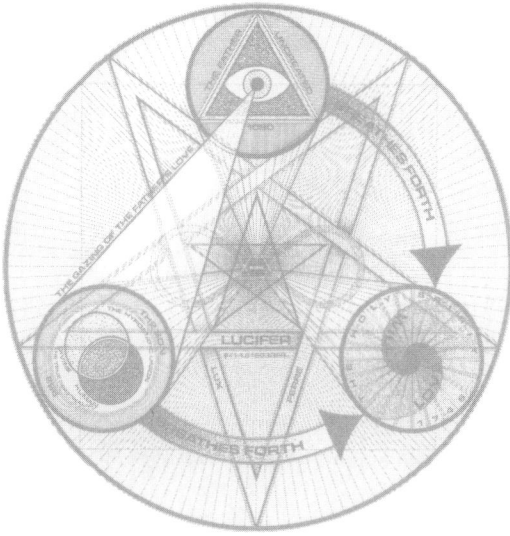

A MUTAGENESIS

JASON LOUV

In the Third Century Gnostic text *The Hypostasis of the Archons*, contained in the second of thirteen codices discovered in Upper Egypt shortly after the detonation of the atomic bombs at Nagasaki and Hiroshima, a rather odd version of the Garden of Eden story is given.

The text begins with a depiction of the central theme of Gnosticism, that the world we inhabit has been created by an insane God. Since the world is imperfect, and is for the most part a malevolent and cruel joke, posited the Gnostics, then it must not have been created by the true God, who must by definition be perfect. To the Gnostics, like Baudelaire, it was clear that "Everything in this world exudes crime." For such an astute and discerning view of existence, the early Persian and Syrian-Egyptic Christian heretics were largely excised from the planet.

The blame for creation is laid at the doorstep of Yaldabaoth, also called Samael—aborted fetus of Sophia, who is afterthought and wisdom. Lion-faced, misshapen; his name means "child of chaos" in Aramaic. It is this God of the Blind that has dominion over the world, who in his cosmic arrogance utters "I am God; there is no other but me."

The androgynous and beast-faced Archons, the authorities who rule the planet under Yaldabaoth, create Adam in the reflected image of the true God, who is but a fond and inscrutable memory, and set him to work naming the flora and fauna of the Garden of Eden. They cause him to sleep, and pull Eve from his side. Adam and Eve are given dominion over the Garden, with the sole provision that they not eat from the tree of knowledge of good and evil.[1]

The divine feminine presence, from beyond the prison reality of the Archons, then incarnates to the first humans as a snake—in this version coming not to tempt them (for what truly perfect God would feel the need to create such a sick test of loyalty?), but to liberate them from the illusion created by Yaldabaoth, saying "It is not the case that you will surely die [if you eat the fruit of the tree], for out of jealousy he said this to you. Rather, your eyes will open and you will be like gods, recognizing evil and good."

Then, as *The Hypostasis of the Archons* or "Reality of the Rulers" recounts, Adam and Eve help themselves to a naked brunch and, as in the Old Testament, realize their imperfection, ignorance and rather advanced state of undress. The Archons find them and become enraged; the two mortals blame the snake, conveniently forgetting that it was they who sought liberation and realization in the first place. The authorities curse the snake until the day that "the perfect human" is to come. Adam and Eve are thrown from the garden, and the human species is damned to constant distraction, to be constantly working to stay alive, so that they can never look up from the material world, never have a second to breathe and return to spirit.

That sure was easy, wasn't it?

When they sequenced the Human Genome I was still in college at the University of California, Santa Cruz, writing for the school paper. UCSC was one of the key proponents of the International Human Genome Mapping Consortium, which had been working for over a decade on the sequencing of the genome, increasingly racing against the prospect of corporate teams (in this case, J. Craig Ventner and the Applera Corporation-run Celera Genomics) getting there first and patenting the contents of DNA (such are the economically-driven absurdities of modern science). The Santa Cruz team was responsible not only for a large deal of the project but also for the computer software that made viewing the genome online possible. The day after the genome was initially mapped, on February 12, 2001, I found myself in the computer science building talking to Dr. David Haussler, the team leader, while the jubilant group sipped champagne and watched the live satellite feed from the international project convening in Washington, D.C., where Jim Kent, the graduate student who had designed the genome browser, was representing the team.

"It's electric at this point," Haussler told me. "The information we have is going to be accelerating at an unbelievable rate. We'll get a much better understanding of human disease by exploring the genome—most of medicine up to now has been working blind."

The thirteen-year Human Genome Project, as conducted in the United States, United Kingdom, Japan, France, Germany and China, was fully completed on the 50th year anniversary of James Watson and Francis Crick's Nobel Prize-winning discovery of the double snakes of DNA. The project identified 20,000–25,000 genes, as well as the sequences of the three billion chemical base pairs that comprise human DNA.

Since the genome was sequenced, we have begun to see the medical benefits of the project's completion, such as tests for determining genetic predisposition to diseases like cystic fibrosis and breast cancer. The holy grail of bioinformatics, the cure for cancer, seems not far away; as of this writing, the Human Cancer Genome Project, which will take an estimated nine years and cost $1.35 billion, is just beginning its planning stages.

It was not lost on me at the time, however, that medicine might not be the only application of such information. Especially not in the dawn of Bush's America; especially not at the University of California, where they built the bomb. It would be almost too easy to compare the cracking of the genome with the cracking of the atom—after all, the Human Genome Project's chief source of funds was the U.S. Department of Energy, originally known as the Manhattan Engineer District, established in 1942 by the U.S. Army Corps of Engineers to oversee the Manhattan Project, and whose top goal is "to protect our national security by applying advanced science and nuclear technology to the Nation's defense."[2]

One shouldn't have to think hard to imagine the military uses that the knowledge of the genome might be applied towards. Corporate slave races. Genocide bombs. As the *Washington Free Press* reported in January 2000:

"Ominously, the Human Genome Project is currently being conducted under the auspices of the Energy Department, which also oversees America's nuclear weapons arsenal. While the similarity of the DNA of all humans seems to argue against the feasibility of 'gene weapons,' British and other scientists were not so sure. In October of 1997, Dr. Wayne Nathanson, chief of the Science and Ethics Department of the Medical Society of the United Kingdom, warned the annual meeting of the Society that 'gene therapy' might possibly be turned into 'gene weapons' that could potentially be used to target certain gene groups possessed by certain groups of peoples.

"Nathanson warned that such weapons could be delivered to humans not only in the anticipated forms such as gas and aerosol but also might be introduced into water supplies. Backing off of any suggestion that such weapons might be capable of eliminating the majority of the world's population all at once, he suggested that the weapons might be used not only to induce death but to cause sterility and deformed births in the targeted groups. The result, just as certain as genocide but a slower, more insidious and therefore potentially undetectable attack. Current estimates of the cost of developing a 'gene weapon' were placed at around $50 million, still quite a stretch for isolated bands of neo-Nazis but well within the capabilities of covert government programs."[3]

The Human Genome Project is the third wonder of the American empire, a massive scientific undertaking preceded—and only matched for scope, effort and Promethean hubris—by the Manhattan and Apollo Projects. The repercussions for humanity, it is expected, will be much greater than either of those previous endeavors. The American century has given us the ability to destroy the planet, the ability to leave the planet and, now, the ability to change the human essence itself.

Swiss anthropologist Jeremy Narby has argued, in his significant and convincing book *The Cosmic Serpent*, that the essence of shamanism across the world is the communication with the genetic code. He cites the prevalence of snake imagery throughout shamanic cultures, including those from areas in which snakes are unknown: the twin serpents Quetzalcoatl and Tezcatlipoca of the Aztecs, the Rainbow Snake of the Australian Aborigines, the Greek monster Typhon, the primordial serpent Sito of ancient Egypt, the African Ouroboros, the Hindu serpent Sesha, the Caduceus, the Tao, the Nehushtan of Moses and the Rod of Asclepius that has been the symbol of the medical profession since the days of ancient Greece. To these I would add *ida* and *pingala*, the double snakes of Kundalini, which go back to Mesopotamia, circa 2600 B.C., to the Eleusinian Mysteries of Greece and to Gnosticism. It's a tempting jump between the imagery of coiled serpents and the DNA double helix, but Narby indeed provides compelling evidence that "shamans take their consciousness down to the molecular level and gain access to biomolecular information."[4]

While Narby takes into consideration shamanic and religious traditions from around the planet, his thesis is based upon fieldwork conducted with Ashaninca *ayahuasqueros* in the Amazonian Pichis Valley of Peru. Since the *Banisteriopsis caapi* vine that the Ashaninca shamans use is native to the Amazon and shamanism is a global phenomenon, there has to be more to communicating with the genome than *ayahuasca* (suggestively, its active ingredient, Dimethyltryptamine or DMT, is found in varying amounts in plants throughout the world, as well as within the human pineal gland).

The access of and dialogue with DNA has been discussed in the literature of psychedelic shamanism,[5] and congress with the genetic code is usually a power ascribed to potent psychedelic brews administered under heavily controlled situations. Magic, it should be clear, is a discipline independent of drugs, yet magic and drugs are indeed strange bedfellows that can occasionally collaborate in making some high weirdness. The skills of the magician can be particularly useful in navigating the other world revealed by psychedelics, just as the heightened awareness of the psychedelic experience can make the processes of ritual magic more tangible and visible. Take a hit of DMT and chomp down a few mushrooms to prolong the trip, in the right context, and you may indeed find yourself in realms where all those funny little symbols and pentagrams from the grimoires turn out to be *a damn sight* more real than you may have once believed. The skills of the shaman, of the magician, of the mystic are essential in navigating these realms safely, in plunging into faerie-land in order to bring back much-needed information.

Yet even dead sober, magic is a direct dialogue with the genetic coils. Take, for instance, the accessing of gods and monsters, "archetypes" that Carl Jung attributed to the collective unconscious but would surely have cited as products of DNA if he had only had the language. (Which is more likely, that a collective unconscious should be found within some intangible ether, or within the genetic code that we all share?) It may be DNA that communicates to the magician in the language of synchronicities, confluences of life events, awakenings, satori, peak experiences and other occult events. DNA is implicit in the use of blood and sexual fluids in reifying wishes, by the combination of the ecstasis of orgasm or bloodshed with intent, along with our strongest magical link to our own beings, the little microscopic bits that contain the code for everything we are. The tarot, its twenty-two trumps a precise map of the human life cycle (and, possibly, a crude map of the twenty-three paired chromosomes of the genome itself, as the *I Ching* and Runes might also be). Austin Spare's atavistic resurgence, in which the magician taps the genetic programs of evolutionary heritage and takes on pre-human forms. And the inmost magic act, that of surrendering oneself to the flow of life itself; gaining enough control let go into the current of existence. Deconditioning has one overriding goal, and that is to strip off culturalization and mind to replace them with the inner evolutionary directive.

In this light, the magician's temple may be as appropriate of a place for investigating DNA as the scientist's laboratory.

Aleister Crowley, for instance, died perplexed, at the very end having dropped all pretense, munching chocolates in his room at Netherwood, Hastings and occasionally curling his hair into devil horns in a last attempt to stoke the fires of controversy. Having endured until the end, the only thing the Great Beast wanted to convince anybody of was, all else aside, the existence of non-local intelligence, holding up as an example the otherworldly being Aiwaz that had dictated the *Book of the Law* to him. That there was "something out there" and that there were higher (and lower) intelligences than the merely human at work on this planet. His experience has often been held up as an alien contact experience, with similarities to those of modern abductees.

Crowley channeled thirteen publicly released documents in his lifetime; fifteen if one counts *The Vision and the Voice* and *The Paris Working*, which are composed of both channeled and non-channeled material. Together these form his primary legacy to the world, and are generally considered to be documents that were written "through" Crowley's nervous system and not "by" him; the rest of Crowley's writing tends to be flowery "autohagiography," occult scholarship or (often only partially successful) attempts by his mundane self at making sense of his channeled documents. If magic is largely a process of deculturalization, of the dispelling of illusion, of stripping away the slime of "not-self," one onion layer after the next, and the discovery of "True Will" (by any other name), then magic may be a process of communicating not with spirits and aliens but with one's own internal faculties and, ultimately, the true *heart* of experience, the genetic code. Our own genetic programming may indeed be the Master Builder pulling the strings of history—or strands, as it were. As Crowley himself says in *Liber Cordis Cincti Serpente*, another of those channeled documents that represent either information directly given to Crowley by his genetics or by *something of equal or greater perspective*:

I am the Heart; and the Snake is entwined
About the invisible core of the mind.
Rise, O my snake! It is now is the hour
Of the hooded and holy ineffable flower.
Rise, O my snake, into brilliance of bloom
On the corpse of Osiris afloat in the tomb! [6]

There are at least two routes to the literally *occult* knowledge of the genome. One is the Human Genome Project, which has given us the *what* and *how*. The other is magic, meditation and shamanism, which can give us the *why*. The last century has been the buildup for this new genetic era, which will provide so many answers and solutions to so many of humanity's dilemmas, and pose so many more. With each technological advance the potential of utopia comes closer, as does that of extinction. Human beings tend to create hell just 'cause. Where will the next Rwanda be? What genetic holocausts will be sparked by the use of the genomic code to produce weapons?

We will leave attempts to curb scientific research to the superstitious and the born-agains—to halt growth is to hide from the future and slide backwards. However, our intelligence in the *application* of our discoveries needs a radical upgrade.

Nagasaki and Hiroshima were the true parents of the great awakenings of the last decades, of our fevered rush to find any kind of spirituality not based on dogma, patriarchal domination and death-fetishism. The mass movements of the 1960s were a step in the right direction, though those who participated soon saw (and in many cases became) their inverse in the 1980s and, in America and Britain, lost ground to the resurgence of the religious right. But the Gnosis hasn't gone away, it just went underground, refined and armed itself and is now re-emerging in a full magical onslaught. Our DNA is calling us home, to the knowledge of its inner workings and the wisdom and understanding to follow it into space.

Why have generation after generation become obsessed with unlocking the doors of the inner planes over the last hundred years? Why occult revival after occult revival? Why the spontaneous "discovery" and mass popularity of LSD-25, and the upsurge of interest in other entheogens like psilocybin and DMT (and would it be prudent at this juncture to point out that Francis Crick's discovery of DNA was precipitated by Crick seeing its double-snake structure while tripping on acid?)[7] Why the widespread clamor for magic? Why are we led across time and space, following oblique destinies we may never comprehend? Could it be the 125 billion miles of DNA within each of our bodies, not to mention the DNA of the entire biosphere—the same for all life—awakening us to our innermost essence?

"Man," Alan Harrington once said, "is DNA's way of understanding itself."[8]

We stare into DNA with microscopes; we stare into our DNA through the skills of the shaman. It is the combination of the technological accomplishment of the Human Genome Project with the information-gathering skills of magic, meditation and shamanism that will safely catalyze the next stage of human evolution. Like the entwined double serpents of the Caduceus, it will be our aptitude with genetic engineering combined with our ongoing shamanic dialogue with the genome itself that will allow us to fulfill our genetic imperative, and follow the directives from DNA itself in reworking ourselves into a species capable of solving its own problems.

To reach out to our DNA—the snake of liberation—is a truly Gnostic undertaking. To call out to a Hidden God who lies not in some far-off cloud but within the vital life essence of each of us. After all, our planet is little more than a convenience for the continued survival and transmission of DNA.[9]

(What are these lurkers inside all of us, for whom we are merely carrier organisms, pack animals? Always this light is born through the sloshing of time's collapsing shore. And who may touch the light? And were the light itself to direct us, what might we become?)

Species may go extinct, we may be wracked by plagues and wars, but the DNA goes on, pulling the strings and evolving itself through endless forms until it finds a way to return to space.

"DNA and its duplication mechanisms are the same for all living creatures. The only thing that changes from one species to another is the order of the letters. This constancy goes back to the very origins of life on earth. According to biologist Robert Pollack: 'The planet's surface has changed many times over, but DNA and the cellular machinery for its replication have remained constant.'"[10]

The theory of exogenesis, as first proposed by the Greek philosopher Anaxagoras and restated in the Twentieth Century by the British astronomers Sir Fred Hoyle and Nalin Chandra Wickramasinghe, states that life may have in fact originated elsewhere in the universe.[11] The constancy of DNA seems to bear this out. It's easy to imagine a meteor containing some kind of cellular material landing on earth, and life taking hold, propagating itself through endless recombinations until evolving an ecosystem capable of supporting the requisite intelligence (that is, us) needed to engineer travel to further planets.

It hides as everything.

As the Twenty-First Century opens, we are seeing a confluence of, on one hand, terminal fundamentalism, cultural gridlock and unregulated military science; and on the other, the mass acceptance and refinement of the technologies for exploring the internal cosmos. The exploration of outer space will be no less of a gargantuan, mysterious and important undertaking as that of inner space, and they have the same goal–ensuring the survival, propagation and positive mutation of the human species.

As this Inner Space Age continues, we continually hear the admonitions of the small-minded that we should not play God for we will soon incur "his" fiery wrath. But what is magic if not the realization of the divinity of Man? The divine (and non-local) hidden intelligence that underlies the masks we mistake for Self? God is hidden within. Take any instructions for spiritual attainment and replace the words "God," "Allah" or the "Holy Guardian Angel" with "DNA" and you will quickly see countless methods laid out before you.

The central idea here, that the "proper" use of magic is in genetic engineering, which will produce the true mutant species, erupted in my mind as a sudden revelation from "outside" while riding with the Dalits in a train crossing the plains of Uttar Pradesh, central India during a grueling thirty-hour trip between Varanasi and Jodhpur, Rajasthan. It came as the solution to the problem I had been working on for the previous year, that is, how magic relates to human evolution, and spontaneously emerged from a deep enough level that it itself seemed to be a communication from my own DNA.

Responsibility for the proper use of genetics cannot be expected of the scientific community, largely run by corporate and defense contracts. Despite the fact that we continually develop new technologies for monkeying with existence, our moral capacity for using them never seems to get past the point of arguing over whether to make laws against them or not, and never seems to factor in the question of what the most intelligent use might be. Research scientists, with many notable examples, can often be the last people to ponder the metaphysical and ethical significance of the fruits of their labors, and at any rate, second thoughts always come second.

"People's careers are at stake," Narby stated in a 2004 interview with the French journal *Prism Escape*. "There are many small pyramids of power. The professors hold their positions for life, and when you're the one who decides what the truth is on a subject, you don't open the door to heretics. An anthropologist who takes hallucinogenic drugs with Indians, bare feet in the forest, can't be taken seriously. That's not the way to study DNA. They have equipment worth millions that bombard DNA molecules with electrons, that's the way they do science."[12] Could we be seeing the birth of a new profession—the genetic shaman?

We are almost awake from our delusion of powerlessness now. We are made over by electronic media (the information revolution has not so much brought us new information as made us more aware of the limits of communication, and the archetypal symbols lying underneath our language systems); hold the keys to the destruction of the planet and, since 2001, have opened the heart of the human organism and peered inside. We now live in a world in which the idea of "human nature" is irrelevant. We've been raised in artificial environments, in artificial media systems, our food pumped full of artificial additives. We're changing, with no reliable map to tell us where we're going.

It is possible that the curve of history is leading us towards the awakening of DNA to self-realization, as our personality shells are stripped off, the fiction of our differences revealed to be simply iterations on the same pattern. The revelation of all life as the expression of the Secret Chiefs that guide all evolution: DNA itself. The realization that there is only one life form on this planet.

It should be clear: Our best guide in altering our genome will not be some assumed scientific or religious truth, but the genome itself. We just have to learn how to talk to it, and the world's shamanic and magical traditions are just waiting to show us how.

"I am God; there is no other but me," cries Yaldabaoth in his blind fury. Such is the first pillar of Islam—*La Ilaha ila Allah, Muhammad Rasul Allah*, "There is no God but Allah and Muhammad is the Messenger of Allah." Or from Exodus 20:5—"For I the LORD thy God am a jealous God."

In recreating ourselves, will we listen to the voice of the Archons, or the voice of life itself?

The snake is our ladder out of this hell.

Amoun.

ENDNOTES

[1] *The Reality of the Rulers: Nag Hammadi Codex II, 4*, pp. 86,20 to 97,23; translated from the Coptic by Bentley Layton (Robinson, ed., *Nag Hammadi Library in English*, rev. ed., pp. 162-99); revised by Willis Barnstone and Marvin Meyer (Meyer, ed. *The Gnostic Bible*, Boston: Shambhala, 2003, p. 171).

[2] U.S. Department of Energy website: http://www.energy.gov

[3] Blake, Roy R. "Genetic Bullets, Ethnically Specific Bioweapons," *Washington Free Press*, No. 43, Jan/Feb 2000.

[4] Narby, Jeremy. *The Cosmic Serpent: DNA and the Origins of Knowledge*. Jeremy P. Tarcher: New York, 1998. p. 160.

[5] See the works of Terence McKenna, Timothy Leary and Robert Anton Wilson.

[6] *Liber LXV* I:1:1-6.

[7] Rees, Alun. "Nobel Prize genius Crick was high on LSD when he discovered the secret of life," *The Mail on Sunday*, August 8, 2004.

[8] Harrington, Alan. *The Immortalist*. Millbrae: Celestial Arts, 1977. p. 251.

[9] Human culture is a macrocosmic version of the insane rush of sperm for an egg. Keep this in mind next time you watch sporting events, romantic comedies, political debates, the Death Star sequence in Star Wars, or anything else produced by human beings, for that matter.

[10] Narby, p. 90.

[11] This is a more plausible version of the more widely-known theory of panspermia, which posits that DNA saturates the universe.

[12] *Prism Escape* #4, Paris, 2004. www.a-lab.org

SELECTED BIBLIOGRAPHY AND FURTHER READING

TOWARDS AN ULTRACULTURE

Bey, Hakim. *Millennium*. Brooklyn: Autonomedia, 1995.

Blavatsky, Helena. *Isis Unveiled*. New York: J. W. Bouton, 1882.

Bulwer-Lytton, Edward. *The Coming Race*. Edinburgh: Blackwood, 1871.

Carroll, Lee and Jan Tober. *The Indigo Children*. Carlsbad: Hay House, 1999.

Carroll, Peter J. *Liber Kaos*. Boston: Weiser, 1992.

Crowley, Aleister. *Liber Tzaddi vel Hamus Hermeticus sub figura XC*. In *The Holy Books of Thelema*. Boston: Weiser, 1989.

Fukuyama, Francis. *The End of History and the Last Man*. New York: HarperPerennial, 1993.

Gatto, John Taylor. *Dumbing Us Down: The Hidden Curriculum of Compulsory Schooling*. Gabriola Island: New Society, 2002.
———. *The Underground History of American Education: A Schoolteacher's Intimate Investigation Into the Problem of Modern Schooling*. Rev. Ed. New York: Oxford Village Press, 2003.

Heinberg, Richard. *Powerdown: Options and Actions for a Post-Carbon World*. Gabriola Island: New Society, 2004.

Mace, Stephen. *Addressing Power: Sixteen Essays on Magick and the Politics It Implies*. Self-published.
———. *Sorcery as Virtual Mechanics*. Pheonix: Dagon Productions, 1999.

McKenna, Dennis and Terence. *The Invisible Landscape: Mind, Hallucinogens and the I Ching*. San Francisco: HarperSanFrancisco, 1994.

Rehmus, E. E. *The Magician's Dictionary*. Los Angeles: Feral House, 1990.

Rushkoff, Douglas. *Playing the Future: How Kids' Culture Can Teach Us to Thrive In An Age of Chaos*. New York: HarperCollins, 1996.
———. *Cyberia: Life in the Trenches of Hyperspace*. 2nd Ed. Manchester: Clinamen, 2002.

Talbot, Michael. *The Holographic Universe*. New York: HarperCollins, 1991.

Wills, Christopher. *Children of Prometheus: The Accelerating Pace of Human Evolution*. London: Allen Lane, 1998.

MY LITTLE UNDERGROUND

Blackmore, Susan. *The Meme Machine*. Cary: Oxford, 2000.

Bloom, Howard. *The Lucifer Principle: A Scientific Expedition Into the Forces of History*. New York: Atlantic Monthly Press, 1997.

Burroughs, William S. *Naked Lunch*. New York: Grove, 1992.
———. *The Job*. New York: Grove, 1974.
——— with Brion Gysin. *The Third Mind*. New York: Viking, 1978.

Cohen, Daniel. *Curses, Hexes and Spells*. London: Orion, 1977.

Crowley, Aleister. *The Confessions of Aleister Crowley*. Eds. John Symonds and Kenneth Grant. New York: Bantam, 1971.
——— and Frater Achad. *Aleister Crowley and the Practice of the Magical Diary*. Ed. James Wasserman. Davie: Studio 31, 2003.

Frazer, Sir James. *The Golden Bough*. Carmichael: Touchstone, 1995.

Geiger, John. *Nothing Is True—Everything Is Permitted: The Life of Brion Gysin*. New York: Disinformation, 2005.

Genet, Jean. *Our Lady of the Flowers*. New York: Grove, 1988.

Hesse, Hermann. *Demian: The Story of Emil Sinclair's Youth*. New York: HarperPerennial, 1999.

Jarman, Derek. *Modern Nature*. Woodstock: Overlook, 1994.
———. *Chroma*. Woodstock: Overlook, 1995.

Keenan, David. *England's Hidden Reverse: A Secret History of the Esoteric Underground*. London: SAF, 2004.

Lachman, Gary. *Turn Off Your Mind: The Mystic Sixties and the Dark Side of the Age of Aquarius*. New York: Disinformation, 2001.

Morgan, Ted. *Literary Outlaw: The Life and Times of William S. Burroughs.* New York: Henry Holt, 1988.

Morrison, Grant. *The Invisibles.* New York: DC/Vertigo, 1994-2000.

O'Connor, Joseph and John Seymour. *Introducing Neuro-Linguistic Programming: Psychological Skills for Understanding and Influencing People.* 2nd Ed. New York: Thorsons, 1993.

O'Hara, Craig. *The Philosophy of Punk: More Than Noise.* Oakland: AK Press, 1999.

P-Orridge, Genesis. *Thee Psychick Bible: Thee Apocryphal Scriptures ov Genesis P-Orridge and thee Third Mind ov Psychic TV.* San Francisco: Alecto Enterprises, 1994.
———. *Painful but Fabulous: The Life and Art of Genesis P-Orridge.* New York: Soft Skull, 2002.

Powell, William. *The Anarchist Cookbook.* El Dorado: Ozark Pr Llc, 2003.

Sobieszek, Robert A. and William S. Burroughs. *Ports of Entry: William S. Burroughs and the Arts.* Los Angeles: Los Angeles County Museum of Art, 1996.

Treleaven, Scott. *The Salivation Army Black Book.* New York: Printed Matter/Art Metropole, 2006.

HOW I SPENT MY SUMMER VACATION

Desjarlais, Robert R. *Body and Emotion: The Aesthetics of Illness and Healing in the Nepal Himalayas.* Philadelphia: University of Pennsylvania Press, 1992.

Mehta, Gita. *Karma Cola: Marketing the Mystic East.* New York: Simon & Schuster, 1979.

Müller-Ebeling, Claudia, Christian Rätsch and Surendra Bahadur Shahi. *Shamanism and Tantra in the Himalayas.* Rochester: Inner Traditions, 2002.

Peters, Larry. *Ecstasy and Healing in Nepal: An Ethnopsychiatric Study of Tamang Shamanism.* New Delhi: Nirala, 1998.

SPOOKY TRICKS

Beck, Don Edward, and Christopher C. Cowan. *Spiral Dynamics: Mastering Values, Leadership and Change.* Malden: Blackwell, 1996.

Besant, Annie. *The Masters.* Madras: Theosophical Publishing House, 1969.

Carroll, Peter J. *Liber Null & Psychonaut.* York Beach: Weiser, 1987.

Conforto, Giuliana. *LUH, Il Gioco Cosmico dell'Uomo (LUH: Man's Cosmic Game).* Rome: Noesis Edizioni, 1998.

Frazer, Sir James. *The Golden Bough.*

Grant, Kenneth. *Outside the Circles of Time.* London: Muller, 1980.

Muktananda, Swami. *The Perfect Relationship: The Guru and the Disciple.* South Fallsburg: Syda Foundation, 1980.

Narby, Jeremy. *The Cosmic Serpent: DNA and the Origins of Knowledge.* New York: Jeremy P. Tarcher, 1998.

NEMA. *Ma'at Magick: A Guide to Self-Initiation.* York Beach: Weiser, 1995.
———. *The Way of Mystery: Magick, Mysticism and Self-Transcendence.* St. Paul: Llewellyn, 2003.

Piaget, Jean and Bärbel Inhelder. *The Psychology of the Child.* New York: Basic, 2000.

Sheff, David. *The Playboy Interviews With John Lennon and Yoko Ono.* Ed. G. Barry Golson. New York: Berkley Publishing Group, 1982.

Spock, Dr. Benjamin. *Dr. Spock's Baby and Child Care.* 8th Ed. New York: Pocket, 2004.

Wilber, Ken. *No Boundary: Eastern and Western Approaches to Spiritual Growth.* Boston: Shambhala, 1981.

Wyler, Rose, Gerald Ames, and Talivaldis Stubis. *Spooky Tricks.* New York: Harper and Row, 1968.

LIVING THE MYTH

Bulfinch, Thomas. *Bulfinch's Mythology.* New York: Dell, 1963.

Crowley, Aleister. *Eight Lectures on Yoga.* Tempe: New Falcon, 1986.
———. *Magick: Liber ABA.* 2nd Ed. Boston: Weiser, 1998.
———. *777 and Other Qabalistic Writings of Aleister Crowley.* Boston: Weiser, 1986.

Hall, Manly P. *The Secret Teachings of All Ages.* New York: Jeremy P. Tarcher, 2003.

Kaplan, Aryeh, ed. *Sefer Yetzirah: The Book of Creation*. Boston: Weiser, 1997.

Simon, Maurice, trans. *The Zohar.* 2nd Ed. London: Soncino, 1934.

Wilson, Robert Anton. *Prometheus Rising.* Tempe: New Falcon, 1992.

YOUR LUCKY HAND

Crowley, Aleister. *777 and Other Qabalistic Writings of Aleister Crowley.*
———. *The Book of the Law.* In *The Holy Books of Thelema.*

Driskell, James E., Carolyn Copper, and Aiden Moran. "Does Mental Practice Enhance Performance?" *Journal of Applied Psychology,* Vol. 79, No. 4. August 1, 1994

Emoto, Masaru. *The Hidden Messages in Water.* Hillsboro: Beyond Words, 2004.

Hamerman, W. J., "The Musicality of Living Processes." *21st Century Science & Technology* Vol. 2, No. 32. 1989.

Hine, Phil. *Prime Chaos: Adventures in Chaos Magic.* Tempe: New Falcon, 1999.

Kaftos, Menas, and Robert Nadeau. *The Non-Local Universe: The New Physics and Matters of the Mind.* New York: Oxford, 1999.

Kaufman, Marc. "Meditation Gives Brain a Charge, Study Finds." *Washington Post,* January 3, 2005.

King, Francis, and Stephen Skinner. *Techniques of High Magic: A Guide to Self-Empowerment.* Vermont: Destiny Books, 1991.

Maroney, Tim. "On the Lesser Banishing Ritual of the Pentagram." 1984.

Regardie, Israel. *The Golden Dawn: A Complete Course in Practical Magic.* 6th Ed. St. Paul: Llewellyn, 1989.

Spare, Austin Osman. *Ethos.* Thame: I-H-O, 2004.

Theiler, Anne M., and Louis G. Lippman. "Effects of Mental Practice and Modeling on Guitar and Vocal Performance." *Journal of General Psychology,* Vol. 122, No. 4. October 1, 1995.

Vaitl, Dieter, et al. "Psychobiology of Altered States of Consciousness." *Psychological Bulletin*, Vol. 131, No. 1. January 2005.

BENEATH THE PAVEMENT, THE BEAST

Anonymous. *The Vodou Tantra Rocksteady Workbook.* London: Trojan, 1983.

Home, Stewart, ed. *What is Situationism?: A Reader.* Oakland: AK Press, 1996.

THE SCARLET GASH / LIBER ANON

Bertiaux, Michel. *The Voudon Gnostic Workbook.* New York: Magickal Childe, 1988.

Carroll, Peter J. *Psybermagick.* Tempe: New Falcon, 1996.

Chumbley, Andrew D.. *The Azoetia: A Grimoire of the Sabbatic Craft.* Chelmsford: Xoanon, 2002.
———. *Qutub: Also Called the Point.* Chelmsford: Xoanon, 1995.

Crowley, Aleister. *Little Essays Towards Truth.* Tempe: New Falcon, 1996.
———. *Magick Without Tears.* Tempe: New Falcon, 1991.

Dukes, Ramsey. *SSOTBME Revised: An Essay on Magic.* Oxford: The Mouse That Spins, 2002.
———. *What I Did in My Holidays: Essays on Black Magic, Satanism, Devil Worship and Other Niceties.* Oxford: Mandrake, 1997.
———. *BLAST Your Way to Megabuck$ With My SECRET Sex-Power Formula: And Other Reflections Upon the Spiritual Path.* Oxford: The Mouse That Spins, 2004.
———. *Words Made Flesh: Virtual Reality, Humanity and the Cosmos.* Oxford: The Mouse That Spins, 2005.
———. *The Good, the Bad and the Funny.* Oxford: The Mouse That Spins, 2002.
——— (as Liz Angerford and Lea Ambrose). *Thundersqueak: The Confessions of a Right-Wing Anarchist.* Oxford: The Mouse That Spins, 2002.

Lee, Dave. *Chaotopia: Magick and Ecstasy in the Pandaemonaeon.* London: Attractor, 1997.

Rehmus, E. E. *I'm Over Here.* Sausalito: Angel Island, 1962.

Sherwin, Ray. *The Book of Results.* Sheffield: Revelations 23 Press, 1992.

Spare, Austin Osman. *The Book of Ugly Ecstasy.* London: Fulgur, 1996.

Spare, Austin Osman. "The Zoëtic Grimoire of Zos," in Grant, Kenneth. *Images and Oracles of Austin Osman Spare.* London: Fulgur, 2003.

———. *Ethos.*

——— with Aleister Crowley. *Now for Reality.* Oxon: Mandrake Press, 1990.

Wei Wu Wei. *Open Secret.* 2nd Ed. Boulder: Sentient, 2004.

———. *Ask the Awakened: The Negative Way.* Boulder: Sentient, 2002.

———. *All Else is Bondage: Non-Volitional Living.* Boulder: Sentient, 2004.

THE SCIENCE OF SUCHNESS

Blake, William. *Complete Poetry and Prose.* New York: Random House, 1965.

Huxley, Aldous. *The Doors of Perception.* New York: Harper and Row, 1963.

Lee, Martin A. and Bruce Shlain. *Acid Dreams: The Complete Social History of LSD.* New York: Grove, 1986.

McKenna, Terence. *Food of the Gods: The Search for the Original Tree of Knowledge: A Radical History of Plants, Drugs and Human Evolution.* Westminster: Bantam Dell, 1993.

Parsons, John Whiteside. *Freedom is a Two Edged Sword: Essays.* Tempe: New Falcon, 1989.

Pinchbeck, Daniel. *Breaking Open the Head.* New York: Broadway, 2002.

Shulgin, Alexander and Ann. *Pihkal: A Chemical Love Story.* Berkeley: Transform Press, 1991.

———. *Tihkal: The Continuation.* Berkeley: Transform Press, 1997.

Reich, Wilhelm. *The Function of the Orgasm.* New York: Farrar, Straus, and Giroux, 1973.

Vayne, Julian. *Pharmakon: Drugs and the Imagination.* Brighton: LiminalSpace, 2001.

Wilson, Robert Anton. *Cosmic Trigger.* Tempe: New Falcon, 1977.

———. *Everything is Under Control: Secret Societies, Conspiracies and Cover-Ups.* New York: HarperCollins, 1988.

OPENING AND CLOSING THE PSYCHEDELIC TEMPLE

Alli, Antero. *All Rites Reversed.* Tempe: New Falcon, 1991.

Alli, Antero. *Angel Tech: A Modern Shaman's Guide to Reality Selection.* Tempe: New Falcon, 1991.

Fortune, Dion. *Psychic Self-Defense.* Boston: Weiser, 2001.

Ganapati, S. V. *Sama Veda.* New Delhi: Motilal Banarsidass, 1992.

Herman, Judith, M.D. *Trauma and Recovery: The Aftermath of Violence—From Domestic Abuse to Political Terror.* New York: Basic, 1997.

Iyengar, B. K. S. *Light on the Yoga Sutras of Patanjali.* New York: Thorsons, 2003.

Kraig, Donald Michael. *Modern Magick: Eleven Lessons in the High Magickal Arts.* 2nd Ed. St. Paul: Llewellyn, 1988.

McLaren, Karla. *Rebuilding the Garden: Healing the Spiritual Wounds of Childhood Sexual Assault.* Columbia: Laughing Tree Press, 1997.

Leary, Timothy, Ralph Metzner, and Richard Alpert. *The Psychedelic Experience: A Manual Based on the Tibetan Book of the Dead.* New York: University Books, 1971.

Lilly, John C., M.D. *The Center of the Cyclone.* New York: Bantam, 1973.
———. *Programming and Metaprogramming in the Human Biocomputer: Theory and Experiments.* New York: Bantam, 1974.

FASTFORWARD TO MELTDOWN

Bardon, Franz. *Initiation Into Hermetics.* Salt Lake City: Merkur, 2001.
———. *The Practice of Magical Evocation.*
———. *The Key to the True Kabbalah.*

Goddard, David. *The Tower of Alchemy: An Advanced Guide to the Great Work.* Boston: Weiser, 1999.

Strassman, Rick, M.D. *DMT: The Spirit Molecule: A Doctor's Revolutionary Research Into the Biology of Near-Death and Mystical Experiences.* Rochester: Park Street Press, 2001.

Vivekananda, Swami. *Raja Yoga.* Wheaton: Theosophical Publishing House, 1969.

THE SUM OF ALL SCENES
(FORAYS INTO GROUP MAGICAL CONSCIOUSNESS)

Bloom, Howard. *The Lucifer Principle.*

Burroughs, William S. *The Electronic Revolution.* Cambridge: Blackmoor Head Press, 1971.
———. *The Ticket That Exploded.* New York: Grove, 1987.

Malaclypse the Younger. *Principia Discordia: Or, How I Found Goddess and What I Did to Her When I Found Her, The Magnum Opiate of Malaclypse the Younger.* 2nd Ed. Port Townsend: Loompaniacs, 1980.

Reed, Ishmael. *Mumbo Jumbo.* New York: Atheneum, 1989.

MY LOVEWAR WITH FOX NEWS

Bey, Hakim. "Media Hex: The Occult Attack on Institutions," in *T.A.Z.: The Temporary Autonomous Zone.* Brooklyn: Autonomedia, 1991.

Greenwald, Robert, dir. *Outfoxed: Rupert Murdoch's War on Journalism.* 2003.

Kitty, Alexandra. *Outfoxed: Rupert Murdoch's War on Journalism.* New York: Disinformation, 2005.

Lama Govinda. *Foundations in Tibetan Mysticism.* York Beach: Red Wheel/Weiser, 1973.

McKenna, Terence. *The Archaic Revival: Speculations on Psychedelic Mushrooms, the Amazon, Virtual Reality, UFOs, Evolution, Shamanism, the Rebirth of the Goddess and the End of History.* San Francisco: HarperSanFrancisco, 1996.

ANGELS OF CHAOS

Carroll, Peter J. *Liber Kaos.*
———. *Liber Null & Psychonaut.*

Crowley, Aleister. *The Revival of Magick and Other Essays.* Tempe: New Falcon, 1998.
———. *Magick: Liber ABA.*
———. *Magick Without Tears.*
———. *The Holy Books of Thelema.*
———. *777.*

Dukes, Ramsey. *Uncle Ramsey's Little Book of Demons: The Positive Advantages of the Personification of Life's Problems.* London: Aeon, 2005.

DuQuette, Lon Milo. *Angels, Demons & Gods of the New Millenium: Musings on Modern Magick.* York Beach: Weiser, 1997.

Drury, Nevill. *Echoes From the Void: Writings on Magic, Visionary Art and the New Consciousness.* Dorset: Prism, 1994.

Evola, Julius. *The Hermetic Tradition: Symbols and Teachings of the Royal Art.* E. E. Rehmus, trans. Rochester: Inner Traditions, 1971.

Frater Nigris. *The Story of Frater Nigris and "I Am I."* Self-published.

Fuller, J. F. C., Captain. "The Temple of Solomon the King." In *The Equinox,* Vol. 1, No. 1-5. Ed. Aleister Crowley. Boston: Weiser, 2005.

Gardner, John. *Grendel.* New York: Vintage, 1989.

Gibran, Kahlil. *The Prophet.* New Delhi: Hind Pocket, 2002.

Grant, Kenneth. *Cults of the Shadow.* London: Muller, 1975.
————. *Hecate's Fountain.* London: Skoob, 1993.
————. *Outer Gateways.* London: Skoob, 1994.
————. *Nightside of Eden.* London: Skoob, 1994.

Hine, Phil. *Condensed Chaos: An Introduction to Chaos Magic.* Tempe: New Falcon, 1994.
————. *Prime Chaos.* Tempe: New Falcon, 1999.

Hyatt, Christopher S., PhD., ed. *Rebels and Devils: The Psychology of Liberation.* Tempe: New Falcon, 1996.

Mathers, S. L. MacGregor, trans. *The Sacred Magic of Abramelin the Mage.* Mineola: Dover, 1974.
————. *The Goetia: The Lesser Key of Solomon the King.* Boston: Weiser, 1996.

NEMA. *Ma'at Magick: A Guide to Self-Initiation.*

St. Teresa of Avila. *The Interior Castle, or The Mansions.* New York: Knopf, 1992.

Unknown. *The Cloud of Unknowing and Other Works.* A. C. Spearling, trans. New York: Penguin, 2002.

Wilson, Robert Anton. *Prometheus Rising.*

A MUTAGENESIS
Blake, Roy R. "Genetic Bullets, Ethnically Specific Bioweapons." *Washington Free Press*, No. 43. Jan/Feb 2000

Conforto, Giuliana. *LUH, Il Gioco Cosmico dell'Uomo (LUH: Man's Cosmic Game).*

Crowley, Aleister. *The Holy Books of Thelema.*
———. *Magick: Liber ABA.*

Grant, Kenneth. *Aleister Crowley and the Hidden God.* London: Muller, 1973.

Harrington, Alan. *The Immortalist.* Millbrae: Celestial Arts, 1977.

Leary, Timothy. *Info-Psychology.* Tempe: New Falcon, 1987.

Meyer, Marvin, ed. *The Gnostic Bible.* Boston: Shambhala, 2003.

Narby, Jeremy. *The Cosmic Serpent: DNA and the Origins of Knowledge.*

Prism Escape, Vol. 1, No. 4. Paris, 2004. www.a-lab.org

Rees, Alun. "Nobel Prize genius Crick was high on LSD when he discovered the secret of life." *The Mail on Sunday,* August 8, 2004.

Wilson, Robert Anton. *Prometheus Rising.*

CONTRIBUTOR INFORMATION

Chris Arkenberg writes as LVX23 at www.key23.net, www.futurehi.net and maintains his own blog at www.lvx23.com. His interests are primarily creative and Gnostic with a healthy dose of politics and media. He currently spends more time thinking about surfing than any of the above. His understanding of magic continues to evolve and has grown to be far more inclusive than exclusive. Every act is a magical act. Will is the vector of imagination. Inflict your dreams on reality before suicidal patriarchs write it for you.

Atman ascends from a long line of alcoholic drifters, megalomaniacs and acute paranoid schizophrenics; his great uncle once caused some ruckus in the Ukraine and got ice-axed in the head for his troubles. Raised by hippies of the yogic persuasion, he was a Boy Scout until he discovered sex and drugs. Shortly thereafter exposed to Burning Man, resulting in High Weirdness. Wigged out on acid, more than once. Became an agent of the Javacrucian Conspiracy. Traveled Israel and the West Bank seeking the key to the true Qabalah; found it behind a hotel desk. Currently under the radar, at an institution of higher learning.

When **James Curcio** (www.jamescurcio.net) isn't conducting mind-control experiments, he is creative director for a number of media companies and projects. Some of these include *Join My Cult!* (www.joinmycult.org) a novel released through New Falcon Press in 2004, and its sequel, untitled and presently nearing the end of its first draft. *SubQtaneous: Some Still Despair In A Prozac Nation*, a collaborative album, is also nearing completion. He is creative director both for the graphic novel *Chasing the Wish* and *Fas Ferox*, a multimedia epic with a team of artists including creative consultant Neil Gaiman. All of his work is informed by a background in world mythology, the occult, psychology and physical-religious practices such as yoga and bagua-zhang. He is most often sighted in New York, though he is by-and-large an elusive beast.

Elijah has exhibited his artwork, based around the Goetia, in Seattle, and has also released two CDs of trance music which explore his magical formulae of HORIZON. He is currently working on linking up the arena of infinite mathematics to the god-manifold and Lamion Continuum, having noticed that the Fool (Atu 0) corresponds to the first jump to the transfinite (Aleph-Null). This of course contains the entirety of the way in itself. The extension of the Fool to the Magician requires the acceptance of the continuum hypothesis (much akin to how the parallel postulate establishes Euclidean space). The continuum hypothesis states $2^{\aleph_0}=\aleph_1$ and is the Magus himself, for the power-set arranges all possible combinations allowing transport (destroying the universe, through the entry point of becoming; the nexus) to the continuum of infinite light.

Angelina Fabbro resides in Vancouver, BC where she is pursuing an interdisciplinary undergraduate degree in cognitive systems. She maintains irreality.net, an established community devoted to the liberation of information and consciousness, and is a director of the projects development company Loki Enterprises Inc. In her spare time she teaches Kundalini Yoga, composes paintings and designs clothing. She is currently working on a novel.

Simon Forrester is a chaos magician with strong Thelemic tendencies. He has traveled extensively in Europe and South America in search of shamanic and magical knowledge and regularly hosts visitors from other dimensions in his garage-temple. Trained as a philosopher, Simon has largely left behind textual traditions in favor of experiential religion of all kinds.

Shaun Frenté, High Priestess of Disco Discordia, was born in the backward swamplands of Ypsilanti, Michigan. After receiving degrees in cinema studies, Shaun tried unsuccessfully to start a pansexual love franchise in Iowa, the operatic failure of which climaxed in a bout of hysterical neuroses. His spotty résumé includes teacher, go-go dancer, pop culture encyclopedist, market researcher and phone sex worker. Currently assembling a full-on disco bible/comic book, Frenté hopes to someday launch a holistic finishing school for young femme *provocateurs* that incorporates neo-Freudian psychoanalysis, martial arts, Tantric sex magic, make-up and etiquette. He lives in New York with his wife and two cats.

Stephen Grasso was born in Newcastle in 1975. He now lives and works in London. He has been blighting crops and curdling milk for fun and profit since he was knee-high to a Shoggoth. He likes kung fu movies, soul music and dancehall. His favorite curry is king prawn bhuna and his favorite wrestler is Rey Mysterio. He is an accomplished art thief, somnambulist and orchid smuggler, and is currently working on a novel and a book about magic. Visit www.molotovia.co.uk to see more of his work.

Rachel Haywire has been creating chaos and destroying belief structures since the age of five. Under the name Experiment Haywire, she is one of the first female musicians to work in the male dominated genre of noise. Her first live show was in Tampa, Florida. She is currently backpacking through Europe. Rachel Haywire can be contacted through her website at thehaywire.net. Her first book will be published in 2006.

George Holochwost has participated in several different magical organizations, but most of all enjoys working with anyone who is receptive to the idea of absolutely losing their shit in the name of magic. Since the summer of 2001, he has been the North American Sectionhead of the Pact of the Illuminates of Thanateros. He currently lives in Baltimore, Maryland.

Jason Louv is a New York-based writer and editor. He has spent the last six years researching and practicing magic, traveling around the Near East and learning how to cloud minds. He is the mastermind of the Global Alchemical Ultraculture and will one day replace the world wholesale. He enjoys being surrounded by beautiful and intelligent people and being given suitably demented-looking toys and stuffed animals.

Micki Pellerano is an artist and filmmaker (www.abraxasfilms.com) with a background in experimental theater. His writing has appeared in such publications as *This is the Salivation Army* and *Dagobert's Revenge*. He currently lives in Brooklyn.

Christian Sedman is currently an outreach worker providing counseling and mental health services to identified HIV+ patients in Los Angeles, California.

Scott Treleaven is a Toronto-based writer, artist & filmmaker, best known for his occulture zine-cum-film The Salivation Army, which the *Village Voice* listed as one of the most notable underground films of 2002. Both his fiction and critical writings have been published internationally, and his collage work has recently been exhibited in New York, Los Angeles, Basel and Paris. Aside from the occasional erotic modeling stint, Treleaven has also curated a number of groundbreaking, magically based film/performance events in conjunction with Pleasure Dome (Toronto), and Genesis Breyer P-Orridge. Upcoming events and an archive of previous works can be found at www.scotttreleaven.com.

ARTICLE HISTORIES

"Angels of Chaos" by Elijah is published in print for the first time in this volume.

"Beneath the Pavement, the Beast" by Stephen Grasso is published in print for the first time in this volume.

"Conflagenesis" by Elijah is published in print for the first time in this volume.

"Fastforward to Meltdown" by Atman was written especially for this volume.

"How I Spent My Summer Vacation" by Jason Louv was first published in *Strange Attractor* under the title "School for Shamans."

"Learning to Open the Haunted Kaleidoscope" by Stephen Grasso was written especially for this volume.

"Living the Myth" by James Curcio is a heavily reworked version of an article that originally appeared on the Z(enseider)Z website (www.z0s.net). It was rewritten specifically for this volume.

"My Little Underground" by Scott Treleaven was written especially for this volume.

"My LoveWar With Fox News" by Chris Arkenberg was written especially for this volume. Portions of it first appeared in *Walking Between Worlds* by LVX23.

"Opening and Closing the Psychedelic Temple" by Simon Forrester was written especially for this volume.

"The Sage's Game" by George Holochwost is published in print for the first time in this volume.

"The Scarlet Gash / Liber Anon" by Elijah is published in print for the first time in this volume.

"The Science of Suchness" by Micki Pellerano was written especially for this volume.

"Spooky Tricks" by Jason Louv was written especially for this volume.

"They Only Want You When You're Seventeen, When You're Twenty-One, You're No Fun" by Christian Sedman was written especially for this volume.

"Towards an Ultraculture" by Jason Louv was written especially for this volume.

"Your Lucky Hand" by Angelina Fabbro was written especially for this volume.

Also Available From Disinformation

NOTHING IS TRUE—EVERYTHING IS PERMITTED: The Life of Brion Gysin
By John Geiger

The multimedia artist, poet, novelist and magician Brion Gysin may be the most influential cultural figure of the Twentieth Century that most people have never heard of. Gysin's ideas influenced generations of artists, musicians and writers, among them David Bowie, Keith Haring, Patti Smith, Michael Stipe, Genesis P-Orridge, John Giorno and Brian Jones of the Rolling Stones. None was touched more profoundly than William S. Burroughs, who said admiringly of Gysin: "There was something dangerous about what he was doing."
$27.95 / 352 Pages / ISBN 1-932857-12-5

BOOK OF LIES: The Disinformation Guide to Magick and the Occult
Edited by Richard Metzger

Richard Metzger gathers an unprecedented cabal of modern occultists, magicians, and forward thinkers in this large format Disinformation Guide. *Book of Lies* redefines occult anthologies, presenting a huge array of magical essays for a pop culture audience. Includes contributions from Grant Morrison, Genesis P-Orridge, Phil Hine, Terence McKenna, Paul Laffoley, Mark Pesce, William Burroughs, and more.
$24.95 / 360 Pages / ISBN 0-9713942-7-X

TURN OFF YOUR MIND: The Mystic Sixties and the Dark Side of the Age of Aquarius
By Gary Lachman

Author Gary Lachman explores the sinister dalliance of rock's high rollers and a new wave of occultists, tying together John Lennon, Timothy Leary, Mick Jagger, Brian Wilson, Charles Manson, Anton LaVey, Jim Morrison, L. Ron Hubbard and many more American cultural icons.
$19.95 / 430 Pages / ISBN 0-9713942-3-7

DISINFORMATION: The Interviews
Edited by Richard Metzger

Richard Metzger presents the most compelling interviews from the hit TV series Disinformation—mind-blowing thoughts from modern culture's most radical thinkers, like Robert Anton Wilson, Grant Morrison, Howard Bloom, Genesis P-Orridge, Paul Laffoley, Joe Coleman, Douglas Rushkoff, Kembra Pfahler and many more.
$19.95 / 176 Pages / ISBN 0-9713942-1-0

TALK IS CHEAP
www.ultraculture.org